POLITY, POLITICAL PROCESS AND SOCIAL CONTROL IN SOUTH ASIA

The Tribal And Rural Perspectives

POLITY, POLITICAL PROCESS AND SOCIAL CONTROL IN SOUTH ASIA

The Tribal And Rural Perspectives

Editors
MANIS KUMAR RAHA
IAR ALI KHAN

GYAN PUBLISHING HOUSE
NEW DELHI-110 002

ISBN : 81-212-0413-5

Published in 1993 by
Gyan Publishing House, 5, Ansari Road
New Delhi-110002

Composed by Computer Bureau B-5, Arjun Nagar, Delhi 110051, and
printed at Goyal Offset Works, Delhi

DEDICATED TO
Late Professor **K.P.Chattopadhyay**
Our Respected Teacher

PREFACE

The traditional village council and the system of social control in the tribal and rural societies of the past, were important forces to integrate these people and to cast control over them. These forces were responsible for bringing social solidarity among these people. In case of any sort of conflict in the society or any sort of faults on the part of any individual in the society, these institutions became active in order to clear these problems and finally cleared those with the satisfaction of all. But with the passage of time, various external and or internal forces, mostly external forces, have started acting on them, and thereby brought about marked changes in these institutions. Forces like urbanization, industrialization, modern education, democratic legislation, modern communication, activities of the political parties, emergence or neoelite groups, etc., have practically moulded the polity, political process, administration and social control of the tribal and rural areas of almost all over the world in a varied degree. But we can particularly say of the tribal and rural societies of the South Asian countries where these forces have brought memorable changes in those systems. In India, the statutory panchayat system has almost replaced the traditional village council and the council of elders, or reduced it almost into nothing. Secondly, different political forces in the tribal and rural areas, during last two or three decades, have influenced these people to agitate against certain activities or politics of the authority which they considered had gone against their interest or would create identity crisis among them. For the same reason many of them started agitating for the autonomy or statehood.

The process of change in the tribal and rural societies in the South Asian countries has almost broken down the traditional politics, administrative and politico-jural systems. To know the present day political activities in the tribal and rural societies of South Asia we must have sufficient knowledge about their traditional politics, administrative and politico-jural systems and the changes therein due to various forces. But unfortunately very little of these systems has been highlighted in the literature on these people. In the rapidly changing socio-political situation of the South Asian countries nobody would disagree that this is a highly important and priority area of study. This is the high time to look fresh into these systems and study these in details to enable the social scientists, academicians, politicians, administrators, planners and others, particularly the state authority, to have a clear understanding about the contemporary political situation in the tribal and rural areas of the South Asian countries and the nature and extent of changes therein. This knowledge is essential to solve various problems of these areas effecting the smooth-running life and activities of the people there as these problems help in creating discontent among them. The growing discontent and grievances of these people have compelled them to agitate, and in some places revolt against the authority. No doubt the authority tackled the situation carefully; but how far they were successful in solving the problems completely is a question. There could be a number of reasons for the failure to achieve complete success, and one of the reasons could be the lack of proper and sufficient knowledge about the people and their socio-economic and cultural life, particularly their polity, administrative and jural systems, the system of social control. This gap in knowledge is because of the lack of sufficient ethnographic materials on the subjects.

The present book, a collection of essays on the polity, political process and social control among the tribal and rural people of some South Asian countries (Bangladesh, Bhutan, Nepal and India) written by distinguished scholars and academicians will, we firmly believe, fill in at least a part of this gap, and as such the scholars, academicians, administrators, planners, social workers and others will gather first hand knowledge about the politico-administrative and politico-jural systems, movements, social control, etc., of the tribal and rural people of these South Asian countries and the changes therein. These, we expect, will help them to sort out the area mostly affected by various external forces and the problems created by these.

Finally, we will feel that our labour will properly be utilised if this book helps in identifying the problem areas and also in solving at least certain problems of the tribal and rural people of South Asia.

ACKNOWLEDGEMENT

From the planning stage to the publication direct and/or indirect help and assistance from a number of persons of different walks of life are received by the author/editor to complete a book. We are no exception. When we first thought of editing a book of this type, till the book is published, we got and are still getting the help co-operation and encouragement of several persons. From our teachers in the university and colleges in the past to our present day authority and colleagues, all tendered some sort of help and cooperation and also encouragement which have made us immensely interested to get this book published. It will be our privilege to gratefully remember the help, cooperation and valuable suggestion given by all of them. But besides our gratitude in general, we need to express it at least in case of some individuals in particular.

We express our deep sense of gratitude to the Director General, Anthropological Survey of India, Govt. of India for his encouragement. We are also thankful to all our colleagues of Central Regional Centre of this Survey at Nagpur, particularly Shri. V.J. Bomanwar, Librarian Gr. II for his ungrudging help in our library work. We are also indebted to Smt. Mala Mukherjee, Shri C.V. Shinde, Shri S.S. Nandanwar and Smt. S.V. Rajam for typing out the manuscripts. We will remain ever grateful to all our contributors as without their active cooperation this book would not have seen the light of the day. We are also thankful to all those scholars who agreed to contribute but unfortunately failed to send their papers for some difficulty. Thanks are due to our numerous friends and wellwishers whose cooperation and valuable suggestions have made us successful in finalising this book and publishing the same.

Finally we express our sincere gratitude to Gyan Publishing House, New Delhi for their keen interest in this book and also for their skill, experience and expertise which helped in publishing this book so early and attractively.

CONTRIBUTORS

Bhattacharjee, Prof. J.B.	Professor of History & Dean of Social Sciences, North-Eastern Hill University, Shillong, India.
Choudhury, Prof. Hasanuzzaman	Associate Professor, Deptt. of Sociology, University of Chittagong, Chittagong, Bangladesh.
Das, Dr. Amal Kumar	Director, Cultural Research Institute, Govt. of West Bengal, Calcutta.
Deogaonkar, Prof. S.G.	Professor, Deptt. of Political Science, Anand Niketan College, Warora, Chandrapur, Maharashtra, India.
Dewan, Prof. Aditya K.	Associate Professor, Centre for Developing Studies, McGill University, 3715 Peel Street, Montreal Que H3A IXI, Canada.
Datta, Dr. Anup	Reader, Deptt. of Political Science, North Bengal University, Darjeeling, West Bengal, India.
Gassah, Dr. L.S.	Deptt. of History, North-Eastern Hill University, Shillong, India.

Goswami, Dr. B.B.	Joint Director, Anthropological Survey of India, 27, Jawaharlal Nehru Road, Calcutta.
Icke-Schwalbe, Dr. Lydia	Professor & Director, Staatliches Museum, Fur Volkerkunde, 806 Dresden, Germany.
Justin, Shri A.	Anthropologist, Anthropological Survey of India, Port Blair, Andamans, India.
Khan, Shri Iar Ali	Asstt. Anthropologist, Anthropological Survey of India Central Regional Centre, 11, Seminary Hills, Nagpur, India.
Lourdusamy, Dr. S.	Director, Institute of Indian Culture, Mahakali Road, Andheri East, Bombay.
Pakem, Prof. B.	Professor, Deptt. of Political Science North-Eastern Hill University, Shillong, India.
Pandit, Shri T.N.	Deputy Director, Anthropological Survey of India, Port Blair, Andamans, India.
Raha, Dr. Manis Kumar	Deputy Director, Anthropological Survey of India, Central Regional Centre, 11, Seminary Hills, Nagpur, India.
Regmi, Prof. Rishikeshab Raj	Professor, Deptt. of Sociology & Anthropology, Tribhuvan University, Kathmandu, Nepal.

Roy Choudhury, Prof. Tapash K.	Professor, Deptt. of History, University of North Bengal, Darjeeling, West Bengal, India. (Director General, Intellectual Forum for Third World Studies)
Prof. Saçhchidananda,	Professor of Sociology & Director (Retd.) A.N. Sinha Institute of Social Sciences, Patna, India.
Sarkar, Prof. R.M.	Professor, Deptt. of Anthropology, Bangabasi College, Calcutta, Editor, *Man in India*.
Shukla, Prof. H.L.	Professor, Deptt. of Linguistic & Comparative, Culture, University of Bhopal, India.
Upreti, Prof. B.C.	Asstt. Professor, Deptt. of Political Science, South Asia Studies Centre, University of Rajasthan, Jaipur, India.

CONTENTS

preserve their culture and life style. In addition to this Dr. Upreti has presented a glimpse of ethnographic picture of the Sherpas at the beginning of his paper which will help the social scientists to plan for future researches among the Himalayan tribes of Nepal.

The Dhimal of Nepal at Cross Road, is the paper of Professor Regmi. The author has very lucidly delineated in brief the ethnography of the Dhimal of Nepal giving detailed but special emphasis on the traditional political system and also the change taking place in sacred and secular aspects of it. The structure and function of the system in general and the role of *majhi*, the secular headman of the village and the *shami*, the sacred specialist in particular, have been dealt in depth. The changing scenario in political system has been described vividly on historical perspective. In this attempt the author is successful enough to show very judiciously the conflict and confrontation in power politics in various stages. Impact of Panchayatraj System, Marxist political activities and even the influence of the Naxalite movement have not been ignored while discussing the political consciousness of the Dhimal. The readers will also get not only a Kaleidoscopic picture of the Dhimal but also the general picture of the Hindu religion and culture in Nepal. This has been elaborated in terms of 'Sanscritization'.

The remaining thirteen papers in this book deal with the traditional and the present day process of the politics, political system and social control in tribal India. Power-politics, leadership, authority structure, socio-political movements and changes therein have also been highlighted by the contributors from different dimensions.

Professor Sachchidananda through his article, *Politics and Political Process in Tribal India: Then and Now* highlights traditional political system that was in vogue among the tribal societies in India and that is in existence now among them. He has traced out the historicity of this system and how the different political, socio-economic and administrative forces have brought about changes in the political system in Tribal India since British era. He has also pointed out how the traditional setup of the tribal people after much reform, is still functioning. The different movements in the

the tribe. Then she emphasized that the clan and kinship provide the background for the social and political representatives of the Munda society. Thus, the *pahan*, the *munda* (assistant to *pahan*) and the *manki/marki* (the chief of *pati/para* i.e. hamlet or territory) play key role in political organisation of the Munda. Besides, the introduction of Statutory Panchayat Raj system has brought about the changes in traditional system and according to author this 'double administration' is less effective and creates a 'lot of avoidable conflicts' in the Munda society.

Shri Khan in his paper *'Traditional Polity of Jatapu: Continuity and Change'* has tried to delineate the continuity and change in the structure and function of the traditional polity of the Jatapu, a tribal group of Orissa. The paper also shows how factions and cleavages have come up after the introduction of statutory council, and at the same time how the people are holding power in statutory council which is constituted on the basis of election of adult franchise. This picture of power and politics among the Jatapu is not only true for other areas of Indian tribes but holds good to some extent for the South Asian countries under study in this volume.

Changes and Persistence in the Political Organisation of the Malayalis of Kalrayan Hills is the paper contributed by Dr. Lourdusamy in this book. In this self-interpreting article, the author has analysed very systematically the political organisation of the Malayalis and depicted the changes in the traditional political organisation which has effected the overall life pattern and the economy of the people. The study highlights the old and new political orders and their significance to the Malayalis and the policy makers. It shows that the changes are drastic so far as the traditional political structure is concerned whereas the persistence is negligible.

Professor Deogaonkar, at the outset of his paper *Political System of the Gonds* gives us a general picture of the political system of this tribal society. He has also discussed all possible ways of social control present among them. At the same time there are societies with the chief, tribal council of elders and monarchical forms of the political system. Thus, he describes the

political system of the Gonds which is headed by the king at the local level. Thus, a feudal type of political system and their functions have been described in this context which the author refers to as the "Vidarbha Pattern" and remarked that this "Vidarbha Pattern" 'is more or less similar in Gonds elsewhere.' The author also opines that 'the political superstructure had its base in the social organisations.' The author quotes Professor Furer Haimendoff in this connection which goes as follows:

> 'the feudal system of the Gond having a territorial and political basis with a hierarchy of feudal chieftains, who occupy a place in a rank system additional to their ascribed status as members of their clan and phratry and cuts at right angles across as vertical division into phratries. Clans and sub-clans divided a Raj Gond society horizontally into a small aristocratic clan of Raja and other chiefly families and the great man of commoners' (Furer-Heimendorf 1979).

This has been highlighted by the author and the mode of function of the feudal system has been taken into account with the co-existence of tradition (as in Aheri of Gadchiroli district) and modernisation (as in Chandrapur district Mangarh area). The Aheri Maharaja "still maintains his feudal position among the Gonds" of Aheri Etapalli and Sironcha.

In his article, *The Dramaturgy of Power and Politics in a Tribal Region,* Professor Shukla has tried to analyse the function of administrative system in the tribal areas in India both in its functional as well as symbolic approaches. The author has shown that the mystification of the administration often disturbs its proper function and control. Such an administrative system compels to adopt an alien structure of administrative system keeping almost no touch or very feeble touch with the social system of the tribal people. This adoptive process or imitative borrowings help the tribal society to acquire new wealth, status and higher prestige. The ultimate result as the author stresses, of such borrowings is that the newly adopted traits conflict with the traditional values of a society. The clash of values never helps in the development process.

Maine, Henry J. S. 1960 (1861) : *Ancient Law: Its connection with the Early History of Society, and its Relations to Modern Ideas.* Revised Ed. New York : Dutton; London and Toronto : Dent - A paperback edition was published in 1963 by Beacon.

Siegel, Bernard J. (Ed) 1959 : *Biennial Review of Anthropology* Stanford University, California.

Sills, David (Ed) 1968 : *International Encyclopaedia of Social Sciences,* Vol.12, The Macmillan Company, Free Press, U.S.A.

Smith, Michael G. 1960 : *Government in Zazzau* : 1800-1950 Published for the International African Institute, Oxford University Press.

Vidyarthi, L. P. 1976 : *South Asian Culture*: An Anthropological Perspective, Delhi, Oriental Publishers.

1978 : *Rise of Anthropology in India,* Delhi, Concept Publishing

2

MODERN POLITICS AND THE TRIBAL QUESTION : A REVIEW OF THE DEVELOPMENTS IN THE CHITTAGONG HILL TRACTS

HASANUZZAMAN CHOWDHURY

Politics which in modern times shapes and is shaped in turn by, the complex forces in the national social formations may be said to have had its points of departure in the dissolution of the primitive commune. The new forces of production, external geographical conditions, clan character etc. had broadly played the decisive role in the dissolution of the respective communes and the determinate forms they assumed later, in the various regions of the world. While in the subsequent processes of historical development the major ethno-racial groups of mankind had more or less caught up with the great historical unfoldings of the economy and society, many more of the smaller ethnic populations have been merely striving to survive with their archaic mode of existence reminiscent of the earliest experience of all mankind. Of some 2000 different peoples now on earth, they are certainly the more numerous but much less populous - 300 millions in total. Many of these contemporary ancestors (or collaterals) of some 5000 million 'modern' population have long been facing the threat of extinction owing to the profound material advancement of the latter. This tragic drama being staged in so many modern States from the most advanced to the least, is only modestly comparable to the similar dramas that mankind enacted during the intra-ethnic, inter-ethnic, class, communal, and regional coercions and conflicts. While largely by virtue of numerical strength all the major ethno-racial groups survived the losses thus inflicted on one by the other, or, on each

In the vast 'non-settlement', or, 'occupation' colonies of Asia and Africa the Europeans undertook to transform the indigenous pre-capitalist modes of production only to the extent that facilitated the plundering of their resources but did not lay the foundation for the development of auto-centric capitalism or capitalist accumulation.[2] In pursuance of such economic policy, the colonial rulers resolutely followed a politico-ideological strategy of driving as much wedges as were possible within and between the subject of ethnic national groups and on the basis of that they practically apportioned those ethnic groups and communities to the new states created at the time of decolonization. Indeed much of the problems of political instability and ethnic conflicts that beset the post-colonial States of Asia and Africa are basically the legacy of such colonial rule. At present, there are at least some 2000 different people in the world living in not less than 163 independent Nation States with total population size ranging from a 1000 million-plus (China) to some 43 thousands (St. Kitts and Nevis) (Grigulevich and Kozlov, 1981 : 228; World Bank: 1987). Perhaps, with the peripheral exception of Europe, the National States of all other continents share the distribution of so many different people on earth, including the large ethnic groups as well as the small tribal communities often very tiny and numbered only in hundreds. The politics of nationalism or national statism brought forth by western capitalism and colonialism led to such distribution of larger as well as smaller people into strictly defined state boundaries wherein the smaller indigenous people are almost universally condemned to the dominance of the larger ethnic populations. For all practical purposes this marked the eclipse of tribalism and the beginning of the tribals' or small indigenous people misfortunes. This may be said to have proceeded in two ways: One, their division across international borders, induced displacement and pushing into harsher or adverse locations, and planned segregation or confinement to reserved areas etc. The other, increased non-tribals settlement in the tribal areas and/or rampant encroachment in the society and economy of the tribal people in the name, or, process of development of the national economy. The consequence has been large scale destabilization of the tribal life even, detribalization in many instances, of those ethnic minorities. According to the UN report some 300 millions tribals of the world are at present confronted with such consequences. Of the said tribal population 'over 50 millions live

in India and many more millions live in Bangladesh, Burma, Thailand, Malaysia, Indonesia and the Philippines'. As to these "forgotten ones, the indigenous and tribal peoples' the UN states that,

> They are almost always the least protected, most marginal of any country's population. Constant and increasing pressure from creeping "development" is displacing more and more tribals. Some find themselves under pressure as outsiders decimate their habitats. At worst, it is bringing about inter-ethnic violence and even the disappearance of entire social groups.... Because they are left out of the main "power structure", the tribals tend to be exploited by the dominant community. Land is almost always at the centre of the tribals' troubles.... (The) inexorable progress of development and the hunger of an ever-expanding consumer society have disrupted their lives.... The onslaught of "development" programmes is posing a threat to the tribals' centuries-old culture, language, customs and traditions. Construction of major hydroelectric and dam projects, however well intentioned, have led to the appropriation of large areas of indigenous and tribal lands and the displacement of tribal Indians from their traditional territories (UNDPI, 1988 : 24).

Colonialism and the Tribal People

Before the advent of colonialism the tribal areas of the Indian sub-continent witnessed minimum of rule or intervention of the central State. This enabled the indigenous tribal people to live within the ethno-cultural bounds of their own ecology in the absence of disruptive contact and/or conflict with any alien cultures from outside. But the incident of Plassey (1757) which led to the colonization of Bengal and then the whole of India, brought an end to the primeval seclusion of the indigenous tribal people. For the first time these people saw alien encroachment upon their lands and jungles, and threat to their culture and society. Though sporadic or unorganized yet the tribal people put up strong resistence to such alien encroachment. Those tribal resistances and rebellions were also contemporaneous of similar actions by other groups or classes in the society at large. Indeed, the tribal revolts

from the hillsmen. However, when under the 'Taluk' system Bengali 'mahajans' started to auction-purchase 'taluks' including the tribal hereditary positions like 'headmanship', 'Dewan' etc., oppressive and exploitative practices also creeped in. The Chakma rose against the passage of these hereditary positions into the hands of Bengalees and ultimately the system was reverted. Thus, "It was resolved by the Government in 1873, that the headmen were to be nominated by the chiefs and appointed by the Deputy Commissioner and that they must be chosen from among the Jhumiyas and must not be non-tribesmen" (*Ibid.* : 254). Subsequently, the system of 'taluk' providing for acquisition of revenue collecting or proprietory rights through auction-purchase, transfer etc. was abolished altogether. Thus,

> In 1900 the so-called taluk system was abolished by the British Government and the Dewans were replaced by a hierarchy of chiefs, Headmen and *Karbaris* who were entrusted with the responsibility of settling petty criminal and civil cases, besides their function to collect revenue. The codified laws applicable to other parts of the subcontinent were not considered suited to the requirements of the unsophisticated and simple tribesmen of the Hill Tracts. So, the Government framed an Act of simple rules under Regulation 1 of 1900 which formed the basis of the criminal, civil and revenue administration of the district. The rules in the Chittagong Hill Tracts Manual made under Regulation 1 of 1900 were intended to protect the rights and interests of the tribal hillmen, their customs and practices, their local or racial peculiarities and prejudices. (*Ibid.* 255-56).

More than administrative efficacy or political rationality it was the colonial rulers' exceptional philanthropic attitude towards the hillmen that is what constituted the most distinctive feature of the CHT Manual, 1900. Indeed, such an attitude was manifest first in the opinion of Captain Lewin, the first Deputy Commissioner of the CHT. Lewin said that,

> Let us not govern these hills for ourselves, but administer the country for the well-being and happiness of the people dwelling therein....What is wanted here is not measure but a man....With education open to them, and yet moving

under their own laws and customs, they will turn out, not debased and miniature epitoms of Englishmen, but a new noble type of God's creature. (cited in *Ibid* : 257).

Indeed, Captain Lewin's most compassionate opinion which can be said to have had found its formal and recognized expression in the CHT manual, was not at all in harmony with the regular practice of the English colonial rulers in respect of the non-tribal subject population. This can perhaps be explained in terms of the fact that having the vast resources of Bengal itself and of the Indian sub-continent as a whole at its disposal, the colonial rulers could spare the most backward people of a remote and inaccessible hill district of its regular and ruthless exploitation. As a matter of fact, compared to any other area this Hill district at that time had very little exploitable resources excepting perhaps the sizeable reserve of potential converts. However explained, the fact remains undebatable that the hillmen in the CHT enjoyed exceptional sympathy, or, sympathetic indifference of the colonial state. In the post-colonial period the same did not happen to continue. Immediately after the partition of India, in 1948 the CHT Frontier Police Regulation of 1881 was repealed whereby the local police force was disbanded and the area was brought under the general police administration of the then East Pakistan. In 1964 the "excluded area" status of the district was brought to an end. These administrative/constitutional changes were in keeping with the Government policy-decisions of exploiting the natural resources and economic potentials of the Hill Tracts. Virtually, in the first decade of Pakistan the area was exposed to modern industrial and economic expansion.[5] This paved the way for rapid influx of non-tribal technical and non-technical labour force, merchants and traders, and middlemen into the area who established their complete sway over the tribal population. The tribals in most instances were left to their natural economy which, however, was fast loosing its natural luster and virginity with the penetration of modern industrial technology and was accordingly turning economically extraverted. Thus, the post-colonial State set in a process of socio-economic and politico-demographic inbalance in the entire matrix of the tribal society. In fact, one single industrial project-the Kaptai Hydro-electric project destabilized nearly the entire community of the Chakma people, the single most populous tribal community in the CHT and adversely affected a number of other smaller communities.[6]

Thus, the penetration of modernity in the form of industrial and technological enterprises aroused deep resentment and frustration among the tribesmen instead of hopes or happiness. In other words, the new administrative and economic measures taken by the post-colonial State led not to a process of assimilation and acculturation of the tribal people but to that of cultural conflicts with the larger National State and society.

Emergence of Bangladesh and the Tribal Question

The administrative detribalization of the CHT and the major techno-economic inroad into the district occurred during the last two decades preceding the emergence of Bangladesh. But the tribal reactions against the same found their cumulative and militant expression in the later period i.e. Bangladesh period. It is assumed that the alleged indifference of the tribal people towards the liberation war of Bangladesh, or, even their collaborative attitude towards the Pakistani occupation forces in 1971 set the stage for an overt antagonism of the Bangladesh Mukti Fauz (BMF/Freedom fighters) towards the tribesmen. Indeed, the alleged attitude of the tribals was extrapolated from the role of the Chakma chief Raja Tridiv Roy who was loyal to Pakistan, held the portfolio of a minister of Pakistan, and had stayed back in Islamabad. This kindled an antipathy in the minds of the BMF toward the tribals, specially the Chakmas. The Indian Government, long beset with the Mizo problem also had a case in the CHT which it considered to provide shelter and support to the Mizos at the instance of the Pakistani authority. Thus the Mujib Bahini (MB, a special force of the BMF comprising the Sheik Mujib loyalists) and India's Special Frontier Force (SFF) had a common cause in the CHT and its people. The commander of the SFF who actually raised and trained the MB and commanded the guerrilla operations against the Pakistani forces in the CHT noted that, "Both Mizos and Chakmas were to play a highly inimical role during our operations" (Uban, 1985 : 68). The contingents of the special Mujib Bahini were sent in different parts of Bangladesh as well as the CHT and Chittagong where they were carrying on strategic operations to halt the escape of the Pakistani forces through Burma and the Chittagong Port. Thus the "Mujeeb Bahini boys who had earlier infiltrated into Chittagong Port and City....captured the radio station....and even announced surrender by Pak troops", had also enabled the Indian SFF to combat the "....Mizos, Razakars, Chakmas and the stranded but armed men of the para-Military Forces roaming the ideal Guerrilla area of Chittagong Hill Tracts." (*Ibid.* :110, 112-3). It was perhaps in this context that the tribal people of the CHT became apprehensive of their future and were thereby constrained to make a formal representation to the newly established Government of Bangladesh for the autonomy of the people of CHT.

In early 1972, a delegation of the tribal leaders led by a Member of Parliament, placed a four-point charter of demands before Prime Minister Sheikh Mujibur Rahman, which included 'autonomy for the CHT', 'retention of the 1900 regulation' and 'a ban on the influx of non-tribal.[7] However, the demands were branded as rather secessionist and rejected outrightly. The Constitution of Bangladesh framed and passed towards the end of the same year (1972) virtually provided for opening up of the district for free movement and settlement by non-tribals. In Article 36 of the Constitution it was provided that,

> Subject to any reasonable restrictions imposed by law in the public interest, every citizen shall have the right to move freely throughout Bangladesh, to reside and settle in any place therein and to leave and re-enter Bangladesh. (GOB, 1986:14).

Indeed, such constitutional provisions may be said to have been warranted among other things by the economic crisis of a war-ravaged society, the problems of general rehabilitation, high population density and pressure of growth in the non-tribal plainland, national integration, etc. But the tribal leaders reckoned a clear threat from all of this and with a view to encounter the same came forward to politically organize the tribal people under the banner of the *Parbotya Chattagram Jana Samhati Samiti* (Chittagong Hill Tracts United Peoples Party/PCJSS) with a military wing called the Shanti Bahini (Peace Force/SB). Although formed in 1972, the PCJSS in pressing its political demands activated its armed wing, the SB in the mid-1970s. It may be noted here that in the CHT the armed uprisings of the tribals is not altogether an unprecedented phenomenon. During the long period of the English colonial rule, there were many incidents of armed conflicts between Kukies, Shendus, Houlong (Lushais) etc. tribes and the English forces between 1777 and 1898. It was only after 1898 that the incidents of armed confrontation came to an end (see GOB, 1971 : 28-32). The CHT Regulation 1900 if not in itself entirely an outcome of those conflicts but certainly mitigated the endemic conditions of those conflicts almost entirely. However, after several scores of years of peaceful existence the tribals have again taken to arms. Under changed political circumstances this time the leadership is assumed largely by the Chakmas and certainly in a more organized politico-strategic manner that suits the trends of modern armed struggle.

Indeed, it was well within the capacity of the leadership and the political Government of Awami League(AL) to settle the tribal question politically at its very inception in the early 1970s. But the AL Government did not do so and on the contrary, left the same to aggravate itself. Even during an election campaign in 1973 the Prime Minister advised the tribal people to forget their ethnic identity and become Bengalee.[8] The tribal leaders expressed their sharp reaction against this call of the Prime Minister both within and outside the National Assembly, pointing to the impracticable advise that blurs the distinction between citizenship and ethnicity. Virtually this, coupled with the increased settlement of non-tribals, led to gradual widening of the gap between the tribals and the Government. Owing to the gap, the tribal leadership had little difficulty in bringing the general tribal population to its side and thereby commanding their support in forging ahead the demands of the PCJSS. Even if this support is indirect, or not politically demonstrated through routine popular movements as occur in the cases of other groups and communities in the political arena of the larger society, there is little scope for denying its existence. Indeed, certain reflections of its existence are observed in the findings of a survey conducted on the formal and informal leaders of the CHT.[9]

The survey covered the leaders belonging to the Chakma and the Mong (the major populous tribe next to the Chakma) communities and the report was produced in 1979. It showed that 92 per cent of the respondents (Chakma leaders only, since they were the sole victims) reported of worsening of their economic condition following the construction of the Kaptai dam. Nearly 84 per cent of the respondents (both the Chakma and the Mong) were against Government interference in matters of tribal social control since according to them, the tribal methods are effective enough for the purpose. Likewise, 78 per cent of all leaders interviewed opined that the tribal chief/king should be given more power. This may be due to two factors. First, most of the leaders (92 per cent) have had no political party affiliation but had primordial loyalty to their king and the culture; and second, under general 'civil' administration, they might have thought, their own interests would be increasingly jeopardized vis-a-vis the increased influx of non-tribal settlers. Although all the formal leaders were more-or-less directly connected with the Government machineries, yet 72 per cent of them as well as 73 per cent of the informal leaders, from both the Chakma and the Mong communities categorically disapproved the settlement of outsiders in the CHT district.

Settlement Issue and Unsettled Problems

Perhaps, the settlement of non-tribals is the crux of the whole tribal question which emerged in the wake of the administrative changes after the departure of the colonial rulers. Indeed, the ethno-demographic characteristics of the district have undergone remarkable changes with the influx of the non-tribals. But the data particularly since the time of first census after Bangladesh are either imprecise or inadequate owing much to the state of law and order situation prevailing therein. Nevertheless, it is very evident that the demographic composition has drastically changed to the discomfort and / or disadvantage of the indigenous ethnic population.[10] Thus the proportion of the total tribal population has declined from 99.2 per cent in 1872, 73.2 per cent in 1961 to that of 53.5 per cent in 1981. On the other hand, as to ethno-religious composition, the proportion of Muslims has increased from 0.6 per cent in 1872, 11.8 per cent in 1961 to 34.5 per cent in 1981. The increase of the Christians from only 4 individuals in 1872 to 19,000, or 2.5 per cent in 1981 is perhaps far less an addition from outside than from the conversion of the indigenous people and the natural increase thereupon. Even the increase of the proportion of the Hindu too, may have been considerably influenced by the factor of natural increase. However, seemingly neither of these two categories of people has aroused the resentment or resistance of the tribals. It is the Muslim settlers whose number has increased from 45,000 in 1961 to 260,000 in 1981, or more than that subsequently, have been the principal source of the whole trouble. As alleged by the PCJSS:

> The policy of changing the demographic character of CHT...particularly from 1978, the ignoble plan of Bangladesh Government to settle thousands of...Bengali Muslims...with financial assistance in the CHT has led to the forcible occupation of Jumma lands by these infiltrators with the direct help from the Bangladesh armed forces. By 1985, the present Government...has settled about 400,000...Bengali Muslims...in the CHT constituting 40%-46% of the total population (PCJSS, 1987 : 1).

Alongside the settlement issue, the Government expenditure of the physical infrastructure and economic development projects, have increased the fear and suspicions of the tribal population which is adequately reflected in the printed statements of PCJSS and its front organizations. Thus, by way of a rejoinder to the President's speech in the National Assembly on 24th January, 1987 which had a reference to the material improvement of the tribals, it is stated that,

> The Chittagong Hill Tracts Development Board has spent a large share of its budget on the development of the rehabilitated non-tribals and the military...so far no development project can be mentioned which has benefited the tribals. On the contrary, by creating the so-called *Jautha Khamar* in the name of development and rehabilitiation of the tribals in the relatively backward areas, the Government is severely controlling their total life-style. Now it is very clear that the development of the Chittagong Hill Tracts and the development of the tribals are not the same thing...The tribals are only a small part of the total population of the country. (Dipen Dewan N.D.)

The alleged measures may have had contributed to the overall deterioration of the situation in the CHT. In its Report of 1985 Amnesty noted that,

> Amnesty International continued to receive reports of human rights violations in the Chittagong Hill Tracts, an area in the southeast of country...Conflict between...tribal inhabitants and Bengalis settled there under Government policy directives persisted and there was fighting between the tribal Shanti Bahini (Peace Force) and the police and

> army. Amnesty International received information on arbitrary arrests and alleged extra-judicial executions committed by law enforcement personnel during 1984. (Amnesty International; Publications, 1985:201).

Amnesty International in one of its published reports has also mentioned about the mass migration of the indigenous tribal people. In the 1988 report it is noted that,

> The conflict in the Chittagong Hill Tracts resulted in thousands of tribal villagers crossing into India in 1986 and early 1987. By mid-February, Indian officials were estimating their number at some 40,000 and the Bangladesh Government at approximately 25,000 (Amnesty International publication, 1988 : 151).

Indeed, the intermittent armed raids of the SB of PCJSS and the Government forces on each other, often involving the unarmed tribal villagers and Bengali settlers, have never ceased. The Amnesty's Report of 1989 notes that,

> In the Chittagong Hill Tracts there were further attacks on the law enforcement personnel and others by the armed tribal opposition Shanti Bahini (Peace Forces) which resulted in a number of deaths and other casualties. (Amnesty International Publications, 1989:163).

The Amnesty reports adequately testify to the fact that the incidents of armed conflicts have not diminished despite the fact that since the formation of a National Committee in May 1984, to establish official contact and hold formal talks with the PCJSS, both sides - the Government and the latter - met several times, or six times to be precise. Indeed the outcome of those meetings have reportedly been nil as the 'five-point demands' of the PCJSS and the 'nine-point outlines' of the Government were irreconcilable to each other. The PCJSS alleged that the talks were rendered fruitless despite the fact that "...in the greater interest of the country and on the request of the Bangladesh Government the JSS had withdrawn its demand for provincial autonomy with a separate legislature, and had placed a modified form of five-point charter of demands to the Bangladesh Government delegation at the 6th formal dialogue." (PCJSS, 1989:2). It is alleged that not only the modified five-point demands were rejected on constitutional ground, but on the eve of the 7th formal dialogue, Bangladesh Government unilaterally passed four local Government bills in the National Assembly, three for the three present districts created out of the CHT and one special Bill for the hill district.[11] According to the PCJSS "these bills are conspiratorial, motivated and contrary to democracy" (*ibid*). Nevertheless, under provisions of those bills, elections to three hill district councils were held in June 1989 which was rejected but not resisted by the PCJSS itself. Nevertheless, the election does not seem to have resolved the problem. It is manifested in the continued armed confrontations between the SB of the PCJSS and Government forces with increased attacks on the non-combatant people, reports of which have become quite frequent in the recent months. Indeed, all these spring from the fact that the tribal question is not yet resolved.

Epilogue

From the above, one thing is clear that certain forcible actions backed among others, by economic considerations of a dominant State came into direct conflict with the articulated aspirations of minority ethnic populations of the hill districts of Chittagong which over a period of some eighteen years, has witnessed little progress toward a political solution but much escalation towards what may be called a local war. It appears that the state is resolute and unyielding to its own policy-predilections: "The people of Bangladesh have to share the available resources in an equitable manner within the severe economic constraints...", and that it is, "...considered to be contrary to the Constitution to prevent any Bangladeshi from settling and buying land in any part of the country" (cited in Amnesty International, 1986 :7). Compared to this, the PCJSS has of late shown greater flexibility in their political demands, though not in armed actions. Indeed, PCJSS has never been secessionist and even by 1989 had withdrawn its earlier demand of 'autonomy with provisions for separate legislature.' In 1988, the PCJSS reiterated that, 'the integration, culture, social organisation, language, customs, proverbs i.e. the national entity of the Jumma people is on the verge of extinction owing to the larger nation's enthnocentrism. But the Jumma people too, have the fundamental right to live in the free and sovereign Bangladesh with human dignity. The JSS i.e. the Jumma people is not involved in any separatist movement' (PCJSS:1988-16-17). It seems that not much efforts have been made to get the best out of that position of the PCJSS. This has been evident in the conflicting relations of the two sides and continued tension in the entire CHT.

It is true that so far as the Government can contain the armed confrontations with the SB within the hill districts of the CHT, it can continue its own programmes in its own manner. But given the geographical (geo-political as well) location of the CHT that kind of attitude may prove to be too costly at the end. It is well known that the CHT is located on the sensitive borders of India and Burma having their own pressures from the Mizos and the Karen Muslims respectively. Even apart from this the fact that an indigenous tribal population is fighting for their rights against the national military and para-military forces is potent enough in itself to arouse international concern at one or other stage of the conflict. In that case, the problem can of its own accord get tangled in multinational tamperings to the detriment of the respective interests of both the Government of Bangladesh and the PCJSS. This makes it imperative that the local, national problem should be resolved within the national society and should not in any case be allowed to slip out of its boundary and thereby beyond its control. The fact that the smaller ethnic populations of the CHT have suffered a loss of their 'special area' status after the creation of Pakistan State and thereafter a total disruption of their social ecology, and then, an ethno-demographic imbalance in the Bangladesh period with unprecedented consequences for the economy and culture of the entire tribal population, provided sufficient grounds for organised resistance as is being given by the PCJSS after what may be called the mode of adaptation of a disgruntled group with the modern bourgeos nationalism whether in a mature or nascent state. Given its combat experience of the last one and a half decades on the military and political fronts as well the base of its armed operations in an otherwise difficult hilly region at the juncture of hospitable international borders, the resistance movement of the PCJSS has also a chance of the survival and continuation for almost indefinite period. But with some pertinent constitutional amendments or special provision for safeguarding the interests of tribal populations the entire arena of conflict can be saved from turning into a zone of such protracted war involving international interests. Even from considerations like the security of the vital industrial installations in the CHT which are indispensible for sustaining the na-

sentatives, the PCJSS) equipped with very modern means of destruction at its disposal constitutes in itself a threat of formidable magnitude. All these considerations, sooner or later may help to find out a reasonable solution of the question at issue, but the sooner it is found out the better.

Notes

1. Pointing to this aspect of the revolutionary role of the early European bourgeoisie Marx and Engels noted that, "The bourgeoisic keeps more and more doing away with the scattered state of the population, of the means of production, and of property...The necessary consequence of this was political centralization. Independent, or but loosely connected provinces, with separate interests, laws, Governments and systems of taxation, became lumped together into one nation, with one Government, one code of laws, one national class-interest, one frontier and one customs-tariffs" (Marx and Engels, 1962(1):38). Conforming to the view of Marx and Engels, it was observed by Lenin that, "The most profound economic factors drive towards this goal (i.e. the formation of a National State) and, therefore, for the whole of Western Europe, nay, for the entire civilized world, the National State is typical and normal for the capitalist period" (Lenin, 1976(1) : 568).

2. This aspect was given a brilliant exposition by Geoffrey Kay whose original premise was that, "...capital created underdevelopment not because it exploited the underdeveloped world, but because it did not exploit it enough." (see Kay, 1975 : X).

3. Thus V.R. Raghavaiah observed that, "...trouble was undoubtedly brewing virtually in every part of the country, among almost every section of the people, like the peasants, intelligentsia, trading communities, the military, the scions of native royal dynasties...The revolts of the tribal people were not isolated on the other hand, shared many features in common with the revolts of non-tribal, agrarian and small trading communities." (Raghavaiah, 1982 : 17-18).

4. On this score Raghavaiah noted that, "One of the main reasons why tribal people in this sub-continent feel disunited, isolated, and thwarted, is the gradual and steady temptation to which they succumbed in the past one hundred years, by allowing themselves to be easily converted by powerful religious Missions, foreign as well as indigenous, not because they really believed that their pattern of faith was inferior to that of others, but because through conversion they fondly hoped to secure economic betterment, freedom from exploitation and relief from the Sowcar's or Mahajan's (money-lender) harassment. The earlier Christian missionaries who felt that the tribal areas served as fertile fields for their proelytizing operations, worked in close cooperation with the British administrators, that the impression was inevitably created that redress from wrongs could be secured quicker and more effectively from the Government through the intervention and influence of these intermediaries" (*Ibid.*, pp.15-16).

5. The newly established modern industrial establishments of the area included: (a) Karnafuli Multipurpose Project (Kaptai Hydroelectric Project) (b) Karnafuli Paper Mills, Ltd. (c) Karnafuli Rayon and Chemicals Ltd. (d) Karnafuli Project Mechanical Division Workshop, (e) Eastern Pakistan Timber and Plywood Industries Co. Ltd., (f) Sterling Plywood Products Ltd., (g) Kaptal Boat Building Industrial Corporation, (h) Azizuddin Cigarette Industries Ltd. (i) Sattar Match Works Ltd., (j) Wagasera Tea Estate. Besides, numerous small scale industries were established which in 1962-63 fell under five broad types viz. (a) Agriculture and Food Products, (b) Metal works, (c) Cane, Bamboo and Wood Products, (d) Pharmaceutical, Chemical and Cosmetics, and (e) Textile Industries. (GOB, 1971 : 154, 157).

6. The construction of the Karnafuli Multipurpose Hydroelectric Project and its reservoir displaced over 100,000 people, i.e. more than one fourth of the then CHT's population, and most of the victims were Chakma. Further, "the inundation threw over 54,000 acres of plough lands out of cultivation. This area constitutes 40 per cent of the total settled cultivable land of the district" (*Ibid*, p. 42). The Project not only completely 'submerged 125 mauzas and houses of 18,000 families' but in addition, "it submerged 10.5 square miles of Reserved Forest. Fertile valleys of the district like Karnafuli, Heingkhong, Chengi, Kasslong and Maini have gone under submersion" (*Ibid*, 126).

7. The four-point charter of demands covered the following: "autonomy for the Chittagong Hill Tracts, together with provision for a separate legislative body; retention of the provisions of the 1900 regulation in the Bangladesh Constitution; the continuation of the offices of the traditional tribal chiefs; a constitutional provision restricting amendment of the 1900 Regulation and the imposition of a ban on the influx of non-tribals into the area" (Amnesty International, 1986 : 4).

8. In a mammoth public meeting on February 16, 1973 at Rangamati the Prime Minister declared that, "To us the people of Hill Tracts are as good Bengalis as other sons of the motherland..." The Prime Minister told the Hill Tracts people that the British rulers and the Pakistani rulers had given them a secondary position by treating them as a tribe. But his Government had accepted them as equal members of the Bengali nation with a guarantee of equal rights and opportunities..."So I shall not dishonour you by calling you tribal people, he said." (The Bangladesh Observer, Dacca, February 17, 1973).

9. The survey findings are shown in the following table:

Opinion of the formal and informal leaders of the Chittagong Hill Tracts on some selected issues and problems.*

	Formal Leaders			*Informal Leaders*		
	Chakma	Mong	Total	Chakma	Mong	Total
	N=52 %	N=48 %	100 %	N=132 %	N=68 %	200 %
Reported that the economic condition of the tribal people was better before construction of the Kaptai dam (pp.127/221)	93	---	---	---	91	---
Reported that tribal methods of social control are effective enough and no Government interference necessary (pp.107/212)	90	80	85	86	75	82
Reported that tribal chief/king should be given more power by the Government (pp.88/184)	83	81	82	75	73	74
Reported to have no political party affiliation (pp.113/193)	100	96	98	84	84	84
Disapprove settlement by outsiders (pp.84/223)	71	73	72	72	75	73

Source: Chowdhury and others (Mimeo.), 1979.

* Formal leaders are the elected Chairman and members of the Union Council, and appointed Headmen. Informal leaders are persons so recognized by at least 10 individuals during construction of the sampling frame of the survey. Figures in parenthesis indicate the page numbers in the study report referred to above.

10. The significance of the settlement issue for the tribal question specially in its demographic dimension can be grasped from the following table:

Ethno-religions composition of population *in the Chitagong Hill Tracts.*

	1872[a]	%	1961[b]	%	1981[c]	%
Tribals (Buddhists and others)	62,527	99.2	281,953	73.2	402,000	53.5
Muslims	381	0.6	45,322	11.8	259,000	34.5
Hindus	142	0.2	47,644	12.4	71,000	9.5
Christians	4	0.0	10,161	2.6	19,000	2.5
Total	63,054	100.0	385,079	100.0	751,00	100.0

Sources : a. W.W Hunter, 1973
b. Government of Pakistan, 1961
c. B.B.S., 1984.

11. The bills are called the (a) Rangamati Parbatya Zilla Sthaniya Sarkar Parishad, 1989, (b) Khagrachari Parbatya Zilla Sthaniya Sarkar Parishad, 1989, (c) Bandarban Parbatya Zilla Sthaniya Sarkar Parishad, 1989, and (d) Parbatya Zilla Special Bill, 1989 (PCJSS : 1989).

References

Amnesty International 1985 : *Amnesty International Report.*

- 1986 : *Unlawful Killings and Torture in the Chittagong Hill Tracts.*

- 1988 : *Amnesty International Report .*

- 1989 : *Amnesty International Report.*

BBS, 1984 : *Bangladesh Population Census 1981- Analytical Findings and National Tables*, Dhaka.

Chowdhury, R.I., and others 1979 : *Tribal Leadership and Political Integration - A Case Study of Chakma and Mong Tribes of Chittagong Hill Tracts*, Faculty of Social Science, University of Chittagong.

Depen Dewan, N.D. : *Chittagong Hill Tracts Situation etc.* Dhaka, President, Dhaka Tribal Students Union.

Engels, F. 1976 : *Auti-Duhning*, Peking, Foreign Languages Press.

Govt. of Bangladesh 1971 : *Bangladesh District Gazetteers-Chittagong Hill Tracks*, Dhaka BGP.

1986 : *The Constitution of the People's Republic of Bangladesh*, Dhaka, M/o Law and Parliamentary Affairs.

Grigulevich, I.R. and Kozlov, S.Y.(eds.) 1981 : *Ethno-Cultural Processes and National Problems*, Moscow, Progress Publisher.

Hunter, W.W. 1973 : *A Statistical Account of Bengal* Vol.No. VI Delhi, D.K. Publishing House.

Kay, G. 1975 : *Development and Underdevelopment A Marxist Analysis*, London The Macmillan Ltd.

Lenin, V.I. 1976 : *Selected Works, Vol 1*, Moscow, Progress Publishers.

Marx, K. and Engels, F.	1962:	*Selected Works, Vol.1* Moscow Foreign Languages Publishing House.
PCJSS,	1987:	*An Account of Genocide and Atrocities Committed by Bangladesh Forces and Illegal Bangalee Muslim Infiltrators in Chittagong Hill Tracts, Information Department.*
	1988:	*JSS Statement on the Dialogues held between the JSS and the Government of the People's Republic of Bangladesh.*
	1989:	*An Urgent Statement of the Jana Samhiti Samiti on the Parbatya Zilla Parishad Bills placed in the Jatiya Sangsad (Parliament) by Bangladesh Government, Central Committee.*
Raghavaiah, V.R.	1982:	Background of Tribal Struggles in India in A.R. Desai (Ed.), *Peasant Struggles in India*, Bombay, Oxford University Press.
Uban, S.S. Major General(Retd)	1985:	*Phantoms of Chittagong* — The Fifth Army in Bangladesh, New Delhi, Allied Publishers Pvt. Ltd.

UNDPI, 1988 : The Progress that Kills in *Development Forum*, Vol.XVI,No.4 (July-August).

World Bank 1987 : *World Development Report*.

3
THE INDIGENOUS PEOPLE OF THE CHITTAGONG HILL TRACTS: RESTRUCTURING OF POLITICAL SYSTEM

ADITYA KUMAR DEWAN

The Chittagong Hill Tracts (CHT) is the south-eastern most district (also the largest district) in Bangladesh; covering about a land area of 13,191 Km^2 (11 per cent of 143, 998 km^2,the total area of Bangladesh). The estimated total population of the CHT in 1987 was 1.2 million (1 per cent of 105 millions estimated total population of Bangladesh).[1] It is inhabited by twelve indigenous groups, numbering approximately 600,000 and a non-indigenous group (Bengalee) about 600,000 in 1987. The indigenous groups are the Chakma, Marma, Tripura or Mrong, Bawm, Lushai, Pankhua, Khumi, Kheyang, Mro, Reang and the Tanchangya. They are different from the majority Bengali population of Bangladesh in respect to race, language, culture, religion and ethnicity. In fact, they are part of the current great population that extends the vast regions from Tibet to Indo-China. The Chakma, Marma, Tanchangya and the Chak are Buddhists; the Reang and the Tripura are Hindus, the Lushai, Bawm, Kheyang and the Pankhua are Christians; and the Mro and the Khumi have their own religion. The non-indigenous groups are the Muslims (majority), Hindu, Buddhist and the Christian and they all speak Bengali and belong to the same racial and ethnic group. The Chakma and the Tanchagya speak a language which is very close to the regional local dialects of the Bengali inhabitants of southern Chittagong which belongs to the Indo-Aryan family of languages. The Marma and the Chaks speak Arkanese (Burmese, Tibeto-Burman); the Tripura and the Reang, Tripuri (Bodo, Tibeto Burman); the Bawm, Pankhua, Lushai, Khyang, Mro and the Khumi all speak Kuki-Chin languages belonging to the Tibeto-Burman language family.

The main occupation of the indigenous people is subsistence agriculture. All the ridge-top-living groups (Lushai, Bawm, Mro, Khumi, Pankhua, Reang and the Kheyang) and some Tripura, Tanchangya, Marma, Chak and the Chakma practise swidden cultivation (locally known as *Jhum* and the farmers are called *Jhumia).* The majority of the Chakma, Marma and the Tripura practise wet rice cultivation in the flat land and they have ownership of land they cultivate. Besides this, a large number of population have adopted both swidden and plough cultivation (mixed farming). A very small number of indigenous people (about 1 per cent) are urban dwellers and their main occupation are service, business and wage labour and petty commodity trade. However, many of the rural indigenous people also practise horticulture and fruit-gardening. The occupation of the non-indigenous people are mainly service, business, fishing and agriculture. They occupy the top civil, administrative and military positions, and as well as 90 percent of all employment in the banks, insurance, transportation, civil service and in industries and factories. Thus all traders, merchants, money lenders, service holders, workers, shop-keepers, landowners, etc. are virtually all Bengalees, and therefore they are owners of major means of production in the CHT.

Pre-Colonial Social Formation

From time immemorial the hills and mountain ranges to the east coast of Bay of the Bengal have been the home of several groups of indigenous people belonging to the main population groups (Sino-Tibetan and Tibeto-Burman) of upper Burma and North-eastern India. The first references to these people are found in revenue records (Committee of Revenue 1784) of the early Moghul administration in Chittagong and then in the early records of British East India Company beginning in 1801 (Macrae, 1801; Lewin, 1869; Selections, 1929; Hunter, 1876; Hutchinson, 1909). The colonial records provide a greater detail of the internal socio-economic conditions of the people. Thus, the historical records beginning with the Moghuls and then with the British unmistakably establish a few facts regarding the indigenous people prior to the establishment of British rule in the CHT.

First, the indigenous people have been living politically independent lives and the area (which now forms the CHT) had never been under any state or Kingdom. Furthermore, neither of these groups, however, had developed any form of kingdom or state structure of their own, nor was there any territorially or jurisdictionally defined boundary of the area they inhabited. However, each of the group had occupied an area tolerably well known but not well defined. Secondly, the Moghul records show that they (especially the Chakma and the Marma) had regular barter exchange and trade relations with the neighbouring people of the plains of the Chittagong sea coast. Their main items of exchange were cotton, sesame, timber, bamboo, ivory, rattons, honey, dugout canoes, vegetables and other forest products. In exchange for these (as there was no money current among them) items, they imported salt, dried fish, spices, sugar, kerosene, cooking oil, cooking pots, jewellery, clothing, water containers, ritual goods (such as brass bells, candles etc.) and iron implements (dagger, knives and blades) etc. Thirdly, the main subsistence pattern of the people was based on swidden cultivation, associated with some secondary activities such as hunting, gathering, fishing and trapping. At this stage, plough cultivation, similar to plains people of Bengal was not practised. Until the last quarter of the 19th century the density of population in the CHT was less than five persons per Km^2 (see Table-1). This had allowed to maintain a balance between the size of population and availability of enough land to everyone for swidden farming without disrupting the normal bush fallow period of 15-20 years. Land was communally owned as there was no private ownership land developed before the beginning of the British rule. Thus, anyone had rights to use land anywhere in the area that the user saw fit. Fourthly, the traditional social organizations of these people was based on autonomous village communities identified by lineage, clan and tribal groups where each group was headed by its own chief who received a yearly gift or tribute in kind (such as rice, rice bear, fowl, etc.) from his people. The surplus appropriated by these chiefs did not lead to any significant inequalities as the surplus collected by them was periodically redistributed through the rites and rituals, ceremonies and feasts of merits. Finally, the major contradictions of the pre-colonial CHT social formations was in part of the existence of inter-tribal warfare, feuding, predation, headhunting, slavery, debt, bondage, plundering expeditions and raids over plains.

TABLE 1

Population of the Chittagong Hill Tracts from 1872-1981 by ethnic groups and density per Km²

Ethnic Groups	1872	1901	1951	1974	1981
Bengali	1,097	8,762	26,150	135,673	304, 873
Chakma	28,097	44,329	124,762	-------	212,577
Marma	22,060	34,706	65,889	-------	122,734
Tripura	8,100	23,341	37,246	-------	54, 375
Mro	2,378	10,540	16,121	-------	17,811
Tanchangya	-------	-------	8,313	-------	17,696
Bawm	305	696	977	-------	5,733
Reang	-------	-------	1,011	-------	4,011
Pankhua	177	241	627	-------	2,278
Kheyang	306	416	1,300	-------	1,422
Khumi	534	1,053	1,951	-------	1,188
Lushai	-------	678	3,341	-------	1,041
Chak	-------	-------	-------	-------	910
Total	63,054	124,762	287,688	508,199	746,649
Total Indigenous	61,957	116,000	261,538	372,526	441,776
% of total pop.	98.26	92.63	90.91	73.30	59.16
Total Non-Indigenous	1,097	8,762	26,150	135,673	304,875
% of total pop.	1.73	0.67	9.08	26.29	40.83
Density Per Km²	4	9	22	39	57

Source :Hunter, 1876: 37-38; Hutchinson 1909: 14-16; Bessaignet 1958:4; Government of Bangladesh 1981:29, 1974:47. Ethnic distribution in the Census of 1881, 1891, 1911, 1921, 1931, 1941, 1961 and 1974 are not available. In the 1872

Census, the total Bengali population was 524 out of 1097. The others were Europeans, Assamese and Nepalese origin employed in Government service.

Therefore, as we can see the social formation of the CHT indigenous people was one based on chieftainship, nominal forms of tribute, swidden cultivation and surplus production of commodities with exchange value for barter trade only. Private property was not in existence and the class formation was based on the collection of tribute through hereditary lines. This form of class / "caste" relation appears to have resulted from trade relations with the Moghuls (tribute tax). The mode of production therefore resembles neither Marx's notion of Asiatic Mode of Production nor the European Feudal Mode. What changes took place under colonial rule? How did they influence the relative autonomy of the Hill Tracts people ?

Colonial Transformation and its Impact

The British were the first foreign group to penetrate the interior of the CHT in the 1860's and in the years that followed. By the end of the 19th century, numerous indigenous groups living in the North-eastern frontier of India and Upper Burma were pacified militarily, subjugated and their territories were integrated into the British Empire and its capitalist economy. In 1860, the CHT was constituted into a separate district within the boundary of the Province of Bengal Presidency and established direct colonial administration in the area. Following the military posts, police stations, hospitals, schools, commercial and trading centres were constituted at the major points of river communication. Secondly, a district administrator, designated as the Deputy Commissioner (DC) was appointed with special power to administer the CHT. This power enabled the DC to remove all non-indigenous people from the CHT area. This special power (not given to the DC's in other parts of Bengal) gave the DC an enormous power in exercising his power and authority in the CHT. The CHT was divided into three main administrative sub-divisions with its main headquarter first at Chandraghona and then at Rangamati. Thirdly, in juxtaposition with this structure, the CHT was also divided into three main "Circles"; the Chakma (the Central CHT), the Mong (the Northern CHT) and the Bohmang (the Southern CHT). Each circle was headed by a tribal chief. In turn, each Circle was also divided into several *Mouzas* (an area consisting of several villages) headed by a *Mouza Headman*. Tribal chiefs were appointed by the Governor General of India and the *Mouza Headmen* were appointed by the tribal chiefs with the consultation of the DC. The main function of the chiefs and headmen were to collect revenue from the swidden farmers. The *Mouza* headman's duty was to collect a certain amount of taxes from each head of the family in the village who cultivated *Jhum* land. Tax collected from the swidden farmers were divided among the headmen, circle chiefs and the colonial administration. The share of each party was this; headmen 30 per cent, circle chiefs 50 per cent and the Government 20 per cent. Besides this function, the chiefs and headmen were given responsibility to manage their own internal affairs (except criminal cases) in respect to their language, culture and religion whereas, the district administration was responsible for maintaining law and order and to ensure overall administration of the district (Lewin 1869, Hutchinson 1909, Bessaignet 1958). Fourthly, the pre-existing practice of slavery, debt bondage, headhunting, inter-tribal warfare etc. were banned by the colonial administration (May 1981:218). Fifthly, 3,215 Km^2 area was declared Government forest reserve (Master Plan 1967 : 6) where swidden farming and habitation were totally banned. Furthermore, nearly 4,047 hectares of valley land (Khisa 1970:25) have been converted into plough land thus reducing the amount of land available for swidden farming in relation to population increase in the CHT (see Table-1). Sixthly, an indigenous police force was created in 1881. The members of the force were recruited from indigenous groups. However, after the constitution of the CHT many people from the plain had started to migrate into the CHT. In the 1890's, more than half of the 3,000 hectares of reclaimed plough lands were occupied by the Bengalee migrants (Mey 1984 : 22). This led to the promulgation of the famous Regulation 1 of 1900 Act. The Act prohibited migration and settlement of the non-indigenous people from outside the CHT and banned all sale, transfer and lease of lands to outsiders. This "Special Status" of the CHT further strengthened by the Government of India Act of 1935 which designated the CHT a "Totally Excluded Area". This gave the local chiefs and the DC more power and autonomy to run the administration of the CHT by which the DC and the chiefs were responsible to the Central Government of India and not to the Bengal Provincial Government. Thus the CHT became a "Centrally Administered Area" within the British Indian Dominion similar to those of other "Tribal Areas" of Northeastern and Northwestern Frontiers of India. Finally, with the promulgation of the Indian Independence Act of 1947, the British rule in the Indian sub-continent formally came to an end in August 1947, by which India was partitioned into two independent States: India and Pakistan. The partition was based on religion by which Hindu majority areas became part of India and the Muslim majority areas formed Pakistan and the other areas (nor Hindu, nor Muslim) were given option to join either of the States. But the CHT was awarded to East Pakistan by the Boundry Commission Chairman, C. Redcliffe. This was done against the will of the CHT people because the CHT representatives had been lobbying the Indian Congress and the British Government for the inclusion of the CHT in the Indian Dominion. This was because they had very little in common with the majority of the Bengalees of East Pakistan whereas they had more cultural, religious, linguistic and ethnic affinities with the neighbouring population of North eastern India and Upper Burma. The inclusion of the CHT with East Pakistan was a turning point in the subsequent history of struggle for survival of the indigenous people of the CHT (CHT conf. 1986 : 27).

Now it is necessary to briefly outline the major implications of British rule in the CHT. Firstly, the annexation of their territories with colonial State led to the break up of relative isolation of indigenous societies and established stable connection with the outer world; it brought them into the mainstream of colonial administrative set up, policy and programs. Secondly, colonization of the CHT put an end to the political independence of each group and domination of the powerful groups over the weaker groups. This led to the cessation of inter-tribal warfare, headhunting, slavery, debt bondage and plundering expeditions over the plains of the Chittagong sea coast. The pacification of these groups also led to the decay of the traditional military organisation, loosening of rigid kinship system, loosening of the legitimacy of the strong chief's office (Mey 1981 : 218) and so on. Thirdly, the political system of the CHT was restructured without radically changing the pre-colonial system because the chiefs, *Dewans, Talukders* and *Roazas* were reintegrated partly with the colonial administration. The same tribal chiefs, clan and lineage chiefs of the pre-colonial tribal elites became the Circle chiefs, *Mouza* headmen under the new colonial system. By restructuring the pre-existing system, the importance of the smaller groups and their chiefs declined. Because, under the new system, the Chakma, Mong and the Bohmang chiefs were empowered to exercise power and authority and to collect taxes within the geographical jurisdiction of his Circle which he did not have during pre-colonial period. Furthermore, the chiefs of smaller groups were not recognized by the colonial administration. Fourthly, creation of forest reserve and conversion of valley flat lands into plough land led to the reduction of swidden lands resulting in the pressure on land and shrinkage of *Jhum* cycle from 15-20 years down to the 8-10 years. But in the swidden land, the rights of usufruct remained unchanged. On the contrary, the introduction of plough cultivation led to the emergence of private property in land in the hills resulting in social and economic differentiation among the various groups and as well as within the numbers of the same group.

Thus, a large section of swidden farmers transformed into peasant cultivators and formed village communities similar to those of the plains of Bengal. Besides the Chakma, Marma and the Tripura, the other groups living on the mountain tops, still practise swidden farming, and none of them have adopted plough cultivation. Thus, the introduction of plough agriculture laid the foundation for a radical transformation in the indigenous social structure and reinforced the creation of private property in land. This was also accompanied by the introduction of money in the hills which facilitated paying taxes increasing commercial and other economic activities in the area. Finally, as a result of opening up the hills to outsiders for trade and commercial activities, many innocent local people fell victim to money lenders, traders, merchants, shopkeepers and so on. Although migration and settlement prohibited under 1900 Act, many Bengalees from the plains moved to the hills as traders, agricultural labourers, boatmen, shopkeepers, carpenters, blacksmiths, goldsmiths, silversmiths, teachers, porters, contractors, money lenders, Government service holders, hawkers and religious preachers. As a result, they dominated the whole economy of the CHT especially in business, service, transportation and in the informal sectors of the economy in the urban areas. The local people especially the swidden farmers and the peasant cultivators became the petty commodity producers and suppliers of agricultural products and consumers of durable consumer goods of the Bengalees. The non-indigenous people became the buyers, sellers and consumers of agricultural products and as well as consumer durable goods. Except in the agricultural sector, the Bengalees had been able to establish (such as wholesale, retail, transport, credits, and services) domination and monopolies virtually in all sectors of the economy of the CHT. (CHT Conf. 1986 : 28).

Pakistani Rule: The Second Colonization of the CHT

Under the Pakistani rule the subjugation of the native peoples and the undermining of their economic base was extended even further. The most important impacts were: (1) abolition of their pre-existing legal rights and "tribal status"; (2) opening up of their lands and resources to national and international bourgeoisie for commercial exploitation and establishment of industries; (3) weakening of their traditional institutions; and (4) migration of non-indigenous people into the CHT. The CHT lost its autonomy and special status as "Excluded Area" or "Tribal Area" under a Constitutional amendment of 1963, which came into force in 1964 (AI 1986 : 4). In 1963, a Bengalee member and Speaker of the Pakistan National Assembly who became the Acting President of Pakistan during the then President's visit to a foreign country, abolished the "Special Status" of the CHT by amending the 1962 Constitution. The establishment of industries and factories in the CHT (during the "Decade of Development" period from 1958-1968) by the Government of Pakistan with the help of foreign aid and leading Pakistani industrialists opened up the land, forest and other natural resources to outsiders. Finally, the traditional indigenous institutions had been severely affected by the introduction of Basic Democracy (BD) in 1959 [2]. The BD system led to the weakening of traditional headman and chief system. Now a BD member has more power and function in the villages than a *Mouza* Headman because all development work programmes of the Government are carried out through the Union Council Chairman and the Council members in collaboration with the Government appointed Circle Officers (Development). Secondly, the income of the headmen and the chiefs had also been reduced to a great extent due to the decline of swidden farmers and swidden farming. This decline was caused by the Hydro-electric Dam built in 1960 which led to the shrinkage of swidden lands, loss of fertility of land and displacement of swidden farmers. Finally, migration of non-indegenous people had seriously affected the traditional life of the indigenous people.

Crime, alcoholism, prostitution, cheating, robbery and other vices had increased in the urban areas with the increased contact with the outside people which were unthinkable during the colonial period (personal observation). In 1947, a large number of Muslim refugees from India came to East Pakistan. Approximately 100 non-Bengalee, Behari Muslims had been relocated in the CHT (Government of Pakistan 1951). The abolition of "Special Status" in 1964 i.e. lifting of legal barriers led to the migration of unknown members of the Bengalee in the CHT. But the major Bengalee migration took place at this time in the major commercial centres, administrative and urban centres. There were major Bengalee population growth in the main urban and industrial centre at Rangamati, Kaptai, Chandraghona, Ramgarh, Bandarban and other weekly market places throughout the CHT (personal observation).

Thus, as a result of urbanisation, industrialization, migration of outsiders, the traditional social structure of indigenous people had been totally disrupted, their economy was marginalized, impoverished a large number of people and subordinated them to the rampaging market economy. They became the object of exploitation by traders, contractors, money lenders, bureacrats, police and other agencies and private profiteers. Due to these factors, they had been further marginalized and pushed to the wall in such a way that for many they had nothing left but to fight for their rights and more fundamentally for their cultural survival.

Bangladesh Rule

The history of the CHT since the liberation of Bangladesh in 1971 is the history of continuous struggle for survival of the indigenous peoples against the policies of the successive Governments of Bangladesh. Over the last seventeen years there have been numerous reports of inter-ethnic violence, conflicts between armed forces and rebels and new settlers migration into the CHT. These have been well documented by various international human rights organizations and international press. (AI, 1986; IWGIA, 1986; ILO, 1986; SI, 1984; Anti-Slavery Society, 1984; Canada-Asia Working Groups; 1987; Globe and Mail, June 22, 1986; New York Times, Oct., 1986; Le Monde (Paris), April 21, 1987; India Today, March, 15, 1987).

Throughout the Pakistani rule which dramatically weakened social and economic organisations of the indigenous peoples, certain leaders of the indigenous peoples supported the Pakistani Government for fear of losing their chieftainship and the associated property and "power" base. With the successful revolution of Bangladesh one of these chiefs left for Pakistan, leaving his subjects to suffer racially and politically. It was perceived that many native people supported Pakistan during the first liberation war. For example, with the help of the Pakistan Army during the Bangladesh liberation war in 1971, approximately 50,000 Bengali Muslims from the neighbouring districts of Noakhali and Chittagong occupied the farmlands of many indigenous peoples who had fled during the war to India from Ramgarh area. When they returned home after the liberation, many of them could not recover their lands. (SI, 1984:11). Sometimes after the withdrawal and defeat of the Pakistani Army and independence of Bangladesh, indigenous people of CHT were reported to have faced unlawful and unjust behaviour. These kinds of actions were the immediate cause for the rise, growth and birth of *Shanti Bahini* (means Peace Force), the main Guerilla force and the formation of Parbattya Chattagram Jana Sangha (PCJSS), the main political party of the indigenous people. Up to this point, the native peoples had no autonomous true political or economic representative due to the colonial policy of "indirect rule" where chieftains were created to service first the Moghul system of trade and then to affect the levying of taxes for the British and Pakistani colonial system both operating within the context of western economic imperialism.

Delegations led by M.N. Larma went to Dhaka to settle the CHT crisis peacefully by asking for autonomous hill tracts and restoration of "Special Status". But this was not granted. The Government of Bangladesh to increase its strength, brought in more army, police, a naval base, several cantonments, air force, helicopter gunships, thousands of migrant settlers etc. So the conflict continued in the areas of the CHT where flat fertile lands are cultivated by the indigenous people. As a result, a large number of people were killed or evicted, and an unknown number of people were arrested and put in jail, thousands of them fled to India and became refugees (currently 54,000 refugees are given shelter by the Indian Government in Tripura State). The land and property of many of those who have been killed and those who have fled to India, have already been occupied by the new migrant settlers.

Now it is necessary to briefly analyze how foreign aid to Bangladesh has furthered the problems of the indigenous peoples in the CHT. During the period from 1972-1984, Bangladesh has received a total of $11 billion in foreign aid from donor countries (QERPBA, 1984 : 27). In 1985, military spending in Bangladesh reached $226 millions; arms imports reached $60 millions, per capita military spending was $2 and per soldier $2,790 (Sivard, 1986 : 34,38,39). Sobhan explains how Bangladesh is so deeply tied and dependent to donor countries. "Our annual development plans, import policies, food policy all have to wait on the political climate and policy decisions made in Washington, London, Bonn, Tokyo and Riyadh" (Sobhan, 1982 : 20). He says that, "there is not a single project designed for expansion of capacity which is not funded by aid." Any sudden decline of its availability would have far reaching consequences for the economy, society and polity of Bangladesh.

This aid dependence has direct implication for the CHT crisis. The imperialists and the comprador bourgeoisie of Bangladesh needed to open up the hills for commercial exploitation to harness the untapped forest and natural resources from the CHT. To do so, the Bangladesh Government needed to control the area and did so by colonizing it. The ultimate aim is to control natural resources and development projects. These policies have resulted in the disruption of natural socio-economic activities and threatened their very survival.

Development Projects and Imperialism in the CHT

Karnafuli Paper Mill: In 1953, the Karnafuli paper Mill was constructed in the CHT with the help of foreign aid at a cost of 65.50 million, including a World Bank loan of 4.2 million dollars (Government of Bangladesh, 1971:156).

Karnafuli Rayon and Chemical Factory: Was set up near the Paper Mill in 1966 at a cost of 1.3 million dollars with the help of Foreign Aid (Bangladesh Government, 1971 : 156).

Karnafuli Hydro-electric Dam: Was built in 1960 with the help of USAID (United States Agency for International Development) in the CHT at a cost of 4.9 million Rupees. Created a lake covering about 1036km^2, flooded 21,853 hec. of (40% of total cultivable lands) agricultural lands. No adequate compensation were given and no alternative land were provided to many of the affected people. (CHT Conf. 1986 : 134, Bangladesh Govt., 1971 : 155).

A Master Plan for the CHT: From 1964-1966, a two year survey was conducted in the CHT by the Forestal Forestry Engineering International Limited of Canada to prepare a *Master Plan* for the future development of the CHT. The Pakistani Government devised a *Master Plan* in 1967 on the basis of the recommendation of this survey (May, 1984 : 10-105).

A Pilot Scheme for Jhum Control: Was implemented in 1967 to control swidden farming in certain areas of the CHT, displacing a large number of the indigenous population (May, 1984 : 105-106).

Horticultural Development Programme: A second step toward *Jhum* control was implemented in certain areas, to transform swidden lands into fruit gardening, displacing a large number of its inhabitants (May, 1984 : 107).

The Chengi Valley Project and the Road Construction in the CHT: Funded ($11 million and technical assistance) by the ADAB (The Australian Development Assistance Bureau) an all weather road (66 kilometres long and 10 metres wide) was constructed in the Chengi Valley but had to be left unfinished due to attack by rebels on the ADAB consultants. All weather roads were also built throughout the CHT by the Bangladesh army with the funds received from Australia, Britain and UNDP (CHT Conf.,1986 : 140; Kamaluddin, 1980 : 31).

The Chittagong Hill Tracts Development Board: Created in 1976, mainly funded by the Asian Development Bank (ADB), implemented many development projects in the CHT. One of them is *Joutha Khamar* (joint farming scheme), which was intended to rehabilitate landless swidden farmers. The second scheme intended to finance the migrant settlers' rehabilitation in different parts of the CHT (CHT Conf., 1986 : 138-142).

Forest Development Projects: The SIDA (The Swedish International Development Agency) implemented programmes for reforestation and forest resource extraction ($6 million project) and forest development but did not renew the contract after 1981 due to press coverage and opposition in Sweden on human rights abuse in the CHT (CHT Conf., 1986 : 139).

UNICEF and WHO: The United Nations Childrens' Emergency Fund (UNICEF) has projects of Drinking Water Supply which helped water supply. The World Health Organisation (WHO) organizes Malaria Eradication Programmes in the CHT (CHT Conf., 1986 : 149 : May, 1984 : 108).

Shell Oil and Foreign Capital: Shell Oil was given contract (25 years) to explore oil and gas throughout the CHT. The CHT has big deposits of natural gas, oil, copper and uranium. Gas is already tapped. Foreign capital in the shape of loans is being injected by Saudi Arabia, $9.2 million and the World Bank, $23 million (CHT. Conf., 1986 : 139).

The Foreign Assistance to Bangladesh

It has been reported that some foreign Governments are directly helping the Bangladesh Government to put down conflicts in the CHT. This is evident that .. in a vivid demonstration of imperialist "internationalism" the Bangladesh regime is being aided...by many imperialist powers' (Revolutionary Worker, 1981 : 9).

Some foreign Government has entirely provided funds for telecommunication project linking the CHT with Dhaka, Chittagong and with other parts of Bangladesh. This project is also a part of general "aid" given to Bangladesh to facilitate radio-linking of all Bangladesh Police Stations with the Central Police Communication Headquarters at Dhaka. A British owned firm has been given a contract to establish this sophisticated telecommunication network that would link army and police forces in the CHT with Dhaka and Chittagong and facilitate army strikes over rugged and often inaccessible terrain (May,1984 : 110; Revolutionary Worker, 1981 : 9 ; Bangladesh Peoples' Democratic Movement U.K., 1981 : 4). This shows that some foreign power is not the only one helping the Bangladesh Government, the foreign private enterprises are also helping to deal with problems in the CHT. (Mey, 1984 : 110). Besides "the United States are carrying through a one million dollar "Security Assistance Programme" which is largely a training programme. The aims of the "Security Assistance Programme" have been defined by a Congressional Presentation as the "encouragement of attitudes sympathetic to US foreign policy objectives." (May, 1984 : 108, 111).

Conclusion

Foregoing discussion helps us to draw the following facts: Firstly, the British colonialism is mainly responsible for opening up the hills to outsiders and leaving the indigenous people at the mercy of the Governments dominated by the feudal lords and national bourgeoisie. This crisis could have been avoided if the CHT people were given a choice to determine their future at the time of partition of India in 1947. Yet this would not have possibly given Britain's policy of indirect rule over the region. They used chiefs as "puppets". The true political opposition at the time were India and Pakistan. Secondly, migration to the hills would not have attracted outsiders if industrialization and hydro-electric dam had not been constructed. Thirdly, some of the development projects in the hills have increased the difficulties and problems of the people because these brought more money, men and new technology in the hills and had practically benefited mainly the non-indigenous people. Finally, the imperialiasm of the west had added insult to the injury by providing advice, training and financing the Government in order to put down conflicts in the area.

In addition to this the indigenous political system of clan and lineage based chieftainship of pre-colonial days was restructured without radically changing the existing system. This is because of the fact that the chiefs, *Dewans* and *Talukdaras* were reintegrated partly with the colonial administration. The same tribal chiefs, clan and lineage chiefs of the pre-colonial tribal people, became the Circle chiefs, *Mouza* headman under the new colonial system. Pakistani rule abolished the pre-existing legal rights and "tribal status". Thus, the traditional indigenous institutions had been severely affected by the introduction of Basic Democracy which led to the weakening of the traditional headman and Chief system. The overall situation further deteriorated after the formation of Bangladesh.

Notes

1. This is my personal estimate.

2. In 1959, President Ayub Khan of Pakistan introduced Basic Democracy (BD) system throughout Pakistan. This was a new political system through which BD members were elected at the local level by adult franchise, and they directly vote to elect the President of Pakistan. There were 80,000 such BD members in the whole country who elected the President of Pakistan before the break-up of Pakistan in 1971.

References

AI (Amnesty International) 1986 : *Bangladesh: Unlawful Killing and Tortures in the Chittagong Hill Tracts.* AI Publications, London.

Anti-Slavery Society 1984 : *Chittagong Hill Tracts: Militarization ,Oppression and the Hill Tribes.* London, Anti-Slavery Society.

Bangladesh People's Democratic Movement (UK) 1981 : *Bangladesh : Planned Ethnocide of Minority. Nationalities in the Chittagong Hills Tracts.* Bangladesh People's Democratic Movement (UK) London.

Canada-Asia Working Group 1987 : *Human Rights in Asia.* Canada Asia Working Group, Toronto.

Chittagong Hills Tracts Conference. 1986 : *The Charge of Genocide.* Papers for the Conference on the Chittagong Hills Tracts, Amsterdam.

Government of Bangladesh *The Preliminary Census Report on Bangladesh Census* 1981. Bangladesh Bureau of Statistics.

1971 : *District Gazetteers, Chittagong Hill Tracts, 1971* Bangladesh Government Press, Dacca.

Government of Pakistan	1951	:	*Census of Pakistan 1951*, Government Press Karachi.
Hunter, W.W.	1876	:	*A Statistical Account of Bengal, Vol. VI.* Trubner & Co. London (Reprint, 1973, D.K. Publishing House Delhi).
Hutchinson, R.H.S.	1909	:	*Chittagong Hill Tracts.* Calcutta.
India Today	1987	:	*Chakma : Shattered Lives.* India Today March 15.
ILO (International Labour Organisation)	1986	:	*Minutes of 72nd ILO Conference*, Geneva, July.
IWGIA (International Working Group for Indigenous Affairs	1986	:	*Bangladesh: Statement for International Conference on Human Rights in Chittagong Hill Tracts*, IWGIA NO. 48 : 2-3, Amsterdam.
Kamaluddin, S.	1983	:	Rain and other Elements. *Far-eastern Economic Review*, May 26.
Le Monde	1987	:	Bangladesh: le drama du surpeuplement *Le Monde* April 21.
Macrae, John	1801	:	Account of the Kookies or Lunctas. *Asiatic Researches* 7/183-198.
May, Wolfgang (Ed.)	1984	:	*Genocide in the Chittagong Hill Tracts, Bangladesh* IWGIA Document No. 51, Copenhagen.
New York Times	1986	:	*In the Hill of Bangladesh. A Conflict Gathers Fury* New York Times, Oct. 23.
QERPRA (Quarterly Economic Review of Pakistan, Bangladesh Afghanistan	1984	:	*Foreign Aid*: Post Independence Aid Reaches 11 billion. *Quarterly Economic Review of Pakistan, Bangladesh, Afghanistan*, No. 4.

Revolutionary Worker	1981	:	Bangladesh: The War against the People of the Chittagong Hill Tracts. *Revolutionary Worker*. Nov. 6.
Sivard, R.L.	1986	:	*World Military and Social Expenditure, 1986* World Priorities, Washington.
Sobhan Rehman	1982	:	The Crisis of External Dependence: Some policy Options for Bangladesh. *Journal of the Centre for Social Studies*. No. 18, Dacca University.
SI (Survival Internal)	1984	:	Genocide in Bangladesh, *Survival International Review*. No. 43, London.

4

STATE BUILDING IN MODERN BHUTAN (1616-1990) : A STRUCTURAL FUNCTIONAL ANALYSIS

TAPASH K. ROY CHOUDHURY

The story of Bhutan's emergence as a state in the twentieth century from its ancient tribal heritage is a story of continuous strife and structural reshufflement. In all strate of the faction-ridden power structure of the Bhutani society the struggle has continued for over three centuries. Organized tribal communities, a few in number (Bose, XV) fragmented the country between themselves and had survived mutual quarrel and occassional foreign invasions on account of geopolitical considerations. Therefore, nothing more important as a social formula than unmitigated communalism held the social elements in Bhutan to unity against disintegration. This unity, nevertheless, was very tenuous and somewhat confused in the absence of any clear under pinning of either geographical or cultural identity. On the contrary, cultural encounter with Tibet, by virtue of pilgrimage, trade, migration etc. induced amongst a section of the erstwhile Bhutanese a feeling of philogenesis to Tibet. The modern Bhutanese, however, disclaim it but the early records acknowledge this sentiment (Rose, 1977 : 50).

The transformation of Bhutan into a modern state system has three clear discernable stages. Initially, from the ninth to late fifteenth century, is the earliest phase of Bhutanis recorded history, the primary concern of the society appears to be either to try to disgorge the migrants, or when the challenge was overwhelming due to hordes of the Tibetans migrating into Bhutan, to devise a functional system by which the immigrants could be accommodated without allowing them to disturb the fundamentals of the

Bhutani tribal order. The second phase has started with the arrival of Ngawang Namgyal in 1616. His success to lay hold over both the clerical order and the laity necessitated organisational reforms in the wilderness of primitive tribal laws and later orthodox scholastic injunctions. His reforms, therefore, proliferated into (i) organisational decisions and (ii) structural re-adjustments. The third phase that leads eventually to the introduction of guided democracy in Bhutan had set in after the introduction of hereditary monarchy in Bhutan in 1907. One of the foundations on which the policy of monarchy was laid was the abrogation of the institutions of *zhabs-drung* and *sDe-srids*. And the other factors which contributed to an equal measure to the stabilisation of monarchy and the introduction of democracy in Bhutan are emergence of an organised bureaucracy and the transformation into money economy from the ancient barter system.

These structural alterations necessitated new organisational policies to consolidate (i) the relationship of the elites with tribal mass, (ii) the relationship of the clerical power elites with their counterparts amongst the laity and (iii) the relationship amongst the power elites from the laity on cross-community basis. Consequently, the structural frame-work had been seriously affected in Bhutan by the organisational decisions and interestingly all organisational decisions arose from functional necessities. Separation of the temporal power from the clutches of the clerics was effected as the first major shift from the original theocratic polity. Presumably, for the purpose of continuations of the process, social mobility had been gradually admitted, more as an empirical reality than as an academic policy, in a rather inflexible and stratified society. The transition from tribalism to diarchy in the seventeenth century and then to hereditary monarchy is, on the whole, materialisation of organisational decisions into structural specifics. What is proposed in the underlying study is to examine the (i) functional necessities, (ii) organisational decisions and finally (iii) structural readjustments in Bhutan in its stride towards modernity.

I

The local elites in the pre-sixteenth century Bhutan were generally settled in three different regions *viz.* Paro, Bumthang and Tongsa, in the form of chiefs of the clans and sub-clans, all of them or their ancestors had migrated into Bhutan either from Tibet or from other adjacent regions. Some Bhutani sources namely *rGyal-po Sindha ra-dza'i rnam thar, Rin-chen gter-mdzod, Rig-'dzin* of Padma Gling-pa and *rGyal-rigas* of Nwagong recounted some of the myths relating to the origin of the tribes whom the leadership represented. Many of the stories were apocryphal but the perpetuation of the myths in the clan life and primitive memory serve to explain the importance with which they were deservedly recorded by the Bhutani authors.

The legendary Sindhu Raja, who was held to have settled in Bumthang in the 7th century A.D. was as much a migrant as other migrants were. Though the historians would still prefer another serious debate on the land of his origin the one point which they could accept without much hesitation was that Sindhu Raja was settled in Bumthang and that on account of the mediation of *Padmasambhaba* he could make a truce with his southern neighbour king sNa'u-che. (Aris, 1968; 52-57). Many such legendary kings were mentioned in the Bhutani sources to have migrated from Tibet and ruled in Bhutan. *Khyi-Kha Rathod, gTsang-ma etc.* had been mentioned with veneration and to *gTsang-ma's* descendents was attributed the credit by *rGyal-rigs* to have established *Jo-bo, eJe, Yas-sDe, sTung-sde* and *Wang-ma* (Aris, 1968 : 57) ruling clans of Eastern Bhutan. The descendents of *gTsang ma* spread over the whole of eastern Bhutan and perhaps beyond it if the diffusionist argument in the mythologies has to be accepted. And subsequently they broke up all ties with the ancestral Bumthang establishment. Tibetan sources (Aris, 1968 : 86) however, gave a different version of the *gTsang-ma* story and located Paro as the place of his banishment. On the basis of the Tibetan sources, which Nwagong probably had consulted, he linked the ancestry of *Wang-gdung* and *Mi'i-rgyal-mtshan* with *gTsang-ma.* But one cannot rely too much on this story on account of the fact that the legend of *gTsang-ma* does not survive amongst the western tribes, nor is his westward expansion authenticated by any other Bhutani sources.

The *gTsang-ma* story is unique in one sense that it has no religious character. According to Aris this uncommon stress on the lay element with regard to the questions of birth and political authority is still preserved among the *gDungs* who live in Bumthang proper. (1968 :115). The prevalance of a few clans under different variations of the *gDung* partronimic has encouraged Aris to argue that the families which grew out of the descendents of *gTsang-ma* had finally developed into clans and thus could have been 'the only patrilinial noble families preserving a lay as distinct from religious character to have survived the vissitudes of theocratic and monarchic Government in Bhutan (Aris, 1968 :115). Another significant element of the *gDung* polity has been observed by Tucci from the *rGyal-rigas* that the tradition of heavenly descent initially treated to be an exclusive privilege of the princely families seemed to have been used later even by non-princely families. (Tucci 1973). This legend of the *U-ra sDungs*, a colateral branch of the *sDrungs* and proposed by Tucci to have originated from *lHo-brag* in the western Bhutan has another interesting myth indicating replacement of divine descent by royal descent from Tibet to claim and legitimise political authority.[1] One of the concerns in these legends therefore was to locate the sources of legitimate political authority and in the process what seemed to have gained in importance was the appreciation of secularity more than religion to develop a stable political culture.

But the rise of the *sMyos* clan in Bhutan and the extension of its authority over the whole of Bhutan through marriages and other social contacts had successfully introduced a competing ideology in Bhutan. The *sMyos* had migrated into Bhutan in the 10th century A.D. from Tibet. Since then, in order to establish its religious and political authority upon the Bhutanese the dominant element in the *sMyos* clan prudently manipulated all marriages to have been negotiated within the clan and in exceptional cases with families outside the clan, which were powerful then.[2] Besides, the *sMyos* introduced two important concepts *viz.* (i) *Chos-rje* (Dharma Raja) and (ii) *Rimpoche* (incarnation), and both of them had been fruitfully integrated later by Ngawang in the evolving political culture of Bhutan. The institution of *Chosrje* was found to be used in Tibet as a 'quasi-independent spiritual hierarchy possessing local authority in a region.[3] The word *Zhabs-drung* which came to use in Bhutan since the days of Ngawang is likely to have originated from *Chos-rje* because of their conceptual identicality. Perhaps on account of that the members of the *sMyos* ruling class did not object to the use of the term *Zhabs-drung* by Ngawang Namgyal either for himself or for the institution which he created later. The other concept i.e., *Rinpoche* became a part of the Bhutani tradition and all spiritual authorities and for some time even political authority were sought to be obtained from only incarnatorial manifestations of the deseased leaders. The role of incarnations, incarnatorial politics and finally their extinction in Bhutan are adequately explained by the fact that the 'incarnation culture' of the *sMyos* had been incorporated in the Bhutani social out-look at large.

Nwagong, the historian had been very candid to admit that all the clans, which formed the ruling elites in Bhutan before the arrival of the *Druk-pas* had to have no kinship ties with the general body of their subjects. The subjects were composed of the descendents of the ancient Tibetan expatriates, Tibeto-Mongolians, Lepchas and later the Nepalese. Almost as a convention the clan rulers sought to have clan principalities with well marked borders, and from their castles which were conveniently located the clan rulers used to administer their respective territories. From the frequency of place names with *mkhar* suffixes, of which twenty four have been counted by Aris (1968: 110) from the contemporary records, different administrative headquarters of various clans have been tentatively identified. Besides territorial jurisdiction the clans used to have their clan deities, either adopted from the ancient people who were their subjects or selected from the deities of the sects of which the clans belonged.

What is crucial at this juncture is to try to understand the reasons why there was relative absence of metathesis in tribal Bhutan, although racial antagonism and power rivalry ought to have led the society to that direction. The tribes in Bhutan in the *pre-Drukpa* days were organised necessarily on communal basis, nevertheless the growth of kingship was not always encouraged from within the specific society. Instead, what has been indicated in the *rGyal-rigas* and *Lo-rgyus,* which partially accounts for the continuation of a peaceful social order, is significantly to seek to coordinate between the need disposition of the society and the role expectation of the personality. Therefore, the king might originate either from within the tribes or from the invaders, provided the members of the subject races were allowed to survive in accordance with the *gestalt* of the society. Nwagong held the view that kingship, once established, was continued in that clan primarily through the descent of male lines and marginally through primogeniture.[4] The situation, somewhat down the social ladder at the level of village chief, was not culturally different from the selection policy for the kingship. Though Nwagong was ambivalent about one institution i.e. *gtso-rgan* (chief elder) which was held for a fixed period by a member of the sub-clan. I do not think that there is any better guidance for the solution of this problem than the verdict of Krishna Kanta Bose that the incumbents for *gtso-rgan* used to come from amongst the chiefs of sub-clans in a district on rotational basis (Bose : XV).

What was not clear from Nwagong was the relationship of the ruling clans with their subjects. Was it vassalage? Because without some identical arrangement a complicated political process in which the clans retained their autonomy and yet the leaders outside the clan had been admitted to their allegiance as kings would not operate. From the statement of the *rGyal-rigs* in one section that the defeated rulers of erstwhile Bhutan were restored to their principalities as vassals by the *Druk-pa* rulers after the vanquished owed allegiance to their order it may be presumed that vassalage was an important element in Bhutan's political culture and that its continuance prevented many disturbances in the society following battles and defeats to produce social tensions.[5] Gradually many of the erstwhile rulers were absorbed in the bureaucracy and monkhood which finally led to the dissolution of the ancient political order.[6]

It was indeed a vertical alliance system that successfully brought all the disparate units in Bhutan within the fold of the *Druk-pa* social policy of homoginisation. Perhaps, a similar patron-clients relation system had operated to stabilise relations between the ruling class with their subjects in *pre-Druk-pa* Bhutan. Rather than destabilising tribal administration by interference the rulers sought to assume real political authority through the process of delegation of administrative power to the ruling community. The right to impose customary taxes by the vassals was therefore retained, though important structural changes within the society necessitated its abolition later. Further, the importance of the *pre-Druk-pa* ruling clans in the later history of Bhutan understandably depended on their conformity to role expectations of the society. This was as much true in the relationship of the invading *Druk-pa* ruling community with the traditional ruling class in Bhutan as it was in the relations of the traditional ruling class with their subjects. Because, it was found that in the subsequent history of Bhutan, when the power struggle for *Zhabs-drungship* and *sDe-srid* began with full intensity, only those ruling families which were throughly integrated with their subjects through ideal need dispositions of the personalities controlling power, could survive the strains of perpetual shifting alliance between the elite leaders in a horizontal system of temporary accord.

II

The real important event which had released some crucial generative forces and had determined the courses of future events in Bhutan was the arrival of *Ngag-dbang rNam-rgyal* (Ngawang Namgyal) in 1616 A.D. Under compulsions of Buddhist sectoral quarrel in which *Ngag-dbang's* claim as the legitimate *Rin-po-che* of the Padma Karpo of the Ralung Monastery of Tibet was challenged by Karma Tenchong Wangpo who migrated to Bhutan.[5] Choice of Bhutan in preference to other places was obviously religious, because he argued that as the chief of the *Brug-pa* (Druk-pa) school he would be able to bring all the Bhutanese under his brotherhood at ease. Besides, some of the erstwhile ruling princes of Bhutan also belonged to this sect. The initial reaction of the Bhutanese, *Ngag-dbang* could guess, would not be that of cordiality: therefore, after wondering in north-west Bhutan, in order to ascertain his acceptability, he settled in the monastery of *sPag-gro* (Paro) and began to receive the princes, monks and members of the laity. His religious services together with discourses on the theological doctrines of the *Brug-pa* order were gradually appreciated by the Bhutanese as intellectual products of a charismatic personality. That he succeeded to persuade the *rNyng-ma-pas, Sa-skya-pas* and the *bka'broyud-pas* to accept *Brug-paism* added further strength to the veneration with which people had already accepted him.

But ideological consolidation could not be achieved unless political consolidation is also achieved in equal measure: hence *Ngag-dbang* had been persuing relentlessly a policy of geographical unification of Bhutan. By his acts he had been laying the foundation of modern Bhutan, but before he could undertake other structural reforms, which he did later, he was interrupted by Tibet. Towards Bhutan, Tibet fondly held the posture as the suzerain power. Though Tibet did not always like doctrinal and liturgical differences with Bhutan but it did not anticipate any political threat from Bhutan. Presumably Tibet's complacence had been seriously disturbed by *Ngag-dbang* and therefore Tibet attacked Bhutan four times in 1632, 1639, 1643 and 1647[6] to disintegrate the power springs of *Ngag-dbang*. But Tibet failed to achieve its objectives, because the terrains were unfavourable to the pre-emtive Tibetan military ventures. On the contrary, *Ngag-dbang* had been able, through his repeated victories over the Tibetans, to get the Tibetans to admit his supremacy over Bhutan and his religious policy in exchange of payment of rice tax to the court of the*Tsang* authorities of Tibet.[7]

Respite from Tibetan invasion after 1647 enabled *Ngag-dbang* to fruitfully utilise his time to introduce momentous reforms in Bhutan. Not only that in the field of administration only his reforms had been confined, instead it was made to be very comprehensive being thoughtfully addressed to polity, economy and culture. One of the major achievements of *Ngag-dbang* was to understand in a climate of exuberant theocracy that for the functioning of a state political administration ought to be distinguished from religious activities. And unless the function of the religious and administrative functionaries were not well defined overlapping jurisdictions might generate almost self-defeating strife and recriminations. So, he visualised that by creating two institutions, which would operate after his death, religion and administration could be taken care of without the interference of the one upon the other. The institutions of *Zhabs-drung* and *sDe-srid* thus came into being. Together with them *Ngag-dbang* also introduced the concept of bureacracy; a group of professionals who could assist the supreme overlords of the religious and political establishments had been organised in hierarchical order.

Zhab-drungship (Dharma Raja), in *Ngag-dbang's* scheme of things, would be held by an incarnation(*Rin-po-che*); for all practical purposes this incarnation culture, brought into Bhutan by the Tibetans and introduced into its tradition, had been used by*Ngag-dbang* to legitimise his control over the *Brug-pa* church. By proposing to associate *Zhab-drunghsip* with incarnation he intended to perpetuate this legitimacy. For the *sDe-srid* his policy had been entirely different; being the chief of the secular establishment a *sDe-srid* did not have to be necessarily a celebrate *lama* and besides, the occupation was temporary, for three years at a time and the incumbent was to be chosen by an electoral college in order to avoid dynastic rule. Interestingly enough, *Ngag-dbang*, in his will, created a council of ministers to assist the *sDe-srid* (Dev Raja) that was to be composed of *Lami Zimpon* (confidential secretary of the *Zhabsdrung*), *Shung-Droenyer* (his own deputy) Thimphu *Dzongpon*, or the Penlo of Tashichhodzong Punakha *Dzongpon, Dev Zimpen*(representative of Deb Raja), the Kalyon (the senior minister) and Paro and Tongsa *Penlops.* In addition to these permanent members of the *Shun Lhan Tsok* (Pemberton 1967 : 53) the *Dzongpons* of Dagana and Wangdiphodrang were also occassionally invited to participate in the deliberations.*(Ibid)*

During his life time *Ngag-dbang* implemented this policy only in parts; he could organise the elections of two *sDe-srid* only, while the *Zhabs-drungship* had not been vacated as long as he was alive. But after his death both over his incarnations and the *sDe-srid* ship such important political forces were released that for two hundred and fifty years the prime concern of the Bhutani elites was to occupy either *Zhabs-drungship* or *sDe-ridship* or both for the purpose of attaining political supremacy in Bhutan. Though the institutions continued to remain in importance for long, and in fact the political institution gained ascendancy over the religious institution almost as soon as the quarrel between the two functionaries had started, yet they faded out from the Bhutani political culture after performing their specific roles not always being very clearly envisaged by *Ngag-dbang*. The subsequent history of Bhutan, therefore, was marked by critical attempts to allow these institutions to sling to order in a seemingly confused state of competition for power.

III

Ngag-dbang died in the year 1651, but this news was kept a secret and what was announced by the clerical officials was that he had gone in retreat. The *rGyal-tshab* obviously sought to continue in power on the basis of fictitious authority, and so, no search for the incarnation of the deceased was also undertaken. Things came to such a pass that on the basis of a forged letter assumed to have been issued by the *Zhabs-drung* the Chamberlain appointed the *sDe-srid* and in fact, by virtue of the same fictitious 'approval' the third *sDe-srid* filled the vacant abbacy after he deposed the Chamberlain. Indeed, a virulent politics came into operation, immediately after*Ngag-dbang's* death, to recognise his incarnation.

The causes which served to hasten the erosion of the authority of this institution in *post-Ngag-dbang* Bhutan were multiple: doctrinal, organisational and personal factors united to undermine the theoretical foundations on which the *Zhab-drungship* had rested. The doctrinal controversy arose from an apocryphal story that after the death of the first *Zhabs-drung, Ngag-dbang* his soul passed into three lamas in the form of *Thu*(mind), *Sung*(speech) and *Ku*(body) and of the three the *Thu Trulku* was officially chosen to be the most authentic *Zhabs-drung*. And practically all the six *Zhabs-drungs* who had been installed into spiritual authority belonged to this category*(ibid)*. The line of *Ku-Trulku* did not develop in Bhutan, as this incarnation took place in Sikkim, and after his death in 1761 no body looked for the continuation of this incarnation. Regarding the *Sung Trulku*, whose reincarnation took place in Bhutan till the last incarnation in that line died in the late 1940 *(Ibid)*, the attitude of the Bhutan Government was ambiguos, although as a spiritual leader of the second order *Sung Trulkus* had always assumed important monastic responsibilities. The last *Thu Trulku*, in other words the *Zhabs-drung* died in Bhutan in 1931 after a controversy arose around the succession of Jigmi Dorji Wangchuk as the second king of Bhutan, in which the *Zhabs-drung* had been suspected to have had a conspiratorial role. The *Zhabs-drung* was retired to Talu monastery (Aitchison, 1920) and after his death this institution was dissolved.

The minority of the incarnations and the intervention of the lama community as power brokers caused the institution to suffer severe organisational set back in the eighteenth and nineteenth centuries. Admittedly, on account of the long 'retreat' of *Ngag-dbang* on the one hand and the persistent efforts of the regents to arrogate, without any social approbation, the temporal and spiritual authorities of *Zhabs-drung* due to their minority on the other, the *sDe-srids* emerged as the virtual arbiter of the temporal destiny of the Bhutanese. After attaining majority the *Zhabs-drungs* could hardly retrieve their temporal authority. Even in spiritual matters the *Zhabs-drungs* did hardly over-come the influence of their former regents, who were veterans and had tested power, and hence, they would always seek to influence the decisions of the *Zhabs-drungs* remaining in close association with them.

The status of the *Zhabs-drung*, even as the supreme spiritual overlord, further eroded due to the emergence of the *lama* community as a powerful *political class* after the death of *Ngag-dbang*. Primarily, the *lamas* were the religious functionaries, but in a theocratic state lamacracy admitted secular activities also, and in the power structure as a class they were either superior to or on equal terms with their secular counterparts. Bhutan's political scenario became more complicated than it would normally be, since the Bhutanese used to send at least one male child for theological education in the monasteries. The students, after the completion of their education, chose freely between a life of renunciation and secular occupations. Consequently, the urge for temporal principles, in which the administrative class had their orientation, could not be too strong. Nevertheless, the lay community which sought for an autonomous existence began to treat the clerical community as a rival for temporal power. Their suspicions were roused by the fact that after the death of *Ngag-dbang* the clerical community usurped the prerogatives of the first *Zhabs-drung* (a) to elect the *sDe-sride* and (b) to identify the *Rin-po-ches.* Interestingly enough, the clerical community had no factionalism amongst themselves from the eighteenth century[8], and, therefore, as totally integrated community they could hold their sway, unless it was imperative, due to circumstances, to form alliance with the leaders of the temporal elitist community. The intervention of the clerical community, therefore, prevented the *Zhabs-drung,* after he attained majority, to exercise his will even in religious matters without any encumbrance.

While the authenticity of an incarnation was normally attested by the High *lamas* in Bhutan the installation of an incarnation as *Zhabs-drung* depended much on the policy of the Government faction. As an administrative convention and, in fact, more in practice, the *sDe-sride* could prevent the installation of an incarnation to the seat of*Zhabs-drung* or could repudiate the legitimacy of an installed incarnation.[9] The controversy started with the installation of the first successor of *Ngag-dbang* namely *Phyogs-las rNamgyal* (1708-36) during the *sDe-sridship* or Druk Rabgye, who accepted *rNamgyal* as the *Zhabs-drung,* though a section of the *lama* community could not approve *rNamgyal* as authentic incarnation of the first *Zhabs-drung.* The plea which they offered for their disapproval was that the incumbent was a *Sung Trulku* of *Ngag-dbang.* The leader of the dissident group, namely Kunga Gyalt-shen, the former 'representative' and the incarnation of the son of *Ngag-dban* was murdered in the controversy. The installed *Zhabs-drung,* having had no other rival, continued to receive education without any interruption. But the controversy was revived by the ninth *sDe-srid,* Geshe Ngawang Gyamtsho(1720-29), and in the course of a long and a bitter civil war, in which the Tibetans finally interfered, the legitimacy of *rNamgyal* as *Zhabs-drung* was terminated. Obviously a frustrated man *rNamgyal* died in Paro in 1736. But the crucial phase of the succession quarrel was approached, when after the death of rNamgyal, the claim of two incarnations, one born in Paro and the other in Tibet, and supported by rival factions of Paro and Panakha, tarnished the image of the incarnations.

The Paro incarnation, Sakya Tenzing was a *Sung Trulku,* while the Tibetan incarnation, Jigme Grag-pa was *Thu Trulku* (1724-61); the relative importance of these incarnations having not been determined in Bhutan then the *sDe-sride,* particularly the 10th, 11th and 12th (1730-44) refused to instal Tenzing as the legitimate *Zhabs-drung.* On the contrary, they landed him into prison to avoid the controversy. During the absence of the *Zhabs-drung* the vacancy was temporarily filled up by two 'representatives', two incarnations of the son of *Ngag-dbang* and one incarnation of Tenzing Rabgye,[10] while the search for the legitimate incarnation continued. The incarnation issue was satisfactorily solved by the 13 *sDe-srid,* Sherub Wangchuk (1744-64) as he installed Jigme Grags-pa(1724-61) as *Zhabs-drung* on the assumption that the *Thu Trulku* was superior to other two incarnations. The controversy was also theoretically set at rest with the Government announcement that the *Thu Trulku* always would be the legitimate incarnation of the *Ngag-dbang.* The *sDe-srid* also released Sakya Tenzing(136-61) and offered him a post of honour.

The controversy over multiple reincarnation in Bhutan underlined two compelling facts that (i) the *Zhabs-drungs* after *Ngag-dbung* were not *sui-generis* and that (ii) there was a transition of charisma from individual to institution. Though two *Zhabs-drungs* at a subsequent date, tried to retrieve the powers of the original *Zhabs-drung* by also assuming temporal authority as *sDe-sride* but they were eventually forced to relinquish the temporal power. The assumption of *sDe-sridship* by *Zhabs-drungs* Jigme Dragpa(1809) and Trulku Jigme Norbu (1851) no doubt occasioned a revival of clerical influence in temporal matters, but the *coup* was short lived and the *Zhabs-drungs* soon realised that they could not perpetuate their control over temporal power in a world of constant hostility. Therefore, they resigned their temporary political acquisations and took shelter in their spiritual preserves.[11]

Assuming that the *Thu Trulku* too was an incarnation, what the lamaistic community could not bring themeselves to accept was that the *Thu Trulku* was complete incarnation of *Ngag-dbang*. Consequently, they were rather reluctant to admit a *Thu Trulku* to complete spiritual authority and therefore regared it that they had been tendering. It indicated that the religious community started looking upon the institution with greater veneration than the person, unlike in the case of *Ngag-dbang*, who was installed in the exalted seat of the *Zhabs-drung*. During the nineteenth century the *Zhabs-drung* became more national than a cognitive entity. As an instrument of change it had become so much barren that this institution could be safely ignored by Wgyan Wangchuk in 1907. The intrusion of incarnations in the field of secular politics was gradually resented by the Bhutanese as illegitimate act. So, the *Zhabs-drungs* trying to hold secular power, had to relinquish their temporal power ; similarly the impact of the new perception of the role of temporal power was found to affect even those incarnation *sDe-srides*, who otherwise were elected in a regular manner by the electoral college. Rinpoche Mipham Wangpo (1730-37), an incarnation of Tenzin Rabgye Chhogley Yeshey Gyanltshen (1730-37), a *Trulku* and Chhogley Trulku Yeshe Ngoedbub (1903-7) and Jigme Singhe (1776-88), an incarnation of Gyaltse Dorji had either to resign, on account of revolt, or were deposed.[12] Only Jigme Singhe ruled for twelve years without facing any revolt. Samuel Davis, somewhat appropriately, summed up the position of the *Zhabs-drung* in 1830 when he visited Bhutan with Turner. He wrote, '..... there is little doubt that the policy of the Government will provide that he be still secluded from any interference in public concerns and wholly confined to the contemplation of the spiritual dignity[13] (Davis, 1830).

IV

The institution of *sDe-srid*, which was a new concept in Bhutan polity and was not ritualised by incarnatorial associations, gained quickly in stability in the other wordly climate of lamaistic Bhutan. Despite elite conflicts and constant civil-wars over incumbents this institution eventually emerged as the real centre of power and the most potential instrument to introduce important social changes in Bhutan. The road to its stabilisation, however, was not very smooth: of the fifty four *sDe-srides* who reigned till 1907, when this institution was terminated, thirty five of them faced revolts, eight *sDe-srids* were assasinated and a few were deposed. Such seemed to be the prestige of this institution in Bhutan society that the ultimate objective of all *Penlops*(governors), and *Dzongpons* (governors of forts) was to secure *sDe-sridship* even by foul means, if honesty failed.

It is fairly reasonable to argue that the context for *sDe-sridship* had released new political forces which had detribalised and demonasticised the traditional factionalism in Bhutan and *Lama* arrogance for spiritual superiority. It forced the society to undergo changes, at least, at two levels *i.e.* (i) consolidation of relations of the provincial elites with their local roots and (ii) elite interaction on the basis of horizontal alliance system to serve factional interest. On the whole, the entire political process, which was formerly moribund, on account of the fact that it was dominated by tribalism of limited political import, had been suddenly lifted to the national level through political factionalism that had transcended the confines of locality or regions. The *sDe-sridship* had internalised and institutionalised the value pattern of culture, which had been gradually moving towards secularisation by renouncing its clerical roots.[14] In its value generative process *sDe-srid* had induced a sense of politico-cultural individualism. As a result a feeling very close to national identity had introspectively replaced the philogenitic associations of the Bhutani ruling elites with Tibet.

From the repeated turmoils which *sDe-sridship* had raised, its importance could be understood in Bhutani society. The magnitude of politicisation that took place in Bhutan over *sDe-sridship* may be comprehended from the following table in which I have computed the frequency distribution of revolts and their consequences.

Table 1

Frequency distribution of revolts and their consequences

Time	No. of sDe-srids	No. of Revolts	Assassinations	Attempted Assassinations	Deposed
1. 17th Cent.	5	3	1	1	x
2. 18th Cent.	17	7	3	x	1
3. 19th Cent.	31	24	4	1	3
4. 20th Cent.	1	1	x	x	1
Total:	54	35	8	2	5

Sources : (I) *Namthars, rGyal-rigas, Lo-rgyus.*
(II) Aris, *Bhutan.*
(III) Hasrat, *History of Bhutan.*

The process of political secularisation, to which the Bhutan society was gradually drifting, is illustrated by the following table where the distribution pattern of the *sDe-srids* between the monks and laity has been studied.

Table 2

***sDe-sridship* held by monks and secular elite leaders**

Time	Monks (1)	Paro Penlop (2)	Dunkha Penlop (3)	Darkar Penlop (4)	Tongsa Penlop (5)	Wandephondrang Penlop (6)	Wangzops (7)
1. 17th Cent.	2	1	x	x	1	1	x
2. 18th Cent.	5	1	1	x	1	x	3
3. 19th Cent.	6	x	1	1	4	x	2
4. 20th Cent.	2	x	x	x	x	x	x
Total	15	2	2	1	6	1	5

Table 2(Continued)

Time	Chhopen (8)	Thimphu Penlop (9)	Shongar (10)	Shung Droenyer (11)	Uncertain (12)
1. 17th Cent.	x	x	x	x	x
2. 18th Cent.	x	6	x	x	1
3. 19th Cent.	1	8	1	1	4
4. 20th Cent.	x	x	x	x	x
Total	1	14	1	1	5

Source: *Op.cit* Table 1.

Notes: (1) *Penlop* is a Governor.
(2) *Wangzop* is a high official in a fort.
(3) *Shung Droenyer* is Secretary to the *sDe-srid*.

That only fifteen out of fifty four *sDe-srid* could assume power from amongst the monks indicated that the temporal leadership was very reluctant to loose its grip over this very vital institution in Bhutan. The quarrel over *sDe-sridship* gained momentum in the nineteenth century, because he was the sole authority on all public economy, the only receiver of the whole revenue, about thirty thousand per annum (Bose: 134) from the Duars, and could trade with a capital of forty thousands *(ibid)*. Further, he could escheat the property of the Government officials after their death and presented horses, silk, salt and hoes to petty land holders and farmers and received much more than the value in retreat'. In fact, the *sDe-srid* were capable of more patronage distribution than any other dignitary in Bhutan. Therefore, he could build up a base of wider social support for this institution on the basis of patron-client relationship. Bogle realised the importance of this institution and communicated it to the chief functionaries of the East India Company in Calcutta in 1774 (Markham, 1879).

Revolts against the *sDe-sride* were endemic and from the British records numerous references of such revolts would serve to indicate that different types of elite alliances had been preferred to stage these revolts. In Table 3 we have computed the information on revolts and diversity of alliances that would account for the success or failure of the revolts engineered by the pretenders.

Table 3
Horizontal alliance of the elites and their revolts against the *sDe-srids*(1651-1907)

Name of the *sDe-srids*	Status	Revolts Organised		
		Secular elites and monks	Monks	Secular elites
1. Umze TenzingDrugyal (First)	Monk			elites Mon Amchhog with help from Tibet and Sikkim
2. Gyalse Tenzing Rabgye (Fourth)	Monk			*Dzongpon* of Wandiphodrong
3. Karbi Geduen Choepl (Fifth)	Secular			
4. Druk Rabgye (Eighth)	Secular	Punakha *Dzongon* with monk		
5. Geshe Ngawang Gyamtsho (Ninth)	Monk	Monks		
6. Rinpoche Mipam Wangpo (Tenth)	Monk			Dondub Gyalpo from Karbisa with Tibet
7. Sonam Lhundub (Sixteenth)	Secular	Monk body with secular elites		
8. Druk Tenzing (Nineteenth)	Secular	Monks		
9. Sonam Gyaltshen (Twenty first)	Secular	Punakha*Dzongpon* with monks		
10. Drug Namgyal (Twenty second)	Secular	Sonam Gyaltshen with monks		

Name of the *sDe-srids*	Status	Revolts Organised		
		Secular elites and monks	Monks	Secular elites
11. Sangye Tenzing (Twenty fourth)	Secular	Tongsa *Penlop* with monks		
12. Umze Parop (Twenty fifth)	Secular	Tongsa*Penlop* with monks		
13. Boep Choeda (Twenty sixth)	Monk	Shongar *Dzongpon*		
14. Zhabs-drung Jigm Dragpa (Twenty seventh)	Monk	Secular		
15. Chhogley Yeshey Gyaltshen (Twenty ninth)	Monk	Punakha *Dzongpon* with monks		
16 Tshaphu Dorji (Thirtieth)	Secular		Thimphu*Dzongpon* and Tongsa *Penlop*	
17. Tenzing Drugda (Thirty second)	Secular			
18. Dorji Namgyal (Thirty fourth)	Secular	Secular elites and monks		
19. Adap Thrinley (Thirty fifth)	Secular	Monks		
20. Choeki Gyaltshen (Thirty sixth)	Secular		*Dzongpon* of Shong	
21. Dorji Norbu with Tashi Dorji (Thiry seventh)	Secular		Thimphu *Dzongpon*	
22. Wanchhug Gyalpo (Thirty eighth)	Secular		Paro and Thimphu*Penlop*	
23. Zhabs-drung Trulku Jigme Norbu (Thirty ninth)	Monk		Wangzop Chagpa Sangye and Shongar *Dzongpon*	
24. Chagpa Sangya (Fortieth)	Secular	Tongsa *Penlop* with monks		
25. Lopon Bachup Damchhoe Lhundup with Japa Tenzing (Forty first)	Secular		Secular	

Name of the sDe-srids	Status	Revolts Organised		
		Secular elites and monks	Monks	Secular elites
26. Kuenga Palden (Forty second)	Secular			Thimphu *Dzongpon*
27. Nagzi Pasang Phunshio Namgyal (Forty third)	Secular			Punakha and Tongsa *Penlops*
28. Tsewang Sithub (Forty fourth)	Secular			Nagzi Pasang, Ex *sDe-srid.*
29. Kague Wangchuk (Forty fifth)	Monk			Nagzi Passing Ex *sDe-srid,*
30. Tsulthrim Yonten (Forty sixth)	Secular			Tsewang Sithub, Ex *sDe-srid.*
31. Tshenyi Lopon Tsuendue Pekar (Forty seventh)	Monk			Paro *Penlop* and Bumthang *Wangdipho Drung*
32. Jigme Namgyal (Forty eighth)	Secular			Paro *Penlop* and Damoche Rinchen
33. Kitsep Dorji Namgyal (Forty ninth)	Secular			Monks
34. Chhogley Trulku (Fifty fourth)	Monk			Tongsa *Penlop*
Total	36	9	4	21

Sources: (I) *Op.cit,* Table 1.
(II) *Reports* of Bogle, Bose, Pemberton, Eden.
(III) Letters and memorandum of the British Frontier officials.

While examining the morphology of leadership we come across another important aspect of the revolts *i.e.* rise in importance of different *Penlops* who frequently exercised their will in the matter of election and legitimisation of the *sDe-sride.* With regard to *Zhabs-drungs* too the same motivation had operated, and, as we had already noticed, this motivation had embittered the *Zhabs-drungs* with the secular elites. It became adequately clear from the above studies that the powerful secular elites sought to fill up both the posts of *Zhabs-drung* and *sDe-srid* from amongst themselves, and so this process stimulated a tendency to conduct all power to flow into one clan or family in defiance of the original scheme of diarchy. From the study of leadership that different regional elites provided, during the period of turmoil, we can ascertain their comparative importance in Bhutan.

TABLE 4
Leaders of the revolts and the number of times they organised revolts

Leaders	1 Punakha	2 Monks	3 Tongsa	4 Paro	5 Thimphu	6 Wangdi-phodrang	7 Other secular elites	8 Karbisa	9 Shongar	10 Ex sDe-srid
Nos. of revolts	5	4	6	3	4	2	4	1	2	3

Sources: *op. cit* tables 1 and 3.

In the course of continuous inter-factional fight for power the Tongsa family gradually gained in strength, ever since the rise of Jigme Namgyal as a political luminary. Jigme Namgyal retired as *sDe-srid*(1870-74) in 1874, but he was succeeded by his cousin Kitsep Dorji Namgyal. But Kitsep's *sDe-sridship* was attended by a family quarrel: his eldest brother, who was the Tongsa *Penlop* at the time of his election tendered his support on the ground that his *penlopship* would not be disturbed after the election, as his governorship was consistently challenged by his brother-in-law. The pretender, in the meanwhile entered into an alliance with Kitsep, the *sDe-srid* and Jigmi Namgyal, both of whom disliked Tongsa *Penlop's* excessive love for power. The situation took a grave trun soon as the *Penlop* of Taga, the *Dzongpons* of Punakha and Wangduphodrang, who were relatives, supported the cause of the Tongsa *Penlop* in order to reduce the influence of Jigme Namgyal and his cousin in the politics of Bhutan (Aitchison, 1920 : 192). The *Zhabs-drung* also endorsed this move (Hasrat 1980 :78)[14] and finally on account of their revolt Kitsep was assassinated in 1879. As a retaliatory measure to suppress the civil war Jigme arrested the *Dzongpon* of Wangdephodrang and killed him, besides, he also kept the *Penlops* of Tongsa and Taga under survillance.

After the death of Kitsep the *sDe-sridship* went again to one of the dependents of Jigme Namgyal, namely Chhoegyal Zangpo (1879-82) who promoted the supremacy of Namgyal in state politics. Jigme Namgyal died in 1881, but his influence prevailed in Bhutan till the supreme political power was transferred to his youngest son Wgyan Wangchuk in 1907. Lam Tshewang, the Thimphu *Dzongpon* and a follower of Jigme Namgyal assumed the *sDe-sridship* in 1882. Tshewang gave to the eldest son of Namgyal the *Penlopship* of Paro and appointed Ugyan Wangchuk as the *Dzongpon* of Wangduphodrang and allowed their uncle to retain the *Penlopship* of Tongsa. This was an important measure to concentrate power in the Tongsa family.

This arrangement, presumably, was not liked by other rivals for power. So, the country drifted towards another civil war which started with the assassination of the Tongsa *Penlop*. Ugyan Wangchuk was at Wangduphrodang then, and soon having left the charge to one of his reliable assistants Ugyan hurried back to Tongsa, apprehended the rebellious forces, killed the murderers of his uncle and established his full control over the administration of Tongsa. In the meanwhile the *sDe-srid* Lama Tshewang having retired in 1884 Gawa Zangpo was nominated by Ugyan as the successor. Zangpo however, turned out to be of no help; on the contrary under the influence of Alu Dorji, the Thimphu *Dzongpon* and Phuntsho Dorji of Punakha he tried to prevent the Tongsa *Penlop* to get his share of the Duars subsidy money from the British.[15] It was also alleged that the *sDe-srid* had appealed to Lord Dufferin for help,[16] but his request was ignored by the Governor General. After two years Zangpo resigned from his post and went to Dote-Drag Gompa for meditation. Then, amidst the usual scenes of compromise discussions Ugyan Wangchuk got rid of his opponents by both contrivance and blood-shed. In the fray the *Dzongpon* of Punakha lost his life and the *Dzongpon* of Thimphu fled to Tibet with his family and followers. Despite the fact that Ugyan was weilding the real political authority in Bhutan he preferred as a political strategy to place his own nominees in the *sDe-sridship*, first Pam Sangye Dorji (1886-1903) after Zangpo had resigned and again *Zhabs-drung* Chhogley as the successor of Pam. Chhogley Trulku was the third *Zhabs-drung* to have the opportunity to conduct as head both the religious and temporal, establishments. Probably, he mis-read the message of his age; so when he tried to retrieve the original authority of *Ngag-dbrang* he overstrained his authority and as the logic would have it under such circumstances he was deposed by Ugyan in 1907. No other successor was sought; instead Ugyan Wangchuk was unanimously elected by the monks and secular elites as the hereditary king of Bhutan. From regional factionalism Bhutan thus entered into a new phase of unified state system under hereditary monarchy and it had succeded to introduce a new dynamism in Bhutani political culture by giving the people a new symbol of political and cultural identity.

The success of Wangchuk family, in the power politics of Bhutan was ensured by two factors, that is to say,(1) the integration of the elitism of the Tongsa family with their mass base and (2) the complexity of elite pluralism in other centres of power. The Tongsa family had originated from the *sMyos* clan of *Sum Pharang Chos-rje* and through his descendent *Padma Gling-pa* the lineage continued through *Mkho-Chung Chos-rje, Dung-Dkar Chos-rje* and finally to *`Brug Rgyal-po'*.[16a] The consanguinal relations of all the sub-branches are like *Kheri Chos-Rje* and *Sibis-Gdung-Chos-Rje* of the *Thugs-sras Kun-dga' dBang -po* branch and *Gtam-Zhing -Chos-Rje, Gyiang -sqang-Chos-Rje, Drod-Phu-Chos-Rje* and *Sqra-Mi-Rtse-Chos-Rje* of the *zThugs-sras rGyal-sras-gSang-dbang* branch. Both the branches originated from *Padma Gling-Pa,* had acted in harmonious relations during the days of civil war. The other powerful elite families from the western Bhutan did not gain any comparable familial advantage. Besides, the relationship with the monastic community after the denudation of the *Zhabs-drungship,* was not much bitter; for on the one hand, the monk body ceased to command a strong power base then and on the other, Ugyan did not challenge the authority of *Je Khenpo,* who was the chief abbot of the *'Brug-pas.* The church only lost its autonomy in money matters and was maintained by Government subsidies.[17] Thus, the erosion of theocratic values in Bhutan affacted the functional role of the two institutions which *Ngag dbang* had created but when they were gradually phased out in the early twentieth century nobody argued for their continuance for the purpose of functional necessity.

V

The institutionalisation of the value pattern of a new polity, during the period from 1616 to 1907, also set the process to originate and regularise an impersonal bureaucracy in Bhutan. From the rudiments of clerical aids that came with the institutional scheme of *Ngag-dbgang* it is difficult to assume that it would develop into fulfledged modern bureaucracy in Bhutan in course of time. But it turned out to be so,because (i) the complexity that grew around the uneasy choice for the Bhutanese between theocracy and secular monarchy and their final option for the latter necessitated the rise of a body of professional rulers and (ii) the economy also entered into a crucial phase of transformation from barter to money economy.

The process started when the first *Zhabs-drung* drew two sets of officials for the personal and administrative convenience of the *Zhabs-drung* and the *sDe-srid*. The *Lami Zimpoen* (household steward), the *Gelongs* (Monks), *Zingaps* (messengers), and *Lopons*(monastic official incharge of Theological Education) were the important officials attached to the office of the *Zhab-drung*.[18] Claude White, the first British Resident at Gangtok named also a group of subordinate officials, namely *Karbari*, *Kuchangs* and *Mandals* whose primary responsibility was to expound the laws of the *Zhab-drung* among the faithful (White, 1909;: 306). The secretariat of the *sDe-srid* consisted of *Droenyer*(Secretary), *Zimpon-nam* (Royal Store keeper), *Wangjop* (Fort official of rank), *Droentshap*(a deputy of Droenyer), *Nyerchen* (Store keeper) and *Dungtsho*(Chief Physician). Further, the *sDe-srid* was assisted by a group of minor officials such as *Solopon* (Steward), *Japon* (Incharge of Tea arrangement), *Thappon* (Incharge of kitchen), *Norpon* (Incharge of cattle), *Tapaon* (Incharge of stud), *Dapon* (Army incharge), *Linpon*(Major) and *Dimpon* (Incharge of Army stores) (Hasrat, 1980: 56-58).

In the absence of any clear policy to appoint these officials at the early stage the *Zhabs-drung* and the *sDe-srid* used to look more for faithfulness than talent in the subordinate officials. Therefore, people with familial connections used to be appointed on terms of prebendage. Absence of money economy in Bhutan then thrust upon the employers this only mode of employment. Besides, the two supreme functionaries of the state were reluctant to share power with people outside their clan or families. Bose rightly indicated the trend in his report (Bose :151) though one cannot be sure, if he had understood the complexity of the emerging political culture.Padro Carrasco's[19] reaction too was basically similar to that of Bose. Regarding the education of the officials Bogle, Pemberton and White had one point in common that before appointment the candidates had to have some religious education. Though observed at different points of time the records nevertheless, indicated that in a theocratic system orientation in doctrinal matters seemed to be more important to the ruling community than in any other temporal affair. Only with the rise of monarchy that the educational policy towards the bureaucratic class had changed meaningfully. Obviously in order to enable the official community to cope with the enhanced responsibility of an organised state system a new educational policy, in which initiations in urgent matters of administration than religion, had been undertaken.

Initially, the Government officials were (prebends); they never had any opportunity to enjoy income in the form of salary. Therefore, they had to depend on their patrons for official rents to be enjoyed purely on usufructurage basis against service. Admittedly the Bhutan Government did realise the importance of a class of officials with professional knowledge, but their bureaucratisation in the proper form was substantially impeded by the economy. The growth of professional bureaucracy, Weber explained, depended on a stable taxation policy which, for all practical purposes, would be progeny of money economy (Weber 1977 : 204). Without it bureaucracy remained personal, depending largely to the services that the bureaucrats could render to patrons more for their personal or clan interest than for the well being of the State at large. But there is no denying the fact that a developed bureaucracy, by transporting community action to the realms of societal action 'societalizes' power relations. To the State building process along secular wave-length societalization hence is a vital element. In the course of critical social transformation in Bhutan, till the beginning of the twentieth century, bureaucracy too passed through different transitional phases, one of which seemed to be clearly identified with the *Rate von Haus aus* (Weber 1977:235) of the thirteenth century German principalities.

One of the evils of personal bureaucracy was the corruption of the bureaucratic community. Pemberton rightly commented that some official, endeavour to amass as much property as possible during the tenure of an office which they are aware, is likely to be but of short duration and as the removal of the superior is generally attended by the dismissal of every subordinate under him at the same time, the incentive to speculative industry exists in every grade (Pemberton 1838 : 57). For Krishna Kanta Bose the experience regarding the bureaucratic community was no more different, and according to him 'whenever any *rayot* or landlord or servant has collected a little money the officers of the Government under whose authority they happen to be placed find some plea or other for taking the whole. On this account the *rayots* are afraid to put on good clothes, or to eat or drink according to their inclination, lest they should excite the avarice of their rulers (Bose : 151-2). The most notorious set of officers identified by them were the *Zinkaffs* (district officials) whose predatory acts would often spell disaster for the peasants.

The supreme moment of change in the bureaucratic organisation in Bhutan appeared when the first two *Druk Gyalpos,* since 1907, tried to reform bureaucracy on the basis of new prepositions. One of the ideas, on which they concentrated, was to recruit members of the community from outside the traditional elite families: their intention was clear, because the monopolisation of the Government machinery by a few families nurtured a feeling of insecurity amongst others. The selected, according to the new policy, were tutored as probationers in the place before being sent to different centres of local administration. At the initial phase the measures were tentative but the third *Druk Gyalpo* further streamlined the process and helped the bureaucracy to develop as an impersonal institutional order. As the first step he established in 1961 a Development Secretariat at Paro and it was placed under *aGeylon Chichap* (Secretary General) differentiating it from the Secretariat proper which was at that time a part of the palace establishment. The palace secretariat was manned by the three principal officers namely, *Gyaldon* (Royal Chief Secretary), *Gyaltse*(Royal Finance Secretary) and the Royal representative in the Royal Bhutan Army, and all these were held to be accountable to the king only.

For two obvious reasons the third king changed these arrangements later for he wanted to introduce some new ideas in Bhutan administration, first by setting up a Council of Ministers in 1968, and then by toning up the Royal Advisory Council into a Parliament*(Tshogdu)*. To the ministers as in a democratic society, many of the departments, which were formerly supervised by the members of the Palace Secratariat, were transferred. One Secretariat, therefore independent on the place, had to be set up to house the first five ministries *viz*(I) Home Ministry (II) Finance Ministry (III)Development Ministry (IV) Ministry of Trade and Commerce and (V) From 1972 the newly created Foreign Ministry. For the purpose of coordination between different ministries a Co-ordination Committee was also set up in 1974 to sort out the problems of overlapping jurisdiction between ministries.[20]

Besides, a number of new posts were created to keep the administration in tune with the change in policy decisions. During the reign of the first two kings the northern part of Bhutan was divided into eleven administrative units, each one of which was placed under one *Dzongpon*(District Officer) and the southern part was placed with the family of Ugyan Kaji of Kalimpong for administration. The third King introduced another administrative reorganisation. He divided the country into two broad divisions and placed each one of them under a *Lhotsem Chichap* (Commissioner). While the southern Divisional Commissioner was assisted by two Deputy-Commissioners, the northern division was first sub-divided into thirteen districts and then in 1976 into seventeen districts(*Dzongs*) each one of them being placed under one *Dzongpon*. For the judicial administration a *Thimpon*(District Judge) was also appointed, by delinking the judiciary from the executive, and the King placed the entire judicial administration under the Chief-Justice of the Bhutan High Court. The *Penlops*, in other words the Governors, who once used to weild real political authority, had been reduced in the process into titular heads and the post reserved only for people of honour. The third King once proposed to introduce a bill in the Bhutan Parliament to create provision for the impeachment and removal of the king, but he was prevented from doing so in consideration of the fact that Bhutan was not prepared for this radical reform.[21] On the whole, the new polity usherd in an era of new administrative polity in which the legislature, executive and the judiciary had been separated from each other for the purpose of equity, efficiency and justice.

For the recruitment of the civil-servants, therefore, a new policy in modification of the earlier one had to be drawn. And on the basis of the report of the Service Sub-Committee of the Coordination Committee, established for that purpose, the Civil Service Rules were introduced for the first time in Bhutan in 1972 regarding the appointment and promotion of the bureaucrats. Till

1969 all lower level officers were appointed by the Home Ministry, but in accordance with the new rule all non-Gazetted Officers would be appointed by different ministries and departments. The Gazetted Officers were however appointed by the King in consultation with the Departments and in case of appointment or promotion to the highest offices in the State the King would appoint them in consultation with the *Tshogdu*.[22] For new appointments and promotions the only condition, in modification of the previous culture, was to look for the quality of the candidates. Though for shortage of adequate number of educated people in Bhutan the Government could not introduce any Public Service Examination, nevertheless professionalisation of the bureaucracy seemed to be the primary objective of the different reforms undertaken in the course of the last three decades.

VI

To understand the quality of the polity and its objectives at the early stage together with the personal nature of the bureaucracy that we have discussed one may justifiably argue that unless the economy had supported such political theory as Bhutan had its perpetuation would have been difficult. And the changes that came in the political outlook of the ruling class in Bhutan, with some concern for secularism and human-rights, too had been organically related to the economic changes that came into Bhutan first by internal reforms and then through the packages of foreign aid from India.

It was purly 'slavery' that the first *Zhabs-drung* had to encounter and therefore in his proposed reforms he hardly tried to modify this position. On the contrary, in order to regularise the operation of slavery for more productive purposes, he had introduced stringent rules. Shortage of manpower and the culture of forceful exploitation of labour, account for the growth of slavery and polyandry in the Himalayan States. Therefore, acquisition of slaves, either through purchase or forceful occupation, was a regular feature in Bhutan. The concept of slavery sometimes governed the principles of family formation, and it was not exceptional that 'three or four males would be enchained by fetters which bound one female. (Pemberton 1839 : 119).

Neither slavery nor the rent policy, in which again *chunidan* (labour tax) was an important element, had been disturbed by

Ngag dbang in the course of his economic reforms. Payment in kind, in the absence of money economy, and by labour was the prop of the primitive Bhutan economy; therefore, by his reforms the first *Zhabs-drung* sought to prevent tax evasion on any pretext, So, inspite of the Buddhist philosophical injunction to show compassion to every form of life, the harsh economic reality induced the Bhutanese to be rigid exploiters of labour under State protection. The only humane measure was that *Ngag-dbgang* had forbidden trading in slaves (Hasrat, 1980 : appendix No. 1). Emergence of the feudal mode of production was a much later phenomenon, and the gradual introduction of money economy made somewhat possible due to the payment of subsidy money by the British after the annexation of the Assam duars[23] and later the Bengal duars from Bhutan, had given rise to a rentier class. Though feudalism did not affect slavery, it did of course affect the Bhutani polity, and the gradual realisation of the importance of temporal acts, as we had studied, even with deference to theocracy, was the product of the feudalising process. From communal ownership of land to privatisation and the admission of the fact that the King was the supreme owner of all landed property in Bhutan clarified the position the King *vis-a-vis* tax and the rentier class *vis-a-vis* rent.

The feudal mode of production continued in Bhutan till the sixties of the twentieth century and even when Bhutan has been gradually initiated into the capitalist mode of production by India's financial assistances disguised feudalism prevailed. Therefore, when the third King, Jigme Dorji Wangchuk sought to introduce land reforms in Bhutan he did touch only the superstructure *i.e.* reducing acrage of individual holding and distribution of some land among the landless. Even for the abolition of *chunidan*(labour tax) the progressive Bhutanese were initially hesitant, and while they had succeeded to propose its abolition in 1968 in the *Toshogdu* only for the womenfolk it did not generate any serious social tension in Bhutani society.[24] But the administration had to take another two years to bring to bear its effect on all forms of slave tax lest their measure, which seemed to them to be still very radical, would generate frustration in the feudal establishment.

But looking at the issues from the point of view of political transformation what transpires in retrospect is that feudalisation had systematically destroyed the strong hold of monastery and theocratic polity in Bhutan, and while capitalism entered in the scene it had ushered in the policy of consumerism, ego-centricism and of placing importance to the material questions of existence. So, theocracy had to recede by steps into that 'retreat' where many of the *Zhabs-drungs* had often retired after having failed to arrest the march of temporality. The effort to titularise monarchy in the late sixties was a product of this process, and even though the growth of political party had not been encouraged in Bhutan the one serious disability in a political culture *i.e.* authoritarianism which is sought to be removed by the democracratic political culture, has been partially removed. Besides, the social transformation seems to be so all prevasive that there is no element in Bhutan now which one can legitimately describe as *'deracine'*.

VII

In the final analysis, Bhutan appears to be a relatively unfamiliar instance amongst the South Asian nations where tradition and modernity, as two sets of cultural *problematique,* have been approached with more authenticity than by plagiarisation of the western *cliches.* Bhutan had never been a western colony as its many South Asian neighbours were: so, this tangible freedom was utilised by the Bhutani elites to augment forces of social transformation from within the society. In the process Bhutan advanced an effective argument that considering the issue of conflict relations between the conservative social order and the modernist tendencies the authentic answer of a country can be formulated, as it has been done in Bhutan, towards accommodation and modification within the framework of its basic roots. Bhutan has realised that the 'aspiration' and the 'consumative' dynamics in the life of a nation can achieve no better result than if they are indigenous and that their operation is not affected by any extraneous influence.

For many South Asian nations colonialism, among other things, has imposed an unanticipated burden of cultural priapism. In its urgency to act as the only agency for politico cultural transformation of its victims; colonialism has disturbed the covariance that always obtains between the attitude disposition of the society and the role expectations of the individuals. On the contrary, 'role expectations', as an autonomous category of value, has been foisted on the society, in disregard of its dispositon, for the purpose of serving colonial interest. The legacy continues to exist, though many of the colonies have become independent, and in the labyrinth of the distorted culture 'authoritaniasm', to identify one element, at the moment continues to survive with all its protean incarnations. Dictatorship of the Kings, the Emperors and later of the colonial administration is being replaced now by that of political parties and the indigent political leadership. Partly on account of the insouciance of the political leadership and partly due to the ignorance of this leadership to understand the banality of their argument to justify their conduct the prospect for democracy in South Asia does not seem to be bright. Besides, what is equally deplorable in the processual changes of the polity is the utter disregard with which the electorate is being treated by the political leadership either in decision making or to examine them as the most authentic generative force for all prescriptions for relevant and organically integrated social transformations of the society. Therefore, the argument in favour of 'dependence' on the developed, which the economist and the scientist community of these nations often tend to advance very arduously, appears to be prophylactic than a sound theory of growth.[25]

Bhutan had no such external compulsion as other former colonies had, so whatever changes came by way of social transformation in Bhutan was a product of functional necessity. Therefore, both in the process of transformation and in the form which the society finally assumes after the turn of events there always remains an extraordinary integrity to the cult of the people. If any part of the traditional institution has been shed it leads to the growth of another that is equally indigenous. Tradition and modernity, as they are assumed to be antagonistic postures of two rival values in other developing countries, are held to be complementary in Bhutan, and in their urgency for economic growth the modern Bhutani elites have never ignored these very vital aspects of Bhutani perception. It took two hundred and fifty years to develop and finally to realise the irrelevance of the institutions of *Zhabs-drung* and *sDe-srid* by the Bhutanese. The decision to demolish these two institutions arose, because the inadequacy of their functional role became patently clear in the changing perspectives of a dynamic society. But the process of change has been so fast, since monarchy was established, that in the course of fifty years that Bhutan could take a correct decision to relieve monarchy of its absolutism by peaceful reforms. Hence, Bhutan, unlike many South Asian countries, has not rushed out of monarchical authoritarianism in order to jump into party authoritarianism.

It has been indeed a complex politico-psychological process that has led to the transformation, as it did, but, on no account, was it achieved by any leadership that had no strong roots in the tradition. Amongst many, two factors have been reflecting the Bhutani sensitivity *i.e.* (i) to draw all the elements of Bhutan's international personality from within the society. Bhutan has been doing too much to project too well its image abroad; perhaps it may contribute to strengthen the cohesive forces in Bhutan, but what it has always taken good care to underline as the fundamentals of its culture are all unfaillingly rooted in Bhutan and (ii) secondly, Bhutan is never rushing through to induct any external idea, whether it is political, economic or cultural, that they think can not be grafted with ease with the politico-cultural host body. These beliefs remain the *thematique* for the Bhutanese, and undertaking to examine the evolution of Bhutani polity one cannot afford to ignore the symbiosis of their *problematique* with the *thematique* to grasp the elements of uniqueness in the Bhutani experiment.

Notes

1. Tucci, O, 1973, The importance of the secular leadership in filling the posts of *soe-srids*, as we have discussed, was a product of this new culture which the members of the Jung families have introduced in Bhutan.

2. Bla-ma gSang-snagags. *aMyos-rabs* and together with it one finds it very useful to read the review of this book by Michael Aris.

3. Aris, M. 1968. In this context Aris observed that possibly under the influence of the Indian *munshis* the Bhutanese started to use the term *Zhabs-drung*. But this is unlikely,because in the Indian languages there is no term which phonetically corresponds to *Zhabs-drung*.

4. Nwagong. *rGyal-rigs* and *Lo-rgyus*. English translation of these indeneneous sources are not available. Therefore, the author has to depend on translations done for him by his friends in Bhutan.

5. Nwagong. *op.cit.* The success of the immigrant regional elites in the matter of integration probably depended largely on how and to what extent they had allowed the traditional terms of relationship beween the local elements and the intruders to continue. Any disturbance in this relationship had been found to have weakened the pretenders in their contest for the *sDe-sridship*.

6. The importance of this phenomenon has not been noticed by scholars like Leo B. Rose who has studied the Government and politics in Bhutan.

7. *gTsang-pa* authorities, some minor officials of Tibet and were not a part of the Tibetan ruling high-command, used to get rice tax from the principalities in the western districts of Bhutan.

8. The informantion of revolts that we have collected from different *Nam-thars* and the different British sources we have arrived at the conclusion that except in the case of Geshe Ngawang Gyamtsho, the ninth *sDe-srid*, against whom the monks revolted, the monks normally revolted against the secular *sDe-srids.* To this position the monks could have been driven by the fact that they had somehow developed an identical interest.

9. Many of the secondary sources on the internal history of Bhutan have recorded the over-all influence of the *sDe-srids* in legitimising incarnations and those which are particularly mentionable are Rahul. R. 1971: *Modern Bhutan*, New Delhi, Rose L.E. 1977: The *Politicas of Bhutan*, Ithaca, Hasrat. B.J. 1980 : *History of Bhutan*, Bhutan Chhogley Trulku Yeshe Ngoedub the *sDe-srid* and a *Zhabs-drung* had been deposed by Ugyan Wangchuk, the founder of the monarchy in Bhutan. For details see author's book *Bhutan and India* (In Press) in which this issue has been treated in details.

10. For the Bhutani sources of information one must consult *bsTan-'dzin Chos-rgyal, Ho'i-chose 'byung* and *rGyal-rigas* Michael Aris has given a tentative reconstruction of the events *op. cit.* p. 260.

11. From the Bhutani sources it is known that *Zabs-drung* Jigme Dragpa, the twenty seventh *sDe-srid* and *Zhabs-drung* Trulku Jigmi Norbu, the thirty ninth *sDe-srid* had been deposed by the secular elites for trying to retrieve secular authority as *Zhabs-drung* per se.

12. *Nam-thars.*

13. To Griffith, another, visitor in Bhutan in the middle nineteenth century the *Zhabs-drung* presented a lamentable picture and he wrote, he had fewer attendants and his room was less richly ornamented than that of *Deb.* Journal *of the Mission whcih visited Bhutan in 1837-39 under Capt. Pemberton. p. 26..*

14. This phenomenon became relatively clear because of the fact that of the fifty four *sDe-srids* only fifteen were monks.

15. Aitchison. p. 192, and Mazumdar. A. D. p. 198. During the civil war the Chinese *Amban* at Tibet decided to intervene *vide.* letter from N.R.O. 'Comor, British Charged' affairs Paking to Lord Dufferein, Vicerory of India, 29 December, 1885 *Dufferein Papers, No. 122, Reel, 525.* The British attitude towards Bhutan was defined by the terms of the Treaty of Sinchula and therefore, India did not encourage any Chinese interference in Bhutan, *vide; Foreign Department, Secret E, August 1886, Nos, 627-49.*

16. *Dufferein Papers No, 122, Reel, 525.*

16(a) Aris. M. 1984 : *New Light on an old Clan of Bhutan: The sMyos-raba of Bla-ma gSang-snagags,* a review article in which Aris developed the geheology chart of the different *sMyos* families.

17. The monasteries have been placed under the Government with the provision that the Government would provide the maintenance subsidy and in exchange the monasteries would renounce their rights to collect taxes and surrender land which they used to possess in the good old days

18. Nwagong: *rGyal-rigas.* The matter has been discussed by Bikramjit Hasrat, 1980, p. 54.

19. Carrasco, p. 1959. *Land and Polity in Tibet,* Seattle, p. 220 Carrasco observed, `officers were not quite recruited from the peasant population at large but only some groups, and the higher positions could be reached by members of dominant families'. p. 197.

20. *Proceedings of the Tshogdu* of Bhutan and different numbers of the *Kuensel.*

21. *Proceedings of the Tshogdu,* 1970.

22. *Proceedings of the Tshogdu,* 1967-69.

23. *Foreign Department; Political Consultation,* November 13,1839 No. 74-75. *Foreign Department, Political Despatch from the Court of Directors,* May 11, 1841, No. 12. *Foreign Department, Political Consultation,* June 14, 1841 No. 83 & 86. For the secondary sources see Deb. A. 1975: *Indo-Bhutan Relations,* Culcutta, Labh. K. 1974: India and Bhutan, New Delhi, Swarug. S. 1965: India-Bhutan Relations, New Delhi.

24. *Proceedings of the Tshogdu,* 1968-70.

25. The theoretical framework for the study of factional politics has been drawn upon the following works. Brass. p. 1965: *Factional Politics in an Indian State: The Congress Party in Uttar Pradesh,* California, Weiner. M. 1967 *Party building in a New Nation: The Indian National Congress, Chicago,* Bailey. J.G. 1969: *Politics and Social Change: Orissa* in 1953, California. Carras, M.C. 1972: *The Dynamics of Indian Political Factions: A study of District Councils in the State of Maharashtra,* Cambridge.

References

Aitchison, 1920 : *Treaties Engagements and Sunnuds Relating to India and the Neighbouring States*, Calcutta, XIV

Mazumdar. A.B. 1979 : *Anglo-Bhutan Relations* . Patna

Aris, M. 1968 : *Bhutan*, New Delhi.

1984 : *New Light on the Old Clan of Bhutan: The sMyos-rabs of Bla-ma qSang-bngags.*

Bose, K.K. N.D. : Account of Bhutan : Political Mission to Bhutan, *Asiatic Researches XV*.

Davis, S. 1830 : Remarks on the religious and social institutions of the *Bouteas* of Bhutan *Transactions of the Royal Asiatic Society*, London.

Hasrat, B.J. 1980 : *History of Bhutan*. Bhutan.

Markham, C.R. 1879 : *Narratives of the Missing of George Bogle to Tibet and the Journey of Thomas Manning to Lhase*, London

Pemberton R.B. 1938 : *Report on Bhutan*, London.

1961 : *Report on Bhutan* (reprinted in Indian Studies : Past and Present).

Rose Leo. E. 1977 : *The Politics of Bhutan*, Ithaca.

Tucci, O. 1973 : *The Ancient Civilization of the Trans-Himalayas*, London.

White, C. 1909 : *Sikkim and Bhutan, Twenty Years of the North East Frontier 1887-1908.*

Weber M. 1977 : *Essays in Sociology*, (ed) H.H. Gerth and C. Wright Mills, New York.

5

STATE STRUCTURE, IDEOLOGY AND POLITICAL SYSTEM IN BHUTAN

ANUP DATTA

Nature of State

In recent years, the concept of 'State' has undergone remarkable ramifications; especially in the emergent Third World States, the nascent character of socio-political institutions, and contours of societal structure have been shaped by the historical-social conditions as well as by economic expediencies of self-survival. The European State system emerged in response to the demands of the right of self-determination; whereas in the existing Third World States, the wave of populist aspirations and claims have led to distinctive formations of the State, based on ideology, religion, social cleavages and primordial identities. Nations were shaped by history, and States were enacted and produced by the specific demands of conglomerate nationalities, of tribes, or ethnic loyalties or class. In some States, there have been a remarkable change of institutional varieties, which have existed before the Second World War. Nevertheless, most of the societies are struggling to cope with the consequences of social and political modernisation (Eisenstradt, 1975: 1-18). In so far as they are committed to a process of social and economic modernisation, the Government institutions have been altered in response to the specific demands or contingencies of social relations.

At the same time their credibility as national societies is complicated by the fact that they attempt to forge links with the past, with their prior experience and culture, while the urges for modernization them to bring about the radical alternation in the erstwhile insititutionalism. Monarchy has not been an usual institution in most of the Third World States. For a country which has remained isolated for centuries, the attainment of a national identity in the modern world has been relatively problematic, while the attempt to modernize is fraught with interminable odds, palpably in contrast and traumatic in the context of a placid, customary, traditional life, absorbed in singing of hymn or chanting of scriptures (Rose,1977).

The Bhutanese of Bhutan

Any study of Bhutan, its state structure, ideology and its evolving political system should be examined in this comparative perspective; while democracy and nationalism have been potent forces, in the South Asian Sub-contient, *i.e.,* Nepal or Bhutan, politics or political system came rather late, in the sense that both the countries, have been under traditional monarchial rule. Although Bhutan was never under colonial rule, the Drukpas or the Bhutanese, of today, were not the original inhabitants of the country. According to ancient sources, Bhutan was known as 'Bhotanta' the term 'Bhot' implies Tibet and 'Anta' denotes, the end (Das, 1973 : ch1). According to the best available records, Tibetan troops invaded the country at the end of the 9the century A.D., expelled the Indian Princes and their subjects, and then settled down in occupation of the land. Another report suggests, that Bhutan formerly belonged to a tribe called Bhotia Telphu, who belonged to the same races as the Kacharis and the Koch, of the adjoining plains of India. The people of Eastern Bhutan, are different from the Drukpa Tibetan stock of people, inhabiting Central and Western Bhutan. The indigenous people of Bhutan are called the Lhoman and the Monpa. The Tibetans - implying southern people. The Tibetan incursions and consolidation between the 9th and the 17th centuries led to the disappearance of the original settlers of the country and emergence of a new ethnic group, called the Drukpas of the Kagpya sect. (Rahul, 1903 : 5). A prominent Tibetan Drukpa Ngawang Namgyal, losing the power struggle in Tibet, succedded in consolidating and uniting the powerful Drupka families and assumed the title of *Shabdung* - establishing a complete theocracy. He created an administrative structure by dividing the country into three provinces, each was headed by a Governor or *Penlop.* Within each province, *dzong-pones* were appointed to administer individual districts. Towards the end of the rule, two faithful monks assisted in administering the country. One is called the *Je Khempo,* or Lord Abbot, who was in charge of religious affairs, while the other *Druk Desi,* was entrusted with administration of civil matters. The *Shambdung* also created a State Council composed mainly of monastic officials to assist in electing these officials in governing the country, while *Shabdung* Namgyal created a unified Bhutan. The theocracy he created was inherently unstable. The State Council became increasingly secularized, with most civil positions, including those of the Druk Desi, the *Penlops,* and the *dzong-pons* filled by civilians. By the nineteenth century, the *Penlops* usually from Paro or Tongsa, became more powerful and rivalry between *Penlops* led to continuing internal turmoil[1]. Thus while there were only seven *Shabdungs,* between 1651 and 1907, there were as many as 56 *Druk Desis* (Das, 1973 : 20). Disarray continued until the turn of the twentieth century, when the *Tongsa Penlop,* Ugyen Wanchuk, emerged as the supreme ruler. Sir Ugyen was installed as the first Maharaja of Bhutan on 17th December, 1907. Despite internal turmoil, factionalism among the Deb Rajas and Tibetan's repeated attempts to annex, Bhutan was able to maintain its unity, and struck a middle case of negotiation with the Britishers, in 1910, signing a treaty with British, amending certain provisions of the 1865 treaty. Under the revised treaty, the British pledged 'to exercise no interference in the internal administration of Bhutan' while the Government of Bhutan, agreed to be guided by the advise of the British Government in regard to its external relations. The annual payment to Bhutan was also doubled to Rs.100,000. Over the next fifty years, successive Kings centralized the power of monarchy, integrated the various factions and regions, into a stable political unity that characterises the present day Bhutan (Rose, 1977 : 32-39). However, the Kings refrained from exercising control on religious matters instead, they recognised the continued authority of *Je Khempo,* in the religious sphere.

Ethnic and Communal Cleavages

The modern Bhutanese society emerged out of distinctively separate ethnic groups. However, it is generally classified into three main distinct groups, the Sharchops, the Ngalops and those of the Nepalese origin. The Bhutanese who dwell in the area east of the black mountains, are supposed to be the major inhabitants of modern Bhutan. Belonging to the Indo-Mongoloid origin, they appear closely related to the inhabitants of north-east India and northern Burma. The linguistic structure of these people is diverse, and the people there speak in different dialects. In dress, fashion and rituals of festivals they seem to be close to the Drukpa-Buddhist cultural patterns, similar to the Western Bhutanese. Essentially constituting the dominant race, they constitute the Government of hierarchial order. It is they who constitute the distinctive patterns of culture. The second group is the Ngalops, who belong to the Tibetan origin arriving in Bhutan between 8th century A.D. and as recently as 1959, bringing with them the Tibetan culture and the Buddhist religion which characterizes Northern Bhutan. Most among them migrated to Bhutan as early as the ninth century, and after the Chinese occupation of Tibet, they adhered to the Mahayana Buddhism, and are close to the Drukpa sect. They speak Dzonkha - the language of the Drukpa religious order. The third element consists of a number of small tribal groups, such as the Drukpas, Lepchas and the Doyas who are supposed to be aboriginals or indigenous inhabitants of the country (Phadnis, 1989: 39-40).

As against this, there is a significant portion of the Nepalese, most of whom are the Hindus, but nevertheless constitute a significant force, brought in during the nineteenth and early twentieth century, to work as labourers in southern Bhutan. Most of them are migrants, speak Nepali and have familial connections, or extended kinship relationship with Nepal, and adjacent Darjeeling and Kalimpong. Although immigration is banned, since 1959, a large number of the Nepalese and Indians are permitted to work in Bhutan as contract labours. They constitute almost 20 per cent to 30 per cent of the total population. According to the Census figures for 1969, there are almost 138,000 permanent Napali residents in Samchi and Chirang who have strong political traditions, different from that of the Bhutanese. The Nepalese of Bhutan are settled in areas, where they constitute the predominant group in population composition. Although the policy of the Royal Government was to restrict them to Southern Bhutan, with little interaction outside, the policy of assimilation with the mainstream, remains the predominant challenge to the Bhutanese authority. Inter-marriage between them are encouraged, and many Nepalese have been given jobs in and around Western Bhutan; the authority by KIDU policy, distributed land, and ownership to many Nepalese, to alleviate the alleged discrimination, and merge the minority communities into the national culture - the basic policy, has been one of accommodation and assimilation, so that the Nepali-Bhutanese are not estranged from the mainstream of the Drukpa culture (Rose, 1977 : 44-49).

Salient traits of Bhutanese Monarchy

It is true that amidst all turmoil in South Asia, Bhutan stood for a few decades, as a symbol of 'integrated society'. It is worth mentioning also that Bhutan has not relapsed into any trap of 'colonial syndrome' it has turned from isolation into a modern State, with a policy of 'equidistance', with the western powers and the socialist powers. Whereas in other monarchic states, a traditional culture has been subjected to radical transformation, leading to the repudiation of existing values, in Bhutan the indigenous control has been strong enough to retain, guide and limit the variety of immediate adjustments in governmental structure and popular political action. Thus, in Bhutan the political culture of the Drukpas, the dominant sect, remains the principal determinant of the Bhutanese political orientation, as she is driven to the direction of political modernization.

What leads distinctiveness to the Bhutanese political system, is the remarkable character of resilence in state apparatus, and her distinct political system.

1. The Bhutanese politics of today is continuously persisting with the political institutions, that were led and founded by earlier rulers, for last one hundred years. Although it shares the agonies and reflections of the new States of Asia and Africa, it has not fallen into any major trap of 'democratisation of politics', or 'politicisation', in broader scale (Rose, 1977: 106).

2. Unlike other constitutional monarchies, whose elites represent alien elements, and whose elites identify with western culture, and absorbed in it -- Bhutan has been traditionally governed by the indigenous elites, connected with her traditional institutions, and bearers of a national culture. However, much divided by differences of region, dialect, custom, theology and language, the elites represent common cultures of ancient national glories, and the symbol of Mahayana Buddhism (Rose, 1977: 107).

3. The Bhutanese Monarchy is never dogmatically or rigidly opposed to the principles of 'accommodation' and 'Consensus'. Though Bhutan is ruled by the Kings, and has no 'written constitution' -- it is not essentially a personalised regime -- the King and the Tsoughidow share power equally. Although the Wanchuks families have dominated the State and politics in Bhutan, the theocratic supremacy is not superseded in the mirages of modernisation and development which characterises the so-called African and Asian States (Geertz : n.d.)

4. The Drukpa hegemony is upheld by a set of beliefs and sentiments, which are not typical of other monorchical States. Although it shares culturally with other South Asian States, it is not marked by extremism, either of the religious monks, or of the political leadership. Unlike many dictators in disguise, the King in Bhutan has been quite responsive to the people's urges and aspirations. Obedience is the prime consideration in the socialisation of the Bhutanese children; they are taught to obey the religious authority and uphold the symbols of the Bhutanese dignity, national prestige and symbolism.

5. The Bhutanese political system lacks a dominant ideology either constitutionalism or 'rigid party rule'. The monoarchial institutions grew out in the earlier twentieth century from a Mahayana Buddhist theocratic ideology -- that provide the underpinning for the system of hereditary kinship. Bhutan, it is argued, had been in a state of anarchial condition, before 1907, and indeed, it is the institution of monarchy, that has lent credence to unity and stability of the country, and resolved the contradictions between the temporal ruler and the secular ruler. The fact that Bhutan has been a non-colonial state, distinguishes her from many nations, in specific respects --

(a) The Bhutanese enjoy a high degree of self esteem and pride in their long struggle against foreigners, the Tibetans, (b) The Bhutanese political life has not experienced very effective role of agitative politics, except for one by the Bhutanese Congress in 1960, and more recently, by the Bhutanese People's Party (BPP) (c) The Bhutanese culture enjoins the attitude that authority, as such, is good and indispensable for the well being of society, and worthy of unremitting deference, obeisance and praise (Rase, 1977: 211-224).

The Basis of Legitimacy

It is difficult to assess that proportion of the total population of Bhutan which accepts the suzerainty of the monarchy. It is also presumably true that a section of the people settled in Southern Bhutan and some tribesmen remain alienated from it. But the large chunk of population certainly accept it, even when they may sometimes be critical of some of the policy measures; perhaps, this could be the reason for the present authority to eliminate semi-autonomous strength of the competing rival factions of the powerful nobles, and to centralize power and prestige in his person and the Bhutanese State. The authority of national Government in Bhutan rests primarily upon a solid base of allegiance and subordination to the offices of the Druk Gyalpo; it also earns legitimacy from the aspirations of the people of Bhutan to maintain their national territory and freedom from alien domination. Except for the Nepalese element in population, most Bhutanese who have strong awareness of the country's polity, are passionate nationalists (Dutta, 1985: 11-12).

The authority of the national Government is further upheld by its acceptance as a spokesman for and defender of national political interests, which is singularly nucleated in Thimpu. King Jigme Singye Wanchuk regretted recently:

"Our greatest disadvantage is that people from outside feel that it must be feudal and backward. The way we have decentralized our decision making process does not deserve the due attention of the outside world. Our future survival will depend on whether we have a highly efficient Government and political system. I will like to leave behind a legacy of a highly efficient Government, receptive to the high aspirations of the people" (Parmananda, 1991: 1422-23).

The Bhutanese is not a 'political society' in as much as involvement with the goals of the total society is not widely dispersed throughout the populace. Men who possess a good measure of one or more qualities for which high status is placed in the Bhutanese society -- family, age, wealth accelesiastical rank and political rank -- are worshipped through out the society, and their judgments and decisions are binding in their local contexts.

Another distinctive feature of the Monarchy's pre-eminent position was his authority to induce cultural as well as economic changes. While the Bhutanese are essentially resistant to change and modernisation, in the restricted sense of bringing westernisation and modernisation, they expect the King to ensure the welfare of the realm; they tolerate, not with reluctance, his deviation from precedent when that do not conflict with the ultimate traditional values, such as obedience to religious monks. The establishment of planned development with the promotion of private sector, and establishment of new institutions, such as Bank of Bhutan, the Citizenship Act 1977, accountability of the King to Tsoughdou and liberalization and reform, by the present King, is looked with reverence, and not with any sinister attempt to radically change the existing traditional moves (Misra, 1981 : 4-6) Whereas, in Euthopia, a traditional cultural has not been subjected to radical transition through the agency of the alien powers, in Bhutan the political culture of the Drukpas, dominant in the modern political system of Bhutan remains the major or primary determinant in political orientation (Levine, 1989: 245-281). It is reasonable at this stage to ask what are the most important features of this cultural environment -- a culture which has attempted to blend forth the traditional values of religion and monastic establishment with the goals and courses of political development.

Political Communication and Social Control

To find an answer of this, one needs to closely scrutinise the legitimate basis of monarchical system, as it is placed in modern context. For Bhutan, the idea of a 'Sovereign Bhutan' was mooted and consolidated under the reign of the former King, who assumed the title, 'Maharaja', and conceived of Bhutan, as a political and social structure, with its independent status -- the present Bhutan sought to accommodate all sections of the populations in a larger national context -- declaring them as all are sons of 'Palden Drukpa', whether he or she is a Nepali, Tibetans, or belongs to other ethnic groups. The modern polity is headed by the King, with enormous powers. The Tsoughdou (National Assembly), which was inaugurated by the Royal order of 1953, is composed of 157 Assembly members which include 107 representatives of the people -- six of them from the Royal Advisory Councils -- 40 Officials of the Royal Government, 10 from the *Rabdey* (Clergy)[2]. Although it enjoys tremendous responsibilites of ratifying appointments, promotion, discussion and deliberation of Government policies, it cannot go against the Royal King, who can persuade or veto any policy resolutions. The powers of the King, are doubly enhanced by the fact that the Druk Gyalpo is both Head of the State, and that of Administration. He is the highest court of appeal. All members of the Government, which includes Council of Ministers, the Lodoi Tsokde (Royal Advisory Council), Secretaries of various Government departments and Ministries, and district officers or zonal Administrators, hold office at the discretion of the King (Parmananda, 1988: 127-128). The Royal Bhutanese Police and the Bhutanese Armed Forces, are under the direct command of the Royal King.

The second concept which is essential to the notion of legitimacy and modernization of institutionalism -- is rationalisation. Rationalisation implies the sustained and systematic efforts to subject man's environment to rational control, more specifically to maximize the efficiency of operation of the various parts of the political system. In regard to the organs of the Government this usually entails a bureaucratic form of public administration, and a division or specialisation of work, the separation of judicial, legislative and executive functions. In Bhutan, in the compositions of both *Ladoi Chepdah* (Royal Advisory Council) and Tsoughdou, the element of checks and balances, are easily identifiable. For any resolution to be passed, two thirds majority, or simple majority is required. In an Assembly, where about one third are officials nominated by the King, and about one half representatives of the people, and the rest, representatives of monastic order, no resolution can probably throw up a direct challenge to the position of the Royal King. In actuality, the traditional belief in the transcendant dignity of the King and authority of the Wanchuk administration, has been strengthened by vigorous functioning of the Tsoughdou and Royal Advisory Councils and perceptible impact of the monarchy, in controlling and regulating different branches of Government (Misra, 1981 : 8-9). The tenacity of the mentality was all the more evident, when Tsoughdou actually repeated the provision of 'removal' of the King initiated by the previous King, from the rules. It was also illustrated by the vigorous way of tightening the civil administration, exposure of corruption in high places, retrenchment of civil servants, who are disloyal or unproductive, by the present King, with the advise of the Royal Civil Service Commission (RCSC), to ensure efficiency and competence in the process of administrative functioning.[3] The course of political modernisation has been streamlined by monarchs, by the introduction of the Citizenship Act, expulsion of foreign nationals of Southern Nepal, and vigorous enforcement of law and order machinery, and quelling of antinational terrorism, introduction of military training of 30,000 volunteers from five *Dzongkhags* to strengthen the shield against terrorist activities in the southern district. The Royal King also cautioned the terrorists, by saying "If a large section of the Bhutanese people feel a closer affinity with people in Nepal, or the Nepalese in India, then with their fellow citizens in the Kingdom, Bhutan -- with its small people -- becomes extremely vulnerable, and its very survival will be surely threatened."[4]

The third concept of political modernization centres round the articulation and aggregation of interests. The lack of organizations for articulation and aggregation of interests in Bhutan is the result not so much of the monarchical ethos, but rather deliberate. It was essentially a product of the trauma which the Bhutanese traditional society was faced with -- especially after the assassination of Prime Minister Jigme Dorji in 1964. It necessarily reflects the difficulties the Bhutanese face in understanding any collective action, particularly in the political sphere (Rustomji, 1978). The Bhutanese society is essentially based on 'elitist politics' and 'consensus'. Whichever and whatever channel the dissent is expressed, it is generally sought to be smothered or accommodated or muzzled in a 'consensus framework'. The mutual distrust and lack of confidence, is generated more by the political climate around Bhutan as well as by the nature of the tiny Bhutanese State. The idea of 'democratizing' the political process -- a free adult suffrage, political participation and election campaign -- probably remains inchoate, so long education, literacy and manpower developments are incomplete and inadequate. Indeed, it is the King who plays the most dominant role in the performance of interest articulation and aggregation. All serious expressions of pressure groups or dissent, are brought to his notice, or sought to be solved by direct intervention of the King.

Political information transmitted to the Government, through different channels, are all under direct or indirect control of the King, the formal intelligence networks, and informal networks who report to him, more or less regularly. Since he is the Supreme Commander of the Royal Bhutanese Armed Forces, he controls virtually all levels of power, with unstinted loyalties. A further source of King's strength is his relationship with *Je Khepmo*, or the Chief Abbot. In the Bhutanese State, being largely based on Buddhist philosophy of tolerance, loyalty and obedience, the Lamas or monks provide a sound credibility to the system of institutionalism. And in such a context, the Royal King,*albeit* not the supreme religious ruler, enjoys the sanction of the religious priests, as well as enjoys confidence of the Bhutanese nobilities. And so long the King can muster suppport from both nobles and religious monks, so long he enjoys the confidence of the large sections of the Bhutanese people, he would be in a position of supremacy. The 1990's and recent demonstrations organised by the Bhutanese People's Party to enlarge mobilisation system and induce democratic process, was prompted by twin factors: one, some subjects were dropped out as citizens, and secondly, because of Government's introduction of *Drighan Namzha* (etiquette) -- *Kho* for men, and *Lira* for women by the Bhutanese of all hues and all ethnic groups--an effort which was interpreted as the 'Bhutanisation', and further estrangement of Bhutanese Nepali -- of the southern districts (Parmananda, 1991 : 1411-1424).

Decentralisation at the Grass-roots

Since the inception of planned development in 1961, the Royal Government has undertaken 'self reliance and the improvement of the socio-economic conditions' of the people, as its principal objectives. The major strategies include self reliance at the destrict level, decentralization of administration, popular participation in the developmental process, and efforts to mobilize internal resources. At the initial stage, the rudimentary character of new administrative mechanism, non-co-ordination and non-functionalism have contributed to the level of poverty, and there were absence of any physical or social infrastructure like roads, health, schools and communication facilities.[5] Realising these basic needs, the macro-level approach was gradually replaced by micro-level planning. The Bhutanese planners have cautiously moved forward to ensure both local participation, without touching the traditional fabric, as well as ensuring communication with the people. First, they attempted to involve district administrations and people's representatives in designing and implementing such local projects, as construction of roads and bridges, schools, health clinics and small irrigation works. Local costs were met by the intended beneficiaries--while the rest was met by the Central Government (Shah, 1989:822-824). In 1985, in order to ensure the effectiveness of Government involvement, at local level, 1/4 of the Central Government work force was assigned to district administrative units, and performance evaluation was prepared (*Ibid* : 822).

Secondly, rural incomes were sought to be improved by offering packaged inputs, extension services, and marketing assistance to farmers in areas, and for crops with rapid productivity. The programme includes six rice growing areas, covering about 25 per cent of arable land -- the promotion of cash crops, viz., orange, apples and potatoes ; the provision of feed and improved breeding stocks for selected animal husbandry projects. What the Government intended to do was to cultivate trust, changing attitudes, and recruitment of personnel, and introduction of new technology. Tashigang Dzongkhag introduced a new approach, called "Impact Oriented Extension Programmes." The new extension guidelines, issued by the Department of Agriculture, divides each *Gewag* into five to seven contact area circles depending upon the households, offering them scope for improvement in agriculture, and accessability. It will help the farmers to learn, adopt and transfer the knowledge to other *dzongkhags,* and improve the 'quality of life' in rural areas.[7]

Thirdly, planning at the central level is increasingly being diverted to improve rural amenities by providing electricity, safe drinking water, sewage facilities, cooking stoves, and insulated houses. If development is to be broadbased, the effective way to do this, is to transfer the fruits of development to rural areas. This will offset both rural-urban migration and is likely to fetch high rate of return. With this end in view, private logging is being banned, and public sector agencies are so regulated that they had to reduce operations. Similarly, in tourism, the unrestricted growth, undermines the traditional fabric of life.[8]

Finally, in the sixth plan itself, the King took a personal interest and visited seven *dzongkhags* of Central and Eastern Bhutan, Tongsa, Bumthong, Lhuntsi, Monger, Tashigang, Pema Gatshel, Deothong Samdrup Jhankar, describing plans with DYT members of the *dzongkhags.*[9] The King insisted that DYT's should be 'dynamic Forums' for exchange of views in the formulation and growth of rural developmental activities, suggesting the modalities of recruitment of membership. Most dedicated, capable and committed persons of the *dzonkhoage* should be chosen as members. The core idea of the Sixth Plan is to invigorate local level participation, from the notional district (dzongkhag) level to the block gewag level. Integrated gewag development centres are to be established in optimum locations. The IGDC are to be spatially distributed, according to both geography and demography. The centres will become core administrative units with a developmental planning committee at the block level. It will help in training cadres and to make more cost effective development investments.[10] The initial dependence of foreign aid should be given way to self sustenance, so that increased internal resource mobilisation can be done. Planned modernisation and development, perhaps, demand not only resource mobilisation but also distribution of growth and ensuring social justice. The decentralisation *of dzongkhas* administration, appointment of Zonal Administrators for all four zones, will automatically streamline the development process, and ensure maximum amount of honesty and compactness in the rural planning process.[11] His majesty's warning that the development activities "tended to lean towards an imbalance " reflect self-introspection, as well as maturity of the development process. The phenomenal increase of *dzongkhag* staff from 303 to 2894, point out also the concentration and urge for decentralization,[12] and perhaps would stall any move towards separatism or ethnic subversions from inside.[13]

The basis on which Bhutanese monarchy, and political system based, derives essentially from the fact that the King is the dominant agent of political recruitment, and his legitimacy derives sanction from his ability to effectuate social and economic changes.[14] Since the mass media are under the total control of the authority and dynamism, in any form, is appreciable to the extent that it inculcates loyalty, submissiveness, and maximising coalescence of interest. The pre-eminent activity of the King, his paternalism, his capacity to induce changes, is blended with his image as symbol of national unity, and protector of Bhuddist cultural and religious tradition, even if that implies disdain for radical changes in political orientation.

Notes

1. Bhutan: Development in a Himalayan Kingdom, World Bank Report, 1982, pp 6-9.

2. Kuensel, July 11, 1987.

3. Kuensel, Aug 29, 1987.

4. Kuensel, Jan 5, 1991.

5. Planning Commission, Royal Government of Bhutan 'Country Economic Memorandum', Vol. I, Main Report, Asia and Pacific Round Table Meeting, Geneva, May, 1983.

6. Kuensel, Issues. 1989, 90-91.

7. Kuensel, February 14, 1987.

8. Kuensel, July 25, 1987.

9. Kuensel, February 21, March 28,1987.

10. Far Eastern Economic Review, Yearbook, 1986, pp.112-113.

11. Kuensel, Dec. 17, 1988. For a recent review of Planning and Development experience,see S.W.R. Samarc Singhe, 'The Bhutanese Economy in Transition', *Asian Survey,* Vol.6, June, 1990.

12. Kuensel, March 25, 1984.

13. Kuensel Issues, October-March, 1990-91.

14. For Development Planning in Modern Context, See Bhutan: Development Planning in an Unique Enviroment (Washington D.C. The World Bank, 1989).

References

Das, Nirmala	1985	:	The Dargon Country (Orient Longman)
Datta, Anup	1985	:	Identity, Development and Modernization ; Self Perceptions of the Bhutanese Monarchy, *Novem-Organum.*
Eisenstradt	1975	:	'The Influence of Traditional and Colonial Political System on the Development of Post-traditional Social and Political Orders in Dieter Evers (ed), Modernisation in South East Asia (Oxford).
Ceertz Clifford n.d. (Ed)	N.D.		Old Societies and New States.
Levine Donald	1989	:	"Ethiopia; Identity, Authority and Realism" in Pye and Verba (ed), Political Culture and Political Development" (Princeton, Indian Edition).
Misra, R.C.	1981	:	'Institutional Achievement, and Problems of the Process of Nation-Building', Seminar Papers, Centre for Himalyan Studies, March 23-25.
Parmananda	1988	:	Political Development in South Asia (Sterling).
	1991	:	(a) 'India-Bhutan Friendship and Bhutan's Problem of National Integration', *Strategic Analysis,* March Vol. XIII, No. 12, p.1422-23.
	1991	:	(b) 'India-Bhutan Friendship and Bhutan's Problem of National Integration', *Strategic Analysis,* March, Also see Kuensel issues.

Phadnis Urmila	1989	:	Ethnicity and Nation Building in South Asia (Sage)
Rahul Ram	1903	:	'Royal Bhutan (ABC Publishing House).
Rose, Leo	1977	:	The Politics of Bhutan (Cornell).
Rustomji Nari	1978	:	The Dragon Kingdom in Crisis (Oxford).
Shah, Sukhdev	1989	:	'Developing Bhutan's Economy' Asian Survey, August.

6

SOCIO-POLITICAL ASPECTS OF THE SHERPAS OF NEPAL : PERSISTENCE AND CHANGE

B.C. UPRETI

The South Asian societies are multi-ethnic and multi-racial. A considerable chunk of population in each South Asian country belongs to tribes. The tribal population has been, by and large, backward, underdeveloped and living in the so countries. These tribes exhibit distinct culture, social life and behavior patterns. While most of the tribes still maintain their traditional culture and life style, the process of modernization and development initiated by the respective countries of the region, has also transformed the socio-economic conditions of the tribes, thereby bringing them in the national mainstream. However, the peculiarities about the culture, social behavior, life style, rituals, etc., have been a great source of attraction to the anthropologists. As a result a large number of studies have been done about the tribes of South Asian region.

In Nepal except the *arai* .region, most of the tribes of the hills belong to the mongoloid racial stock. The mongoloid element is strongly expressed in their physical features and cultural traits (Fuchs, 1982 : 33). The tribal population of mongoloid origin have generally medium stature, brachycephalic head, broad face, high chickbone, flat nose and light-yellow or light-brown skin (Fuchs, 1982 : 42). Some of the important tribes belonging to the monogloid group are the Gurungs, Magars, Tamangs, Thakalis, Sunwars, Limbu, Rai, Sherpas, and others. Their traditional profession has been agriculture, pastoral works, animal hunting and trade. These tribes are said to have been originated from Tibet and further north and east to that. Their culture, language, religion, liege style have been quite similar to those of the Tibetans. The Rais, Limbus and the Khambus are considered to be the early settlers among the tribes. Though the Tibetan cultural influences have been dominant many of these tribes have also began to follow the cultural traits of the south. Thus, some of them are passing through a stage of cultural transformation. Although the degree of influence of the south-primarily that of Hindu culture - may be different among different tribes (Fuchs, 1982 : 93)

Among various tribes of Nepal the Sherpas have been the most prominent. It has indeed become a distinct group in the social and economic life of the tribal Nepal. The Sherpas have earned world fame because of their mountaineering skill, and they have quite successfully professionalized this skill.

Sherpa Settlement

The Sherpas are highland people residing in the northern districts of Sagarmatha zone, along the Dudh Kosi river and in the Hlmu and the upper Trishuli valley.(Bisk, 1987 : 160). They are the people of mongoloid origin who have migrated in the Himalayan region of the kingdom from Tibet.

The term Sherpa is said to have originated from the word 'Sharva' which means people living in the east (Bista, 1987 : 160). The mains areas of the Sherpa settlement are Solu, Khumbu and Pharak. Solu is situated at an altitude of 8000 ft. It has temperate climate suitable for agriculture. Khumbu is a broad valley at an altitude of 11000 to 15000 ft. The whole area of Khumbu remains covered by snow for more than half of the year. The cultivable land is naturally limited in this region. Pharak is a narrow belt on either side of the river Dudh Kosi. Apart from these main centres of settlement, Sherpas also reside in Rolwaling, Likhu, Khola, Khimati Khola, Inukhu Khola and Taplejung. In the present times, however, the Sherpas have settled in other parts of the kingdom as well, particularly in the Kathmandu valley.

Generally, they have two types of settlements -- winter and summer. During the winter seasons they come down to warmer area and travel widely.

Society, Religion and Culture

The Sherpas have a homogeneous society (Haimendorf, 1975 : 26). All are considered equal within the society. It is by and large an unstratified society and in that respect it differs from the Hindu society or even the Bhotis living in the neighbouring regions (Haimendorf, 1975 : 151). Earlier there was no status differentiation in the Sherpa society but with the settlement of the Khampas in this region the element of status differentiation has come up. The Sherpas consider the Khampas as people of a lower status in comparison to their own status. Moreover, with the changes in the economic activities of the Sherpas status differentiation is taking roots within the Sherpas themselves.

The Sherpa society has been influenced by the outside changes. Yet the traditional pattern of the society has been maintained. The sherpas live a free life. They enjoy full right to select their own life pattern. The joint family system is not operative by and large.

The Sherpa folks enjoy freedom in selecting their life partners. Festivals, religious ceremonies, and other get togethers provide opportunities for selecting life-partners. The only restrictions is that cross-cousin marriages are prohibited. Marriages last for many days. It is an occasion of eating, singing and dancing. The Sherpa marriages are mostly monogamous but polygamy and polyandry are also practised (Haimendrof, 1984: 44) But now they are in decline (Hain dorf, 1984:46). Divorce is possibly through mutual consent of husband and wife. One interesting thing about the Sherpa marriage is that the social status of a Sherpa is enhanced as soon as he brings his wife home. Now onwards he is called father of anssom instead of being designated by his name. Therefore, he should have atleast one child born before his wife comes to live with him. Naturally the birth of first child is prestigious (Bisto,1987: 167).

Woman has equal status in the society. She is self reliant and shares all the burdens of family equally. When men folks are out for the purpose of trade or trekking she alone is responsible for the proper lookafter of family, animals and agriculture. The climatic conditions and life pattern have made Sherpa women hard-worker and brave.

The Sherpas are religious people. The observe a large number of rituals (ortner, 1978). Most of the Sherpas belong to Nigagma-pa sect of Tibetan Buddhism. But some being to the Sakyapa sect as well. In every village there is one *gompa* (monastery) where Buddhist monks and nuns stay. Some important *gompas* of this region are at Tangboche and Chiwang. Tangboche is considered to be the best maintained monastery. The Sherpas are nonviolent and slaughtering of animals is prohibited among them. But they can eat meat if an animal is slaughtered by some one else. Earlier the Tibetan butchers were child in the Sherpa villages for this purpose.

The Sherpas speak their own dialect originated from the Tibeto-Burmen language (Gaize, 1973; 48). After their mobility and trade link is with the southern parts of the kingdom they have also started speaking Gorkhali and other religion dialects. The Sherpas engaged in tourism profession, have also earned a workable knowledge of English which is necessary from the point of view of their profession.

The Sherpas observe a large number of colourful festivals. Festivals are indeed occasions. Most important festival for the Sherpa is *Losar* -- the new year festival-observed in the month of February or early March. On the occasion of *losar* all the Sherpas who had gone out during the winter season, return to their villages. It is time of feasting, eating, drinking and dancing. *Dumze* is another important festival and celebrated for seven days in the month of July when the agricultural work is just over. This festival signifies health, prosperity and welfare of the people of Nepal. *Mainirimdu* is celebrated twice in a year by the monks of the monasteries. Monks perform religious dances in different costumes and by using masks of various deities.

These dances are watched by others. Apart from these big festivals there are a number of small festivals of social relevance celebrated by the Sherpas. *Nyungne* is a festival when drinking and dancing is prohibited and people keep fast for three days and monks for fifteen days. It may be pointed out here that in the absence of the means of recreation the festivals had specific significance from the point of view of individual enjoyment and merry-making.

Traditional Economy

The traditional economy of the Sherpas has directly been related to the mountain environment. The constraints of nature has also limited the economic activities of the Sherpas. Traditionally, there were three main areas of their economic activities: agricultureal, animal husbandry and trade. There were regional variations in economic means. For instance, in the Khumbu region trade and animal husbandry were major professions rather than agriculture, while the solu-Sherpas are mostly engaged in agriculture. In this region winter crop is also possible.

The cultivation of potatoes is major agriculture activity of the Sherpas, which constitutes a major part of their diet. Other crops are buckwheat, radish, barley and millet.

Animal husbandry is an important profession even to those Sherpas who are engaged in agriculture. The main pet animals are Yak, *Dropkyo Drum*, etc. Animals provide them better meat which is prestigious part of the Sherpa food. It is also used in lamps in the monasteries. Long hairs of the Yaks are used for weaving blankets and making ropes. The soft wool obtained from them is used for preparing clothes. Animal breeding is also an important profession. Earlier the crossbreed animals were sold in Tibet. The owners of Yak heads have to travel from pasture to pasture in search of food for the animals.(Harimendorf, 1975 : 52-56).

Trade was yet another major traditional profession. The Khumbu Sherpas had an upper hand in the trade. It may be noted that among the hill tribes only the Sherpas and the Thakalis were involved in business (Gaize, 1975; 33). The Sherpas acted as middlemen and had benefited in this regard because being habitual to high altitude atmosphere it was possible for them to cross the Nanghala pass and travel in Tibet. They would sell food-grains, potatoes, butter, handmade paper, hides and cotton clothes in Tibet in exchange for tea, salt, sheepskins, furs, ornaments, religious books. Namchebazar was the main trading center. The Sherpas had a monopoly over Nepal's trade with Tibet which was also confirmed by the Rana rulers of Nepal (Haimendrof, 1989; 22). The trade with Tibet was so flourishing that it had developed into a well established commercial system. However, after the Chinese occupation of Tibet and the subsequent closer of Nepal-Tibet border, trade with Tibet had also declined. As a result the Sherpas had to search alternative means of livelihood.

Aspects of Economic and Social Change

The development of tourism, trekking and mountaineering provided unique economic opportunities to Sherpas. Their settlement in the highland areas again benefited them in this regard. Being skilled in long distance travel in mountainous and snowclad regions the Sherpas are considered to be the excellent guides and partners by the foreign tourists. The Sherpas are employed not only for travels in Solu-Khumbu but all over Nepal. The opportunities of employment in tourism and trekking has indeed brought tremendous changes in the economic and social life of the Sherpas.

In some of the Sherpa villages, nearly half of the families are engaged in tourism. In 1985 the Sherpas owned about 30 per cent of the total trekking companies in Nepal (Fisher, 1986 : 40).

The rapid development of tourism has encouraged the rich Sherpas of Namchebazar to engage themselves in hotel business. A large number of hostels, lodges and trekking shops have been established in the Solu-Khumbu region. These trekking shops provide toned food, warm clothes, photographic materials and other essential goods to tourists. Wayside shops and teastalls have also come up. The tourist activities have been further encouraged by the construction of airstrip at Lukla (Phark), 30 minutes flight from Kathmandu from where Namchebazar is two days journey, and the development of Sagarmatha National Park. The attitude of the Sherpas towards the tourists has also changed. Their traditional culture of providing hospitality to travellers has changed. Now some of them try to get maximum money from the foreigners to whom they consider rich and prosperous.

The Sherpas prefer to join tourism in comparison to other professions. The Khumbu Sherpas even hire Solu-Sherpas to work in their fields as they themselves are busy in tourists activities (Marie, 1979). The Sherpa porters earn about 35 per cent of tourists trekking dollars coming in Nepal in a year, (Fishers 1986; 40). Earlier a Sherpa had to go to his *Sirdar* with a bottle of change to seek permission to carry a load but this situation has now completely changed. Other professions which the Sherpas have joined, are teaching, hotel business, contracts (Haimendorf, 1987; 70). They have settled in Kathmandu and other places.

With the changes in the economic activities, social atmosphere of the Sherpa villages is also undergoing a change. Their food habits have changed. Most of the Sherpas are now rice eaters. Other edible things are also available in Namchebazar house utensils and other articles have been replaced by plastic goods or modern articles. The clothing style has also changed. The modern jeans, jackets, wind-cheaters, etc., have taken the place of traditional clothes. The young Sherpas seem to be more attracted to westernized living style. Infact, their association with the foreign tourists has influenced them most in this regard.

The development of the modern education system is yet another important aspect of social change among the Sherpas. Earlier education was imparted by the Lamas in the monasteries. The first modern school was established in 1961 at Khumjung by Sir Edmond Hillary. Later on, its branches were opened at Panboche, Thami, and Ralwaling. The Government educational institutions are also in operation. Now almost every Sherpa village has a school.

The development of tourism has also created certain social problems as well. The family life of the Sherpas has been affected by the tourism. Because of absence of menfolks for a long time other members of the family have to live alone.

Liaison of the young Sherpas with the foreign girls has led to the breaking of many Sherpa families. A number of cases of the Sherpas marrying the foreign girls have been noticed. High casualty rate among the Sherpa guides and porters is also a serious problem. It has been disastrous to many families. The rapid development of tourism has also generated environmental problems in the Himalayas and also affected an otherwise peaceful village life of the Sherpas.

Politics, Political participation and Political Role of the Sherpas

The political system in Nepal has always been centrifugal in nature. Right from the establishment of the Gurkha rule in 1769 till the recent political change in Nepal after a democratic movement launched by the political parties, the Nepalese political system has remained highly authoritarian and politics has largely been confined to a few privileged groups of the society who have enjoyed political as well as economic powers embodied by their higher social status being connected with the higher caste groups of the society. The Kathmandu based ruling elite enjoyed absolute control of political power. During the reigns of the Gurkhas and later of the Ranas common man had no freedom. Although for a brief interlude, the Parliamentary democracy came into operation in 1959 which seemed to precipitate in the politics of the Kingdom but the system was abrogated in December 1962 by King Mahendra who himself assumed all powers. The Panchayat System which was established in 1962 as an alternative to the western type of democracies which also remained authoritarian to the core for it did not allow organized political activities and freedom. Although some changes occurred in the nature and structure of local politics and political participation but by and large the authoritarian nature of the political system continued and the politics remained confined to a few privileged groups.

One exception to this kind of political orientation has been the topography of the kingdom and the lack of means of transportation and communication till recently due to which it was not possible for the central power to exert their political control in the isolated regions. Where there were no means of communication, the communities residing in these pockets enjoyed autonomy in the matters of local village politics. Although the supreme authority continued to be the Kathmandu based rulers, these communities enjoyed de-facto autonomy in the matters of village administration and revenue collection. This was particularly true to the tribal groups which apart from living in isolated regions maintained destinct socio-cultural patterns. Like various other tribal groups the Sherpas also enjoyed some kind of freedom in managing their local affairs.

In the Sherpa community, as in the case of other tribes, village politics and administration was established on the traditional pattern in which the persons responsible for managing local affairs, inherited their positions on hereditary basis.

In the traditional Sherpa society, three positions were important in the village politics and administration, i.e.-*naua, chorpen* and *choumba. Naua* had control over village land collection of revenue. *Chorpen* and *choumba* were responsible for the management of village temples and religious affairs. The village conflictws and disputes were locally resolved and there was no day to day interference in the management of their affairs, unless the revenue collected by the village authorities would not reach to the State treasury in time.

A change occurred in the administration and politics of the Sherpa villages when the Rana rulers appointed paid officials in the Sherpa region for the collection of revenue. This brought certain changes in the traditional pattern of local authority. It also symbolized the increasing control of the central authority. Nevertheless, the traditional village elites were still influential in the local affairs and played a dominant role. This system was followed after the overthrow of the Rana rule in 1951.

After the introduction of the Panchayat System in 1962, village and district Panchayats were also established in the Sherpa region and the Sherpas were thereby brought into a broader political system. It provided an opportunity to the Sherpa to participate in the village politics, although it did not bring any significant change among them in respect to political participation. Their participation in the national politics remained almost negligible. Apart from systemic constraints and difficult topography of the Sherpa region, they also lacked high caste status and educational background which had indeed become essential prerequisites for entering into the politicoadministrative structure. Moreover, the harsh living conditions and limited means of livelihood kept them busy in managing their own household affairs. The other factor was that the Sherpas being a trading community, had hardly a stable life so as to find sufficient time for taking interest in the politics. Till Nepal-Tibet trade was in operation, they were more interested in maintaining their trade connections with their Tibetan counterparts, and were little interested in the affairs of the southern region.

However, as the trade with Tibet declined after 1960 and the Sherpa region gradually opened for tourism and trekking purposes more and more Sherpas adopted the profession of tourist guides and trekking companions in the Himalayas. As a result they began to establish contacts with the people in Kathmandu and other parts of the kingdom. Many of the Sherpas also began to migrate to Kathmandu valley and other southern regions, and settled there. Some Sherpas also started business in Kathmandu. It was natural that they also began to take interest in the local and national political affairs. Some rich Sherpas who had established tourism and trekking business, were also brought into the national Panchayat politics by the ruling elites although in order to serve their own interest. This however, provided. the Sherpas an opportunity to participate in the politics outside the Sherpa region.

With a gradual and limited political-socialization of the Sherpas along with the other tribes of Mongoloid origin, they are becoming politically conscious. Their main grievances seems to have been the domination of a particular group and the State protection to it, and the underdeveloped and backward conditions of the tribes of the Himalayan region. They are conscious about their meagre participation and representation in the national politics and administration. They also feel that the Government has done little to improve their economic lot. There seems to have resentment against the discriminatory policies for the authority. So long the political system was rigid and closed these resentments were latent but as some form of liberalization took place in the Panchayat System after the 1979 movement, the Mongoloid tribes started expressing their resentments.

In the recent years a kind of pan-tribalism is taking roots in Nepal (Phadnis, 1990 : 123). Of course it is still in its nascent stage. In 1980 during referendum people of Mongoloid origin held a conference demanding proper representation of Mongoloid origin in politico-bureaucratic structures declaring Nepal a secular state (Phadnis, 1990 : 123). and starting Nepal samvat instead of Vikram samvat (Basal, 1983 : 96). A Sagarmatha Sherpa Seva Kendra has also been established to look after the economic and political interests of the Sherpas. Although the Sherpas are still not fully politically mobilized, it is hoped that with the liberalization of political system they would also be drawn in the political mainstream of the country.

In sum it can be said that the Sherpas are hardworking people and they have acquired work fame because of their mountaineering skill. They do not sit idle and pay no mind to work hard even in worst weather conditions. There is a saying that a Sherpa does not become poor by eating but by becoming lazy. In the modern times, the social and economic life of the Sherpas have changed. With the changes in their economic life, their political participation is also increasing, and they are becoming politically conscious. In fact, the Mongoloid tribes have began to organise themselves as a pressure group in order to improve their economic conditions, ensure greater political participation and preserve their culture and life style. They still follow their traditions. In fact, they have popularized life style in Nepal.

References

Baral, Lok Raj 1983 : *Nepal's Politics of Referendum,* New Delhi, Vikas Publishing House.

Bista, Dor Bahadur, 1987 : *People of Nepal,* Kathmandu, Ratna Pustak Bhandar.

Fisher, James F. 1986 : 'Tourists and Sherpas I *Contribution to Nepalese Studies,* 14 : 1.

Fuchs, Stephen	1982	:	*The Aboriginal Tribes of India*, New Delhi Macmillan India Ltd.
Gaize, Frederick H.	1975	:	*Regionalism and National Unity in Nepal*, New Delhi, Vikas Publishing House, P. 15; R.S. Chauhan, 1989, Society and State Building in Nepal, New Delhi, Sterling Publishers.
Haimendorf, Christoph	1975	:	*Himalayan Traders: Life in Highland Nepal*, London, John Murray.
	1984	:	*The Sherpas Transformed* (Social Change in a Buddhist Society of Nepal) New Delhi, Sterling Publishers.
Marie, Bjonness Inger	1979	:	*Impact on High Mountain System*, Kathmandu.
Ortner, Sherry	1978	:	*Sherpa Through Rituals*, Cambridge.
Pawson Ivan G.	1983	:	Effect of Modernization on Nepal's Khambu Region: Changes in Population Structure (1970-1982), *Journal of Mountain Research and Development*, November-December.
Padnis, Urmila	1990	:	*Ethnicity and Nation Building in South Asia*, New Delhi, Sage Publications.

7

THE DHIMAL OF NEPAL AT CROSSROAD

RISHIKESHAB RAJ REGMI

Nepal can be traditionally divided into three geographical areas... they are:

1. Himalayan region on the North,

2. Siwalik mountains and the hills in the middle, and

3. Plain Terai region on the South, facing the border of Uttar Pradesh and Bihar of India. The Southernmost part, the Terai, has traditionally been very sparsely populated in the past due to a hot humid climate and the prevalence of a virulent type of malaria. Most of the parts of the *Terai* consisted of dense forests. But, in recent years as a result of effective malaria eradication, much of the forest has been cleared for cultivation. As a result of increasing pressure of population in the mountains and other parts of neighbouring regions, the *Terai* is becoming a densely populated agricultural belt. Damak municipality is a multi-caste township in the Jhapa district of Nepal Terai where a very old agricultural community (tribe) called Dhimal inhabited since a long time past. They are supposed to be the first settlers of this area. Though their concentration is found mainly in the flat and fertile villages of Jhapa, they are also found in Morang district of Nepal. The Dhimal tribe estimated at eight to nine thousands in all, are at the cross-roads of continued cultural identity and assimilation with other communities like the Rajbanshis, Tharus, Brahmins, Chhetries, Limbus, Gurungs, Rais and the Newars inhabiting the adjoining areas.

Dying Language

The word Dhimal seems to have originated from 'Himal' denoting the snow-peaks. It is probable that the Dhimals were once the inhabitants of the Northeastern belt of the country. During the course of my study most of the old Dhimals told me that their original home was somewhere in Lhasa amid the rugged mountains. However, in absence of inexorable evidences like the written documents and manuscripts their original abode is difficult to be exactly located. It is the strong opinion of many Dhimals, whom I personally met, that they were the real inhabitants of Northeastern belt of our country and were physically changed since the migration due to different natural environment in the Terai. They have preserved their own dialect and can communicate in it among themselves. Their language belongs to the Tibeto-Burman group. They have no script of their own. Their language is however dying day by day because of its lowering practice and use.

Previously they were hunters and then they became food gatherers. In course of time these nomadic people were led to settle down permanently. The plain was suitable for agriculture. Forest was there for the use of fire and huts.

They generally practise traditional methods of cultivation which is still primitive and yield low harvest. They are completely dependent upon agriculture for their livelihood.

Traits

Many members of the group pointed out interesting facts to prove that they are the brethren of the Limbu community. As a matter of fact, while tracing the geneological character it can be ascertained that the Dhimals descended from the Mongols who were the forefathers of the Limbu community. They have patrilocal society and trace their descent through the male line. Being exogamous group they might have inherited traits akin to the Limbu as a result of cross marriages. Some social customs and religious beliefs and rituals are similar to those of the Limbu community. The social status of the Dhimal group is the same as that of the Tharus, Rajbanshi and the Majhis of Jhapa.

At present the Dhimal areas are overcrowded due to recent migration in the Terai from the Hills. Thousands of hilly people of various ethnic groups, driven by the lack of cultivable land and increasing population, have penetrated the Terai belt. The language, dress, food and various other social customs are rapidly changing. The Dhimals cannot remain unaffected by them. The urbanisation, opening of east-west highway, establishments of small-scale industries are fast bringing them in the main stream of national life.

Marriage and Divorce

The Dhimals are very simple and laborious people. They generally have simple and single family. Sometimes joint extended family is also found. These people call themselves Hindus. This seems to be a result of their contacts with the orthodox Hindu community.

The marriage ceremony takes place according to their own customs. They are endogamous people. Generally a man marries a girl of his own ethnic group. Monogamy is the general rule. Polygamy is rare. Usually marriage takes place by negotiation. Sometimes love marriages with other caste also do occur. But the clan (*gotra*) of the boy and girl must not coincide, as they follow clan exogamy. A Tengmali Dhimal boy cannot marry a Tengmali Dhimal girl. They do not have preferential marriage system which means the marriage between cousin brother and sister is not permissible. If any member of the group violates the traditional social custom or cultural heritage he is looked down upon by the Dhimal society. He is censured as the breaker of social sanction and order. Children born from the women other than Dhimal are accepted in the community with the same social status equal to other members of the tribes, but not respected.

The Dhimals have altogether twelve clans (gotra) linking their origin with various totems. These are the twelve clans (1) Dongenunia (2) Din (3) Tengmali (4) Tegre (5) Bangmali (6) Talipa (7) Haradeya (8) Rathum (9) Kochele (10) Nunia (11) Lebang (12) Kashyar.

Divorce is permitted for reasons of adultery, barrenness and incompatibility with his/her spouse, but the separation can take place only after mutual consents. In some cases, the party desiring the dissolution of marriage has to pay compensation to the deserted party. It is known as the *Jari* payment in the local custom.

Widow marriage is permissible and in vogue. The feast must be given as early as possible to mark the ceremony. The kins and relatives are invited. With the feast marriage gets socially sanctioned. Children borne of such couple can inherit the paternal property.

Beliefs

The Dhimals are very much afraid of ghost and sorcery as they bring calamity to their lives. So they usually try to destroy the evil spirits by means of magical rituals. They seek help from religion and magic at times of distress. They do not worship stone images nor do they propitiate ancestral God in the form of an idol. But these days under the influences of Hinduism a few of them have begun to worship the Hindu deities.

Unlike Hindu tradition the corpse of the Dhimals are not generally cremated but burried in a nearby forest. The period of pollution lasts for three days followed by a purificatory ceremony on the fourth day and a feast. In this respect the Dhimal tradition seems to be exactly like that of the Limbus who represent the ethnic groups which have been transformed into castes at a comparatively recent date but have retained some traces of the tribal stage of development. The causes of migration of the hilly people have considerably caused a slump in their aesthetic value and culture. Other migrants of different ethnic stocks in the Terai are immense in number and are a bit accultured. So these tribal people have started to adopt their way of habits and culture. For example, they have started speaking Nepali, wearing *saris.*

Using cosmetics, giving up their traditional dress, visiting to Hindu temples, drinking tea and eating bread as a fad, burning dead bodies after death, putting vermillion on the forehead during marriage.

They have started to admit their children to the schools. The East-West highway passing by the side of their homes has brought about a revolution in their life and thinking. They have come in contact with the people of other regions and getting integrated with the rest of the country. Economically they are self-sufficient as most of them possess plenty of land. The young generation is now attracted towards education and other vocations. They are meanwhile conscious of their cultural heritage.

Village Officials: Secular and Religious

At present the Dhimal community is undergoing tremendous change in their norms, values, customs and beliefs but at the same time they are also adopting these recent values and customs due to the impacts of new innovation and circumstances. Even in such a stage of change the role and authority of the *Majhi* (Village chief) and the *Dhami* (Priest) still continue in a traditional manner and their directions are followed in social and religious affairs. The traditional role of *Dhami* and *Majhi* is shrinking, and they are taking new roles of the village social workers.

In every traditional Dhimal village there used to be a village headman who was specially assigned the charge of protection and development of the village. In the Dhimal villages, the *Majhi* gets the respect of the village chief. In this society, some social systems like *Chourasi* and *Choumajhi* (like caste council) used to have stronghold until 1950. In such a system, and important village chief called *Majhi* alongwith some youths and oldfolks of the village used to be present to arbitrate on disputes. Though the *Majhi* had the sole authority, every other member of this institution (*Chourasi* and *Choumajhi*) could have his full say, to assist him to come to a decision. In a way, they had such democratic systems which had enjoyed the full support and acceptance of the society along with vested judicial power. All kinds of cases, ranging from a simple domestic quarrel to theft, divorce, division of property, rape and murder were discussed and settled in such councils previously.

The tradition of *Majhi* is inherited by some particular families even to these days. The custom of approaching the *Majhi* for his advice during celebration of festivals and settlements of disputes is still found in the Dhimal villages. Minor cases of domestic affairs are still settled by the *Majhi*, older-folks and members of the village development committee. Though these old conventional values and norms were accepted until sometime back, they are losing their hold gradually. For example *shirlohanka* or the raising of head is the system where compensation is paid to the aggrieved accoording to the judgement of *Majhi*. In this process, when two persons have a dispute or quarrel and one insults or hurts the other, the aggrieved seeks such judgement. Some respected villagers are called by the *Majhi* for consultation. The aggrieved is paid or given a bottle of wine with cock before all, by the offender. Then the wrongdoer raises his head before the village society, acknowledging his offence or guilt.

Another case of compensation on rape of a Dhimal woman can well be cited as an example where *Majhi* offers his judgement. When a Dhimal commits rape forcibly of any woman, the *Majhi* has a right to award and enforce suitable punishment. On judgement, if the man is found guilty, he is made to touch the feet of the molested woman by his forehead before all the witnesses and beseech pardon from her. In some cases, the man is made to pay, as fine, some amount of money and a bottle of wine to the elder social workers of the village. The man has to take a public oath that he would never again insult the woman in any way and do such crime.

If some Dhimals get married by absconding with another man's wife, he has to pay compensation in cash according to the demand of the first husband before the *Majhi* and other villagers. This system is known as *Jari* compensation. The *Majhi* plays, not only a vital role in dispensing social justice, but he also conducts and leads the village religious affairs. He must lead the most important religious festival, *Sirijat* and *Dhang Dhange mela* which commences in the month of June/July, marking the beginning of summer. But today judicial and political roles of the *Majhi* no longer exists in the village as before, though he still occupies the religious role.

After the prestigious rank of the *Majhi, the Dhami* is recognised as the next. *Dhami* represents the priestly class. They are respected and their services are required in various types of community rituals, festivals and feasts. The *Dhami* performs mainly the social role of religious leader and priest. His demand is very high because of his knowledge in dealing with the personal and community (collective) problems through magico-religious practices. In the community shrine of the Dhimal tribe, the *Dhami* has a prominent role to play. During festivals like *Sirijat Puja, Ashade Puja,* and *Naubangi Puja,* the *Dhami* is specially felicited by the villagers and given presents. The *Dhami* shoulders the responsibility of assuring security and protection of village from external and internal (supernatural) threats, and offers animal sacrifies of fowls and other animals to different deities.

In the past, the Dhimal were forest nomads, always surrounded by ferocious wild animals. These wild animals like, rhinoceros, wild elephant, wild cows and buffalos were tactfully avoided or killed for safety. When the tribe reached the stage of settled agriculturists, they were in need of a *Dhami* who could protect their agricultural fields from these wild animals by some magical powers. So they created the institution of *Sirijat* and *Naubangi* worships with colourful celebration. The *Dhami* worship the deities on these occasions for the protection of agricultural crops, every year, and great festivals were held by all the members of the tribe on such occasions. To these days also, whenever pests and worms, web of spiders are seen in the paddy fields and in jute crops, the *Dhami* is called, who utters magical spell and incantations, and the worms are found to die, and thus the crops are protected. He also counters the evil-spirits afflicting the sick and protects him from such evil forces. It is stated that generally the *Dhami* orders his '*Gaiyas*' (invisible cows that act under his supernatural power) to protect the village from such afflictions. There are many types of the *Gaiyas*, such as the *Milk Gaiyas, Dhuipa, Hulman, Sul, Taba* and the *Taran Gaiya*. These *Gaiyas* have their special kinds of functions.

Thus the Dhimal tribe even when under living harsh developed conditions in the wild environment and forests, have had the institution of the Dhami who could guide them and protect them from diseases, attack of wild animals and poor agricultural production due to attack of pests.

In the past, economic condition, Government services (power) and political strength did not play any vital role on the social set-up of the Dhimals, but religion had the most significant role to play in their social hierarchy, as was seen in their community festivals and worships. In order to occupy a prestigious high rank status, knowledge, cleverness, cleanliness, tactfulness, having many kinsmen, a large family, membership of the village development committee (political power) and wealth in the form of land were most essential in the Dhimal tribe.

Changing Political Forces and the Dhimals

It is said that as early as in 5th centuary A.D. King Soiyak Lodohang ruled the Dhimal tribe (Iman Singh Chemjung). Then the Sen Kings and in 1770 A.D. the King of Sikkim, Fungcho Nymgyal conquered these kirat lands, including the village of the Dhimal tribe. This area was completely conquered by King Prithivinarayan Shah, Gorkha King in 1774 A.D. After the unification of Nepal, what was the social system of villages of the Dhimals is not known, but their oral traditions gives us an idea of the system of village headmanship or the *Choumajhi* system. This social system retained its root till the revolution of 1950, when the autocratic Rana rule was thrown by the people. Until then, the Dhimals had the same archaic type of village social organisation, where disputes and quarrels were settled by the headman and his associates peacefully.

In the Dhimal tribe, some social systems like, the institution of *Choumajhi* used to have a strong hold until sometime back. In such system, an important village headman called *Majhi* along with all the youths and old-folks of the village used to be present to adjudicate on disputes and award impose punishment. All kinds of cases ranging from a simple domestic affair to theft, divorce, division of property, rape and murder etc., were discussed and settled in such parajudicial system.

The traditional post of the *Majhi* and its authorities are inherited by many families even today. The custom of approaching the *Majhi* at the time of festivals and other occasions by the villagers for seeking his advice and suggestions still persists. Minor cases arising from domestic quarrels are still settled by the *Majhi* with the help of older folks of the village and the social workers. But though the old conventional laws and rules, norms and customs used to be fully accepted and obeyed by the people until sometime back, they are increasingly losing their ground slowly. During this time the link between the people and the Government was limited to collection of land revenue.

After 1950's revolution, democratic Government was established, and there was slow change in their life. Many families from other ethnic groups began to migrate from the plain areas. They started acquiring lands by purchasing in the Dhimal villages. Malaria was gradually eradicated and many forest areas were cleared. As there were many people from different ethnic and caste groups, quarrels between their kinsmen as well as with other immigrants from hills started in full swing on land issues.

This revolution brought a new consciousness among these tribal people. The contact and relationship between the Dhimal and the Limbu (other tribe) increased more and more. These two similar type of ethnic groups who claimed to be of the same dynasty and brothers, hold meetings (*Chumlung*) in several places, sometimes in the hills and sometimes in the Terai because the Limbus live mostly in the hills. This sort of *Chumlungs* took place in the years--1951, 1954, 1956, 1962-63, 1978 and in 1989. No written documents regarding these *Chumlungs* are preserved by these tribal people. They know why and how the *Chumlungs* were arranged. In these meetings, they unanimously adopted a resolution to stop the system of cashnut marriage, and offering of 'bride price' and avoiding costly feasts. They agreed that from that time "negotiated marriage" will be their chief custom. The other aim of holding *Chumlungs* was to find out the history of their community. The attempt to unite the Dhimals and the Limbus through such *Chumlungs* was to find out the history of their community. The attempt to unite the Dhimals and the Limbus gave way to political shape when a Dhimal *Majhi* contested in general election of 1959 as an independent candidate but was defeated. The elected Government of the Nepali Congress, headed by B.P. Koirala, under Parliamentary system, was dismissed by King Mahendra in 1960, giving way for new partyless Panchayat system.

During the 1960's decade the Dhimal tribe spectacularly advanced towards attaining political consciousness. These people in underground, were always spearheading for political change. During the individualist Panchayat system very few Dhimal people were involved but had nothing to gain. They gradually changed their outlook and their ways of life. In 1980, during referendum when King had opted for the partyless Panchayat or Party system, very active Dhimal youths and activists went in canvassing for Party system. Many young people were tirelessly active in the Marxist political activities, as these youths were influenced by the activities of the *Naxalite* extremists just near the village, in the border of West Bengal of India.

After 1981, a young Dhimal contested for the National Assembly and was elected. In this way they completely aligned themselves in the political mainstream of the country in national level. They, secularised themselves in politics, religious and social life, thereby integrating themselves with the main culture of the Nepalese traditions and patriotism.

Thus, despite their apparent isolation, the Dhimal people are exposed in multiple ways with the outside world. This contact with the exterior is maintained by a series of institutions that operate at different levels and in different patterns. Such agencies are the village development committee (previously Village Panchayat), the visiting travellers the East-West Highways, traders, Government officials of Land Revenue Department, Health assistants, agricultural technicians and the police.

The police *chowki* (station) of Damak and Dhimal villages has its headquarters at Chandragadi. The nearest local police force operate from Damak (a town, now the centre of municipality). The police are not permanently posted in the villages, they come only occasionally on specific circumstances, and in search of murderers, or in cases of accidents and theft. These police also maintain law and order of the whole settlement area. There are also some special days, as market days, and community festivals, when the police are found to attend.

These are few kinds of situations in which the Dhimal and the police come in contact, at this level of conflict. But such situations are created from outside. The Dhimal villages are not a politically independent territory. They are a part of the bigger Nepalese society. The rules of the Government are framed by the Government and enforced by the police. The relation between the two, however, sometimes becomes tense. Some of these people do not trust the Government. In general a few of them consider it as a kind of enemy, but in some instances of developmental needs and land distribution, they see it as a patron, with whom they must interact in a formalised manner to fulfil their needs. The relationship then, is one of opposition in terms of values and institutionalised set-up, and on the other of friendly co-operation for gaining assistance. But they do not have friendly and close relationship with the Government or the officials. They sometimes speak against the Government in communal and personal level. Some members of the Dhimal tribe have not understood the moral legitimacy of the Governments's laws. They see the laws of the Governments as a 'tyrant power', which force them to conform to certain patterns of behaviour. The law is seen by many as something imposed from outside. They avoid the whole legal process, and other Government officials. The rational understanding of laws as the basic norms of social integration and protection is not clear among some of them.

Two basic concepts that are fundamental for analysing this attitude are - the concept of community and that of the Government. The community is affected by the law, but persists in using its own cultural modes to deal with any conflict. The result is tension between the two levels, as the different systems of values come into contact. The people become afraid and there is always a tendency of suspicion and avoidance in the relation between them and the Government officials and police.

The tribal community are attempting to raise their status by educating their children, Sanskritising their rituals and urbanising their ways of life. Although there is some apparent tension in the structural pattern of the village community, they have yet preserved so far their culture unity structurally. In fact, recent political changes and administrative reforms in Nepal have made a deeper inroad into the Dhimal community and its traditional village policy, with the increasing influence of the court of law, new Parliamentary election system and constitutional kingship.

Social change

The immediate effects of political changes and independence after 1950 among the Dhimals were almost none or very nominal from the point of view of increasing or lessening of village integrity. But in post-1950 period, spread of western type of education and new economic opportunities, opening of the East-West highway, migration of the Hindu high castes from the hills, largely expedited by the opening of the Terai for new settlement of migrants, together have had a tremendous impact on the traditional socio-cultural and political systems in Damak, and in the Dhimal society in particular. These forces have introduced new institutions and roles, and values and behaviour patterns, to support these roles.

Independence, and of late introduction of various socio-economic reform after creation of the Panchayat system, have brought along some other factors in the wake, namely, the abolition of the rights of land held as intermediaries or the Zamindari system, abolition of *Birta* (1959), road development, educational facilities and consciousness about the country beyond the boundary of the villages. The changes that have occurred in the recent past are found to have their root in the economic infrastructure, though these have affected their political religious lives as well.

In the sphere of social life, the outlook of the Dhimal people in general have undergone certain changes. As a result, the traditional observances in day-to-day life are no more taken seriously. For example, the taboos for a pregnant woman are flouted so long as it does not directly lead to any actual physical harm of the woman.

The cultural changes among the higher castes on the hand, point towards secularisation, the changes in the Dhimal culture, on the other hand, have been Brahmanical in nature. Srinivas's theory of 'Sanskritization' (1952, 1967, 1968), one of the most midely accepted theories of social change in the South Asian context, seems to be in well tune with some of the aspects of such social changes.

Sanskritization among the Dhimals has been a process that was set in motion over thirty years ago. The pre--1960 Sanskritization of the Dhimals was very limited. The culture of the Dhimals is largely based on what may be called as *'animism'* and worship of non-Sanskritic Gods and Goddesses. But on account of their coming into contact with the high caste Hindus, their gradual consciousness and freedom from traditional bondage, spread of new ideas through the radio, newspapers and cinema, increasing rate of literacy among the new generations, and dissemination of the ideas and values of urban-culture through the migrated higher castes, have together produced positive effects on their traditional way of life. Now they are not only following their traditional religious practices, but have also imbibed some new ideas and values of Hindu religion in their way of life.

To begin with, there are some rich and conscious Dhimal families, who have started identifying themsleves with the nexus of hierarchical social relations of the Hindu caste system.

The most interesting change in the Dhimal commensal practice has been the banning of the 'buffalo sacrifice' during funeral rites, a practice 'which was a must', as in the Limbu system. There has also been little changes in the Dhimal habit of keeping domestic animals, specially cows and buffaloes. Before 1970 when this author visited some Dhimal villages, he found that they did not keep domestic cows and buffaloes, for milk was not used by them. At present, milk of cow is considered a sacred item of offering to various deities, as found in the Hindu practice. Moreover, they are selling milk to hotels and restaurants in the Damak market for cash to meet their needs.

Many Dhimals have started the religious worship and activities such as, Satyanarayan Puja and reading of Purana (recitation of the Holy Texts), having been influenced by the Brahmins.

Many Dhimals have abandoned the traditional Dhimal burial custom and instead, have adopted the Hindu practice of cremation of the dead. Some of them have also started following the Brahminical practice of observing thirteen days of pollution after a death in the family, in place of their own traditional three days observance. Some Dhimals even engage Brahmin priests, in lieu of the Dhimal *Barang* (Priest) for performing funeral rites.

The system of marriage customs are also changing. In some places smearings of vermilion on the forehead of bride and Hindu system of '*Kanyadan*' have been started.

The Dhimal system and custom of paying 'bride-price' during the marriage is changing. Formerly the marriage rituals and feasts continued for three days. Now, it is completed within two days. Along with the changes in wedding rituals, it is found that the circle of marriage relationships has been considerably widened than before. Two new additions are that-their new guests are even some higher castes who take pig's meat and liquor with them. Inter-caste marriages are also increasing among the Dhimals now.

The present author also feels that the theories of 'Sanskritization' and 'Westernisation' forwarded by Srinivas, Chon and others provide only a partial understanding of the socio-cultural changes that are taking place in Damak villages. In Damak itself Brahmin culture seems to be secularising, but not all Brahmins are participating equally in the process. In case of an educated Brahmin, secular values may be expressed in his 'not wearing a *janai* (sacred thread), or drinking liquor' but this does not mean that older Brahmins have adopted these secular practices.

Regarding socio-cultural changes in the Damak villages the older higher Hindu castes still follow the traditional values.

Their seemingly accommodating attitude towards the elements of secularization, such as liquor drinking by their youths, is accepted by them as the forces of social changes beyond their control, rather than a choice freely and willingly made. At the same time, the young educated Dhimals are not 'Sanskritizing' in the same sense, that the older Dhimals are doing, while almost all the Dhimals have adopted certain Nepalese national values, which are Sanskritic in origin. The conscious educated revolutionary youths of the Dhimal society, neither see themselves within the caste-hierarchy, nor unlike their elders, find any religious meaning in Hindu religious practices, such as, reading of the *Purana* or *Satyanarayan-Ko-Puja.*

Similar secular values shared by higher caste Hindus and the Dhimal youths are a product of the 1950's revolution and they are receiving education now. Before 1950, Sanskritic education was open to and valued only by the Brahmins and friendship between the Brahmin and the Dhimals was based on the relation of tax-collector and tax-payer ties at best, and creditor-debtor relationship at the worst. But at present, contact between the groups has been restored in much friendlier atmosphere. Although the number of the Dhimal children attending schools is still smaller than the Brahmin children, nonetheless, they learn together, play together and are being encultured into similar value together.

The present socio-cultural changes in the Dhimal village are almost revolutionary in nature. In a broad sense, the pre-1950 political milieu in South Asian sub-continent, generated by the independence of India and the nation-wide revolution against the Rana rules of Nepal, provided a background for these changes. As a result of these changes, the people who changed their previous patterns, either economic or socio-cultural, were well-rewarded for their efforts. In the post 1950 national social-political milieu, different news media, such as the Radio Nepal, newspapers and magazines coming from the urban centres of India and Nepal, played a key-role in the national integration and its secularization process. Messages regarding the importance of education, the evils of the caste system, and so on, were constantly hammered into the people's mind. A new era of awareness, in terms of State's responsibility towards its own citizens spread among the masses. Before 1950, Government took active interest in the welfare of its people.

The first priority was given to education and many schools were established to educate the people.

Furthermore after 1960, when the Panchayat system was introduced, the opening of Nepal to outsiders brought not only new ideas of education and the Government, but also affected the traditional economic system as well. Previously the village economy of Damak area tended to act in a relatively 'self-contained' fashion (Bailey, 1964: 230).

The later Government decision to participate in the international economy brought the villages in contact with market-economy. This brought further changes in the life-style of the people, while at the same time, it made the village economy vulnerable to the effects of national and international political events and pressure. Under their cumulative impact, radical changes are now taking place in the Dhimal villages and the country as a whole.

Bailey's (1964) concept of 'moving frontier' affords a useful perspective and to view post-1950 developments and the problems associated with it. In Damak village and elsewhere in Nepal, the State's call for and support for establishment of educational institutions and programmes enthusiastically accepted by the people as a means of achieving a higher standard of living. Then with the State's support, the frontier of knowledge' in post-1950 Dhimal villages were expanded considerably and concomitantly changes in values, aspirations, goals and perception also emerged.

In the same way, 'economic frontier' too moved from pre-1950 into these villages. The post-1950, rather after 1960, contact with the market-economy brought the remote villages closer to the outside world and as a result clothes and shoes, radio and watches made in Japan and India and other European countries as well as from China were brought by the villagers. Kerosene oil produced thousands of miles away in the Persian Oil-fields made its headway into these villages. But at the sametime, the link with the market-economy impeded the growth and development of their traditional technical knowhow (e.g. making of Khadi cloth or shoes) and other resources and cottage industries. While it substantially altered the life-style of the people, it also made their life dependent upon outside sources and supplies, over which they had no effective control. The opening of Terai as a new 'economic frontier' accorded a small minority of the people as a means of keeping up with increased household expenditure and further enabled them to establish a reciprocal relationship in the functioning of the market economy. For the majority of the people, however, the relationship with the market-economy was only minor and did not benefit them ever in a marginal extent.

It is now observed that there is a growing trend to educate boys and girls among the Dhimals.

Changes are also found in dress, diet and standard of living. The old varieties of diets are being gradually replaced by the new ones. Formerly, the lunch and dinner included cooked rice, some kind of curry-mainly of fish, pulses with occasional liquor. Now use of green vegetables and kitchengarden products is increasing. Many untensils of aluminium and of stainless steel are used, replacing brasswares. They are also spending their money for buying hair-oil and other beauty-aids.

Some other elements of urban culture in the life of these people are also found in the use of modern medicine, their hobbies and cultural activities and in adopting modern agricultural techniques and implements, to some extent. The marked change in their attitude is the faith in family. There are four women who have done laproscopy operation, about a dozen are using birth-preventive pills. There are ten men who have also done vasectomy thereby entering the modern era. With these new additions in their cultural activities, it has been seen that they are now discarding some of their own traditional festivals like, *Sirjat Puja* and *Dhang Dhange Mela*, because of high economic burden. Their joint families are now breaking away, as well as the parental landed properties are also fragmenting into small holdings.

Thus the social, religious, political and economic life of the Dhimals have changed and are still changing. These changes have brought their social system within the orbit of a much wider society than before.

Whatever may be the changes they are undergoing, they have not undermined the traditional pattern of their social structure. The adjustments made in the contour of the society have been gradually absorbed, so as to fit with the changed pattern, without breaking up their traditional institutions. Various counteracting forces under the impact of both urban culture and Sanskritzation are so operating that there is gradual absorption of the new values in their social and cultural system. They have been able to retain their traditional culture even in this situation of close contact with other communities. Their traditional social institutions are not disintegrating, but with some strain they are adapting themselves with the organisational needs of the present time. Their value system is still maintained by their cultural consistency. They have reacted with their own pattern emotionally according to their value system for the stability of their culture. Traditions, institutions and values of their consistent cultural pattern have helped them to maintain their socio-cultural identity uptill now, of course, with certain adaptations and modifications.

References

Berremen, G. 1972 : *Hindus of the Himalayas: Ethnography and Change,* University of California Press.

Burrow, J.W. 1966 : *Evolution and Society,* Cambridge University Press.

Bailey, F.C. 1957 : *Caste and Economic Frontier,* Manchester University Press.

Banerjee, S.K. 1963 : *Land Alienation :Causes and Affects Thereon,* Calcutta.

Bose, N.K. 1953 : "Hindu Method of Tribal Absorption" in *Cultural Anthropology and Other Essays,* Calcutta Indian Association Publishing Co.

Caplan L. 1970 : *Land and Social Change in Nepal,* Routledge and Kegan Paul, London.

Chemjong, I.S.	1952	:	*Kirati History*, Gangtok.
Dahal, D.R.	1979	:	*Dhimal Lokjivan Adhyayan*, Royal Nepal Academy, Kathmandu.
Diwas, T.	1982	:	*Dhimal Lok Dharma Ra Sanskriti*, Royal Nepal Academy, Kathmandu.
Gould, H.	1961	:	'Sanskritization and Westernization' *Economic Weekly*:13.
Jones, Rex.	1979	:	Sanskritization in Eastern Nepal, *Ethnology*, XV : 1.
Majumdar, D. N.	1937	:	*A Tribe in Transition*, Longman and Green Co. Ltd.
Nepali, R.K.	1978	:	*Dogare Ra Karikoshika Dhimal*, H.M.G. Home Ministry.
Regmi, R.R.	1972	:	'The Dhimal at Cross Road', in *Nepalese Prospective*, January.
Regmi, R.R.	1972	:	Dhimals of Eastern Nepal, in *Ancient Nepal:* 17, Department of Archaeology, Kathmandu.
Regmi, R.R.	1978	:	*Ex Srot Teen Dhara Sajha Prakashan*, Kathmandu.
Srinivas, M.N.	1971	:	*Social Change in Modern India*, Berkeley, University of California.
	1952	:	*Religion and Society Among the Coorgs of South India*, Oxford University Press.
Steward, J.	1955	:	*Theory of Cultural Change*, Ulbana, University of Illinois.
Sharma, J.L.	1978	:	*Hamro Samaj*, Sajha Prakashan, Kathmandu.
Vanisttart, E.	1894	:	'The Tribes, Clans and Castes of Nepal' *Journal of the Asiatic Society of Bengal* LXIII: 4.

8

POLITICS AND POLITICAL PROCESSES IN TRIBAL INDIA : THEN AND NOW

SACHCHIDANANDA

I

Politics is concerned with the form of power, its control and manipulation and the social relations in which they are expressed. The examination of the internal political organisation of any group is complemented by a study of the external political relations of groups with their neighbours. This constitutes the political system of the whole region. Systematic relations of hostility or alliance may exist between political units which are not embraced within a single organisation. This leads to a set of political relations involving distinct tribes and their non-tribal neighbours. Power is expressed in various patterns of dominance and subordination both within the group and in political relations involving alien communites. These patterns change from time to time. Thus, over a period of time, change is manifested in the nature of politics and political processes in a particular region.

Amongst the peasant communities in tribal Bihar, the population in the village in the pre-contact period was divided between two status groups (Sachchidanand, 79). The first represented the descendents of the original settlers and the other comprised later tribal migrants in the village. The first group constituted the clan of *Khuntkattidars* or the joint owners of the village. It was from their ranks that the secular and the religious headmen of the village were chosen. The other group was known as *Parja* or subjects who had to pay a tribute to the *Khuntkattidars*. Thus the *Khuntkattidars* formed the dominant group and all important decisions regarding the village were taken by them. In the clan of *Khuntkattidars* there were two lineages from which the headmen were drawn. From the senior lineage the religious headman was selected and from the junior lineage the secular headman was chosen. There was intense rivalry between these two lineages for dominance in village affairs. This cleavage was seen until lately in many Munda villages (Schchidanand, 1978 : 178). In course of time, the secular headman scored over the religious headman and came to be regarded as the more important between the two. With the advent of the colonial rule, the secular headman became the intermediary between the village and the Government (Sachchidanand, 1978 : 178). Among some tribes he was given the power of revenue collection and in some cases certain police powers also. The decisions in the traditional village panchayats were supposed to be just but in some cases there were reports of miscarriage of justice under the influence of dominant sections of the village community.

In many tribal areas, particularly in middle India, there was intense interaction between the tribals and the non-tribals, in economic affairs, in the religious field and at the political level. More often than not, the long history of the interaction has been one of tension and conflict. The tribal way of life contended for the position of dominance but in the unequal fight it had to reformulate its goal and to struggle first for co-existence on the basis of equality and later for sheer survival. In the process, there was considerable adjustment and accommodation. However, the interaction was characterised by a good deal of discrimination, exploitation and oppression of the tribals.

Another phenomenon which transformed political life in middle India in the pre-colonial period was the process of state formation. This was in evidence among the Gond, Chero and the Bhumij. There were four factors (Singh ,1985: 37) which promoted this process among these communities. These tribal communities were marked by settled agriculture and an organised political system. The extension of cultivation through a network of irrigation schemes was necessary for building and sustaining these states. There was reclamation of forest lands on a large scale for cultivation. The second factor was the process of Hinduisation of the tribal communities in middle India. The network of temples, wandering Hindu mendicants and the penetration of the kurmi peasantry from Bengal, promoted state formation among the Bhumij. A similar process was in evidence among the Gonds of Madhya Pradesh and among the Chero and the Kharwar. The third factor was the role of an acculturated tribal elite which tried to clamp its rule on the people. The new rulers imitated Rajput princes and built forts. They also had the usual court paraphernalia and a sizeable army. However, the consolidation of the process of state formation could only be completed by attacks and invasions of more powerful non-tribal imperialist forces. This process also coincided with the emergence of fedual structure which divided the tribe into different status groups. Some of these groups were divided into various sections. The Chero society in Palamau is an example of such stratification. The Bhumij were also divided into a number of strata based on corresponding distribution of power and economic interest in land and defined in terms of ritual status (Singh, 1941). The aristocratic stratum that emerged in the once egalitarian tribal communities have survived the demise of these tribal states.

The tribal states became the agents of Sanskritisation. They also adopted the Kshatriya model. They became the natural reference group for the tribal masses. They were also instrumental in attraction to their area not only the Brahmanas but also up country businessmen and diligent non-tribal cultivators to boost agricultural production. It is thus that the Koiris and the Kurmis came to Chotanagpur and the Kubis from the Maratha country were attracted by the Gond rulers of Madhya Pradesh. While both endogenous and exogenous models of State formation were in evidence, the process produced similar results. In the new states there was the need to manage a multi-caste and multi-community population in which there was an economic interdependence between a tribe, non-tribal peasant and the artisans. All this necessitated a new politics for these tribal areas.

II

The gradual extension of the British authority in middle India generated a new type of politics in the tribal areas involving both tribals and non-tribals. Smarting under the pains they were suffering under the colonial rule, they resorted to resistence movements whose nature changed from time to time. The introduction of the colonial system in tribal areas in middle India resulted in displacement of the Zamindars following the sale of Zamindaris for failure to pay rent and depriving their men of service land. Some of these disgruntled landlords combined with the tribals and created disturbances. One example of such unrest was the Chuar rebellion which was at its peak in Chotanagpur from 1795 to 1800. The Chuar sought only the restoration of land and not political independence.

They plundered the alien Zamindars and robbed the Bengali and other people who had come to purchase land in their areas. Sometime before a Santal leader known as Tilka Manjhi raised the banner of revolt against the British in 1781. He organised guerilla warfare in which even Santal women participated. He attacked Bhagalpur in 1784 and created panic among the people there. In some other areas similar resistance was manifested. It is in Chotanagpur that we find a series of resistance movements under traditional tribal leadership. In the Tamar rebellion in 1789 the Mundas were up in arms against their landlords. The unrest in the area reached its culmination in 1819-20. These uprisings mark the resistance of the tribe against the break up of the agrarian system.

The Kol and Bhumij insurrections of 1831-32 represent the peak of the process. In these uprisings the tribals played the dominant role. They were led by the tribal aristocracy which had suffered at the hands of the colonial rulers. The tribal state system sought to preserve the tribal autonomy which the colonial system tried to subvert, though unconsciously, due to lack of understanding of the rights and privileges of the tribal chiefs and village headmen. The British equated the Chotanagpur chief with the Bengal Zamindar and the tribals with tenants, subjects to the same pattern of duties and obligations. The colonial system further introduced a new system of administration, levied a host of new taxes and appointed a large number of petty officials. The tribals had to pay not only quit rent but fines for crimes, excise duties on spirits and various *salamis*. They were also forced to render free labour. The traditional system of land control also broke down. Not only did the hereditary tribal chiefs lose their estates but the tribal cultivators lost their land. The upsurge was against all outsiders, the *Thikadars*, moneylenders and petty businessmen (Singh, 1985;126). The insurrection made the authorities aware of the depth of the tribal disaffection. A number of steps were taken to modify the pattern of governance of the area and for redressal of local grievances.

In the North-East there were also some tribal rebellions. The Khasis were engaged in depredations in the plains from 1787 to 1825. The Singho, Mishmi, Lushai, Khampti and the Dafla raised the plains and killed people. From time to time, British had to send expeditions to punish these groups.

In 1857 many Chero and Gond Zamindars took part in the revolt. In Hazaribagh some Santals resorted to plundering while some Bhuia chiefs saw in the Mutiny an opportunity to recover their lost land. In Gujarat the Bhils, Kolis, Thakarda and the Naikda rose in revolt against established authority.

The tribal movements in the next phase were characterised by peasant cum revivalistic upsurge. Armed uprisings were associated with an urge for social reform. The movements were not by chiefs but by commoners. The main issues were the alienation of tribal land, erosion of their rights in forest, levy of taxes and illegal cesses and the exploitation and oppression by moneylenders and petty officials. The period was marked by the breakdown of the tribal agrarian system consequences were disastrous. The autonomy of the tribal system withered away. Communal ownership came to be replaced by individual ownership. The solidarity of village community gradually gave in. The contact with the Hinduism and Christianity intensified ideas of divine inspiration and the Hindu concept of purity made an impact on the tribal mind. Christian missionaries promoted the concept of peasant proprietorship and emphasised peaceful and constitutional means of change as against violent means to which the tribals were more accustomed.

The first example of such a movement was the Santa *hul* (insurrection in 1855). The Santals were joined by the Mal Paharia and a number of artisan and low Hindu castes. The movement was led by the two brothers Sidhu and Kanhu. These leaders were inspired by a divine call. They directed the *dikus* and the Britishers to clear out the Santal land. Their fury was against the *mahajans* and the petty officials. They were not against the artisan castes who lived in their villages. The Santal insurrection was crushed with a great deal of trouble. The rebellion was marked by the scenes of inhuman cruelty. Villages were burnt and property looted. Most brutal outrages were committed on the moneylenders at whose hands the Santals had suffered most.

With the spread of Christianity the agrarian question turned a new leaf. Once the mutiny was suppressed, the missionaries began promoting the cause of the Christian tribal tenants against the landlords. Gradually these tenants became aggressive. Thus, for the next forty years from 1958 the *'mulki larai '* or the 'Sardar Agitation' raged in the Ranchi district. This was aimed at curbing the excesses of the landlords and protested against forced labour. It drew inspiration from the heroes of earlier tribal revolts. The means they adopted for the long drawn struggle was peaceful. They adopted prayer, protest and petition as methods. They distrusted the *dikus* and the Indian judges and magistrates who were supposed to be hand-in-glove with the Zamindars. They sometime did not pay rent and tried to take away such lands from landlords which they claimed to belong to their ancestors. They raised funds for fighting the legal battle necessary for the restoration of their lost rights and lands. The Zamindar's oppressions were resisted and sometimes clashes took place between Zamindars and the tenants. In 1867, a huge petition was made to the British authorities at Calcutta against local officers and the Raja of Chotanagpur. In 1881, some christian Sardars set up a kingdom at Doesa a former seat of the Raja of Chotanagpur. From 1890 the Sardar movement turned against all Europeans, both missionaries and officials, as the latter were no longer helpful in their struggle. The constitutional methods had not yielded any results and the leaders felt cheated by these Bengali lawyers at Calcutta who had assured them of complete success.

The ground was thus prepared for the Birsa movement. The movement aimed at the establishment of Munda Raj. Its ideology was influenced by the Hindu and Christian idioms. It led to the establishment of a new cult which found adherents in many parts of Ranchi district. The rebels attacked police stations and officials and churches and missionaries. The undercurrent of hostility against the *diku* was not manifested in the struggle. Birsa was imprisoned after the first uprising in 1895. However, after his release two years later, he began preparations for the struggle on a larger scale. The second Birsa uprising early in 1900 caused great consternation among British authorities in view of the stiffness of the struggle and the extent of its sweep. "The Birsa movement was agrarian in its roots, violent in its means and political in its ends" (Singh; 1983). In his speeches Birsa underlined the agrarian factors and sought a political solution to the problems facing his people i.e the establishment of the 'Birsait raj' under the new King (himself). Birsa was a charismatic leader and was hailed as a Prophet. The religious aura with which he surrounded himself further enhanced the effectiveness of his command. He was extremely shrewd, a good organiser and a pursuasive speaker. No hero in Munda folklore has been commemorated in such moving terms such as Birsa. He is a fountain of inspiration for all struggles for the tribal autonomy in the region.

Of the many Bhagat cults among the Oraon, the most famous is the Tana Bhagat cult. It began as an agrarian revitalisation movement but later on assumed political overtones. It was founded by one Jatra Bhagat around 1914 in a village in the Gumla district. It worked through the idioms of purity, temperance and teetolalism. In course of time, under the influence of the Congress movement, the Tana Bhagats were drawn towards the idea of Swaraj, Gandhi Raj, non-payment of taxes and *Ahimsa*. The tribals seized upon these idioms to express their protest against the agrarian ills from which they suffered. They refused to pay land tax because they thought that Gandhi Raj had arrived and the land belonged to them. Twenty thousand farmers lost their land and became staunch followers of the Congress and Gandhi. Large numbers of them courted imprisonment in the Non-Cooperation Movement and they walked long distances to attend sessions of the Congress held in different parts of the country. They spread the message of the *Charkha* and the tricolour National flag. They hoped that the lands they had lost would be restored to them as soon as freedom was attained.

Gandhiji's tour of Chotanagpur in 1925 produced waves in the tribal areas. A Santal leader in 1928-29 proclaimed himself as the disciple of Gandhi and exhorted his people to give up meat and liquor. The Santals refused to pay Chowkidari tax and displayed the Congress flag. Among the Ho, Haribaba in 1930 proclaimed himself as another disciple of Gandhi. His message was propagated with dance and feast and the slogan was "The British are no more and victory to Gandhi Mahto" (Singh, 1963). The movement was crushed with the arrest of Haribaba and his colleagues.

It is thus clear that by the twenties and thirties of this century many of the tribal movements originating from agrarian protest and expressing themselves in the idioms of revitalisation developed links with the national freedom movement led by the Congress under the leadership of Gandhi and Nehru. They began operating on expanded horizons and were involved in the movement for Independence. Local grievances and problems were at the roots of dissatisfaction but their protests mingled with the national struggle.

III

Tribal politics from the twenties onwards witnessed a change in its character. Agrarian causes and revitalisation concerns were relegated to the background. These were replaced by demands for separation and autonomy. There was the search for an identity. Chotanagpur was the best example of the rise of such movements as it was fairly advanced among all the tribal regions in middle India in point of literacy, political consciousness and industrial progress. The spread of Christianity gave them a sense of history and accentuated the notion of private property in land. It led to the spread of education, promoted western values and emphasised a sense of separateness from the rest of the community. The father of Indian anthropology Sarat Chandra Roy helped them in the articulation of their demand for tribal autonomy. It was in 1912 that efforts were made for forging the unity of people of Chotanagpur, whether Christian or non-Christian. However, the pan-tribal sentiment was weak. Soon after this talk about the Montague Chelmsford Reform were in the air and need was expressed for the preservation of tribal identity in the changing political context.

From 1920-38 the *Chotanagpur Unnati Samaj* dominated the scene. It laid stress on the formation of the tribal sub-state extending over parts of Bihar, Bengal and Orissa. A memorandum was also submitted to the Simon Commission demanding autonomy and special privileges for the tribals. Uptill now Catholics had kept aloof from the *Chotanagpur Unnati Samaj*. They formed a separate organisation called the *Chotanagpur Catholic Sabha*. For the first time the Christian Church lent its support to a purely political organisation. In 1937 election, two of its candidates were successful. In 1938, the *Chotanagpur Adivasi Mahasabha* became the joint organisation for the different groups working for the tribal cause in the region. Jaipal Singh became the Chairman of this organisation in 1939. With his foreign training and experience, he capured the imagination of the tribal masses and became the unquestioned leader. He tried to bridge the gulf between the educated Christians and the tribal masses. The immediate motivation for the formation of the *Mahasabha* was the experience of first general election held in 1937 in which the Congress had swept the polls. The poll results made the tribals close their ranks. Being an astute politician, Jaipal Singh exploited the Bengalee--Bihari controversy raging in Bihar at the time and the Muslim League politics (Singh, 1963: 200, 201). The Bengalis felt that their interests in Bihar were not safe and they could therefore combine with the tribals to form a separate state. The Muslim League in the mid 1940s toyed with the idea of forming a corridor passing through the tribal areas in middle India to link East and West Pakistan. To have the tribal on their side gave the financial support to the *Adivasi Mahasabha*. The *Mahasabha* was led by professional political workers, some of whom were highly educated and articulate. They operated in both rural and urban areas. The *Mahasabha* demanded the formation not of a sub-state but its complete separation from Bihar. A series of violent incidents occurred at this time which underline the militant nature of the movement. The *Sabha* was routed by the Congress in the Assmebly elections of 1946. The link with the Muslim League was broken and the Bangalee--Bihari controversy tapered off.

On the eve of Independence, changing social, political and economic contexts continued to alter the prevailing tribal non-tribal equations and generated new passions and conflict. Suspicion and distrust prevented them from forging lasting bonds of co-operation and interdependence and an uneasy co-existence prevailed.

IV

Soon after India achieved Independence, the new Consititution came into being. In the framing of this Constitution a number of tribal leaders and social and political workers in tribal areas were involved. Added to this was the commitment of the Congress party for closer integration of the tribals with mainstream of national life. However, they were also concerned with the protection of the tribes from exploitation of all kinds and for their social, educational and economic development. To meet these ends, a number of protective and promotional provisions were made for the tribals in the Constitution.

Adult franchise and the democratic political process, accompanied by regular elections for legislative bodies changed the character of the tribal politics. Although the tribal polity all over the country was democratic in character and village panchayats worked on the principle of consensus. The concept of one man one vote and decisions by majority were alien to tribal thought. "In course of the rapidly changing context of national life the tribals have been catapulted from their relative isolation into the vortex of competitive politics (Dube, 1972, 30). Due to the spread of education, exposure to outside influences and uneven distribution of resources, an articulate and effective political elite has emerged in several tribal areas. It has acquired a taste for politics and is vigorously contributing to the growth of a new political idiom. It has learnt the game of politics from non-tribal political workers. But it does not stop with the conventional rules of the game. It makes its own rules as the play progresses. The elite cajoles regional political leaders to obtain concessions from them. It is conscious of the pressure it can bring to bear on the local leaders and is capable of making calculated moves to gain the acceptance of their demands. In case, in a particular region, such an elite has not come up, national, regional, and local parties fill up the vacuum. The tribal problems are being politicised. Much of the tribal unrest in India is undoubtedly a product of manipulative politics.

In recent times the entire gamut of tribal problems has to be seen in the political perspective. Politics is seen as the principal avenue (*Ibid*:30) through which the tribals can find solutions to most of the problems that have plagued them for centuries. Some of these problems have developed a sharper edge due to the development programmes in the tribal areas. There has been a revolution of rising aspirations. There have been new additions to the long inventory of the tribal needs. The tribal leaders are aware that in contemporary politics, the amount of pressure that one can build up, determines his place and share in the decision making process. It is only their participation in this process that they can ensure the preservation of their self-respect and can obtain a larger share of scarce resources for economic development of their area. In many areas, they have discarded the role they have been playing as members of national parties in the political process. In areas of the tribal concentration, they have built up local parties highlighting neglect of their areas by other parties. There has been a shift in their political attitudes and strategies. From politics of compliance and affirmation they have moved over to the politics of pressure and protest. In their efforts to capture the imagination and the votes of the tribals they are adopting radical postures and fomenting militant agitatior The fires of discontent are being fanned by interested tribal and non-tribal agencies. The politicisation of the tribal scene is a natural culmination of the democratic process. The political culture of the tribes is undergoing rapid transformation.

The tribes are coming out of their subject political culture in which they did not question the validity of political decisions taken about them at higher levels. They believed that their own role would be one of their compliance. They were concerned only with the output functions of the political system and did not care about the input processes. The new political culture in the tribal area is characterised by Dube "as a cross between what Almond and Verba would call 'parochial political culture' and participant political culture' (*ibid* : 31). It is inspired by sub national tribal identities. The broader national identity is lost sight of. When there is a clash of interest between the smaller and larger units there is a tendency to sacrifice the latter. This concentration on purely regional or tribal interest imparts parochial overtones to the emergent political culture. It may be argued that the realities of the situation have led to such thinking. At the same time the tribal elite are taking an active part in framing issues and formulating policies and thus a participant political culture is being born. Thus, there is a concern both for the output and input processes of the political system. Such a trend may be welcomed as it will strengthen the roots of democracy. It is however, difficult to harmonise national and tribal interests at all times. Many of the issues are extremely sensitive and the mishandling of any one of them is likely to rouse violent passions.

It would be useful at this juncture to examine the emergent political culture in the context of nation building in India. The political trends discernable in tribal India are both conjunctive and disjunctive. After Independence, there was a trend toward tribal solidarity all over the country. At the same time, the tribes as a whole are being viewed by others as a distinct category, sharply differentiated from the general population by various mechanisms of safeguards and protective discremination. Tribalness has become a powerful political factor. To exploit its full potential, tribal groups at different levels of socio-cultural development and representing different cultural ethos are being linked at the political level. This might underscore intertribal conflict and frictions. To that extent it is to be welcomed. But it cuts the other way also, as it separates the tribals from the rest of the country and as such stands in way of nation-building. Separatist movements result in mass violence and senseless destruction of public property. They mix up social and economic issues and make their solution difficult. In recent years, however, the politics of violent agitation and separatism has yielded results and it has therefore spread to areas which were comparatively peaceful. One cannot expect political restraint from the tribals when they see that more matured parties and politicians use the same methods to further personal or party interests. The tribals can no longer remain insensitive to the political culture of the country as a whole. If we find that tribal political culture is oriented towards violence, intolerance, and unreason, we have ourselves to blame. The tribals are adept pupils of seasoned political masters and have learnt the game from them to the last detail. We shall examine the situation in Chotanagpur and in the North-East to illustrate conceptual frame outlined above.

V

Till the advent of freedom, tribal politics in Chotanagpur was confined within ethnic boundaries. The failure of Adivasi leadership in the elections of 1946 led to serious rethinking among the leaders. It was realised that it would be advantageous to include non-Adivasis living in Chotanagpur in their organisation. To press this point of view Justin Richard organised the United Jharkhand Block late in 1948. After resisting this idea for sometime, Jaipal Singh accepted it and the Jharkhand Party was formed in 1950 in Jamshedpur (Sachchidanand, 1972). In the 1952 elections the Jharkhand Party was in alliance with the socialist party. Besides winning the bulk of the tribal seats, the party also registered success on some non-reserved seats in Chotanagpur, with the result that it became the largest opposition party in the assembly. The election slogan of the party was the creation of separate Jharkhand State. The elections were managed very efficiently (Singh, 1985) by the Jharkhand Party. The tribals hailed elections as a festival and the percentage of polling was pretty high.

However, during the visit of the States Reorganisation Commission in 1955, Jaipal Singh declared himself to be against the dismemberment of Bihar. In the 1957 elections, the party lost some ground and the Congress gained some reserved seats from them. In the 1962 elections the party suffered further loss of seats. It secured only 59 per cent of the 32 reserved seats. Spectacular gains were made by the Swatantra Party. After the 1962 elections, the Jharkhand leaders felt that their cry for a Separate Jharkhand state remained unfulfilled. The tribal masses' faith on the leaders was fading away. The leaders were tired of sitting in the opposition. Development programmes had also made same impact on the mind of the people and the demand for Jharkhand did not evoke much response. Thus psychological climate had already been created for the merger of the party with the Congress. When the then Chief Minister of Bihar, Sri Binodananda Jha, approached them for joining the Congress, they jumped at the idea. (Sachchidanand, 1976). They would get an opportunity of sharing the fruits of power and also contributing to tribal development. However, they did not realise that with the merger they would lose their identity and that would aggravate the resentment of the tribal masses.

Soon after the merger its architect Sri Binodananda Jha lost his office under the Kamraj plan. Jaipal Singh who was a minister in the Bihar Government for only three months was replaced by his deputy, S.K. Bage, by the new Chief Minister, K.B. Sahay. The rank and file of the party was never happy with the merger decision and after losing office Jaipal Singh was also sulking. In fact, merger decision was never ratified by the council of the party.

In the fourth general election in 1967 the erstwhile Jharkhand leaders suffered the blast of the anti-merger wind. S.K. Bage forfeited his security deposit and many tribal leaders lost their seats. Even Jaipal Singh narrowly escaped defeat in his parliamentary seat. The Congress recovered its lost ground in Chotanagpur. The Jan Sangh Party also registered significant gains. Independent candidates were successful in one-fourth of the seats. It was for the first time that besides the Congress another national party had established a firm footing in the tribal areas. This was possible by the mobilisation of non-Christian votes.

After 1967 a number of splinter groups, new parties and organisations sprang up to fill the vacuum created by the demise of the Jharkhand Party. The most important of these groups was the *Birsa Seva Dal* organised under the leadership of the young educated tribals. Their slogan was to win Jharkhand by the use of force *(Jharkhand hamara hai and Jharkhand larke lenge teer ke bal par).*

The BSD was an urban based party and although its constitution spoke of the commonalty of interest of the tribals, backward classes and other exploited sections of the population, its objectives were geared to promoting the interests of the tribal people. From 1967 to 1969 it passed through a militant phase. Meetings, processions of youth armed with bows and arrows were its modes of mobilisation. It demanded creation of a separate State, expulsion of outsiders from Chotanagpur, agrarian refoms and stringent measures against money lenders. By 1969 the BSD was rent by splits. For the next two years Naxalite activities were noticeable in Chotanagpur. There were many incidents involving murder, dacoity and violent clashes.

Late in 1972 politics in Chotanagpur took another turn with the Kurmi Mahto and some Santal leaders joining to form the Jharkhand Mukti Morcha. Its objective was the formation of a separate Jharkhand State, ending the exploitation of the tribals and securing preferential treatment for the sons of the soil in the matter of employment. 'The Morcha combined in its operations elements of agrarian radicalism and cultural revivalism'(Singh 1985 : 212). Its leader Sibu Soren acquired something of charisma and was regarded as a god. Elements of ancient tribal self-government were revived. The *baisi* (tribal courts) functioned without fees, and meted out speedy justice. A voluntary force was raised, tribal traditions of collective farming and preservation of jungles, pastures and common land were revived and a common grain pool was created. There was an effort to put a stop to drinking of liquor and taking of bride price. The Morcha emerged as a major political force in the industries and mining belt of Chotanagpur and in State politics after the 1980 general elections. It reached an understanding with the Congress which led to the parting of ways with the Marxist Co-ordination Committee and the Kurmi Mahto. The Congress continued to be the major force in the tribal region. It improved its position further in 1985 elections. However, in the 1990 elections, the Morcha and the Bhartiya Janta Party raised their tallies at the expense of the Congress.

The elections in recent years have revealed that there has been a shift from ethnic politics to regional politics. The voter's participation in the tribal constituencies is lower than in the non-tribal constituencies although the turn out has increased over the years. This shows that the politicisation of the tribals has been less intense than in other areas. It is seen that the tribal constituencies reflect the differences among the tribes themselves, their demographic distribution, levels of modernisation, intensity of self-awareness and their relationship with State and central authority.

The demand for a separate State has become more insistent in recent years. 438 delegates representing 48 organisations in Chotanagpur came together on a platform organised by the Jharkhand Co-ordination Committee in 1987. The idea was to organise an Assam type agitation calling on legislators to resign and then organising a provisional Government. Some leaders even talked of an armed struggle. The Jharkhand state is to comprise of 21 districts of the four States Bihar, West Bengal, Orissa, and Madhya Pradesh. However, the movement could not achieve any success outside Bihar. From time to time, *bunds* were organised but it did not evoke much response. None of the legislators resigned. In April 1989, the three day *bund* wintnessed large scale arson and sabotage. It was for the first time that the movement had turned violent. In all this agitation the All Jharkhand Students Union played a prominent part but only one of its leaders was successful in 1990 assembly election. The Bharatiya Janta Party improved its electoral strength on the basis of its promise regarding the formation of *Vananchal*. It is however not known how different is this concept from that of Jharkhand.

The pattern of leadership in Chotanagpur has undergone sea change. Earlier leadership was rural-bred, charismatic and tradition oriented (Vidyarthi, 1972 : 443). It tried to revitalise the tribals on the Hindu model. The coming of the Christian missionaries upset this pattern. Till 1962 tribal leadership remained in the hands of western educated urban-bred and Christian tribals. These leaders worked in close co-operation with the missionaries. However, the missionary influence began to wane after the merger of the Jharkhand Party with the Congress. In course of time a sizeable non-Christian leadership also began to emerge in Santal Parganas, Singhbhum and Ranchi districts. In areas under the influence of the Bharatiya Janta Party, the leadership was exclusively Hindu.

The Christian non-Christian divide became more evident with the emergence of *Adivasi Vikas Parishad* . This organisation seemed to be pro-Congress anti-Christian and opposed to the policies of the Jharkhand Party.

The movement for Jharkhand in recent years has been strengthened by businessmen and industrialists operating in Chotanagpur but hailing from outside Bihar. Some other intermediate and lower Hindu castes have also supported the movement. However, there is sizeable opposition from the upper caste Hindus, erstwhile landlords and professionals who have organised themselves into the "Sadan Parishad." The support or opposition of the non-tribals to the demand for Jharkhand is important since the tribals form less than 30 per cent of the population of the area

Traditional tribal leaders have been marginalised. Positional leaders like members of the statutory Panchayats, MLAs and MPs have become prominent. Some tribal leaders have come into contact with politicians from outside and acquired an extrovert personality. They have two faces, one for their constituents and the other for their peers in other groups. Most of the leaders believe that the tempo of tribal development could be speeded up through greater politicisation. The participation of the tribals in national and regional politics has to some extent weakened the solidarity of the community life of the tribals. Some of the tribal leaders, however, like their counterparts in other areas, are more interested in feathering their own caps than in serving the community. Thus, in some cases the tribals continued to be exploited by both tribal and non-tribal leaders.

VI

The tribal situation in north-eastern India is vastly different from that of middle India. There the historical background is also different and the interaction with non-tribals was very much restricted than in middle India. Some of these areas were lightly administered and more often than not, left in charge of tribal chiefs. On the basis of their political history the area can be divided into three categories (i) those which were more or less completely untouched by British administration as a consequence of which their traditional culture and political administration remained undisturbed. Arunachal Pradesh may be put into this category,

(ii) areas like Naga hills which were a continuous source of irritation to British authorities and remained in constant conflict with the British, (iii) areas now included in Meghalaya and Mizoram which after some initial resistance came under effective British administration. The impact of cultural and political changes in the area depended on the degree of the effectiveness of British administration and the influence of Christian missionaries (Sinha 1972 : 336).

The political history of the region since Independence has been marked by the successive dismemberment of the State of Assam in which most of the tribal people were included. Each of these big tribal groups had a hill district known after it. Christianity came in the first quarter of the 19th century. About 90 per cent of the Mizo are Christians and the majority of the Khasi, Garo and Naga have also been converted.

Although, there were sporadic rebellions against British authority, the many of the tribals of the north-east were never directly involved in the mainstream of the national movement. The tribal people were never very happy under foreign rule. As early as 1829 the Khasi chiefs had revolted against interference with the traditional rights on land and forest and the impositions of new taxes. The Zeliang Naga revolted in 1933. This, however, was a secessionist movement. In each of the hill districts there were social and political movements. In 1899 the Sen Khasi movement presented a strong challenge to the ascendency of Christianity. It was in 1923 that Khasi nationalism took a complete shape with the formation of Khasi National Darbar. In 1933, the Khasi chiefs made a strong plea for recognition of their federation which pledged its loyalty to the British Government. In 1946 the Garo National Council demanded that powers of taxation and administration of justice should be vested in it.

After Independence, the Government of India realised the critical situation and the political aspirations of the people in the hill areas of Assam, in the background of the assurances said to have been given by the outgoing British rulers. A measure of autonomy was given to the hill districts under the provision of the Sixth Schedule of the Constitution, but it fell far short of the aspirations of hill people. The Nagas took the path of armed struggle which they had suspended on the eve of Independence. The political parties in the other hill districts continued their agitation first for enlarged powers for the District Council and then for statehood. The States Reorganisation Commission gave its verdict against the formation of hill State.

Nagaland

In 1951 Phizo became the President of the Naga National Convention and organized a plebiscite in which thousands of Nagas gave their thumb impressions in favour of Independence. In the first general election in 1952 the Naga nationalists organised a total boycott of the elections. In 1956 the underground Naga Federal Government was formed, with a complete outfit. When violence escalated, the church leaders gave a call for peace. Ultimately negotiations were started to bring about a political settlement. In August 1960, Pandit Nehru announced in Parliament the decision to make Nagaland a separate State. After due preparation, the new State came into being in December 1963. The anger and fury of the underground now turned against the State Government. To ease the situation the church leaders took the decision to form a Peace Mission (Aram, 1972 : 336) consisting of Jaya Prakash Narain, B.P Chaliha and Rev. Michael Scott. The Peace Mission succeeded in bringing about a ceasefire in September 1964. The talks between the Naga underground and the Government continued till 1967. The ceasefire had ushered in an era of peace and development in Nagaland. From the elections of 1969 Naga people participated with great enthusiasm. The elections were free and fair and polling was as high as 76.39 per cent. In 1977 the polling was to the tune of 83.26 per cent. However, the existence of an opposition party and its full significance in Nagaland is yet to be realised (Thakkar, 1972 : 328). The opposition itself has not been able to understand the contribution it could make in the legislature.

Peace returned to Nagaland in the last quarter of 1975 when the underground leaders signed the historic Shillong Accord, outlawing any underground activities and joining the mainstream of political life in the state.

Meghalaya

During the 1957 general elections the local parties in the Khasi and Garo hills district swept the poll on the basis of the demand for the hill State. This was because of high level of political consciousness in this region. "The preponderance of cash crops, better communication and higher percentage of literacy had raised the level of aspirations among people "(Sinha, 1972: 242). In 1960 the All Party Hill Leaders Conference amalgamating all local parties was born. In the 1962 elections 53per cent of the hill people voted for the hill State. In the Mizo Hill 72 per cent of the Mizo voted for this. In 1965 the Pataskar Commission was appointed to make recommendation about giving autonomy to the hill people. The Commission rejected the idea of a separate administration for the hill areas. The Hill Leaders' Conference rejected the recommendation. In 1968 there was the plan for autonomous hill State within the general frame work of Assam. However, there was great distrust among the tribals for Assam Government and they persisted in their demand for a separate State. Ultimately a separate State of Meghalaya was created in January 1972 consisting of the Khasi and the Jayanti Hills and the Garo hills.

Mizoram

In Mizo society there was a big gulf between chief and the masses. To counter the power of the chiefs, the Mizo Common People Union was formed in 1946. On the eve of independence the British administrators, the missionaries, the chiefs and the businessmen tried to sow the seeds of discord between Indians and the Mizo (Goswami, 1979). The right wing of the Mizo Union, the chiefs council and the few others formed the United Mizo Freedom Organisation with the intention of secession. They wanted to opt out of the Indian union. The Independence Day celebrations at Aizawl in 1947 was very much disturbed on this account. In 1954 the UMFO changed its strategy, gave up secession demand and opted for a hill State. It merged with the Eastern India Tribal Union in 1957. In 1958 there was a severe famine caused by the destruction of crops in Mizo hills. Some disgruntled elements including dissidents from both the existing political parties formed the National Mizo Famine Front for organising relief. It was at this time that Laldenga joined politics. The Mizo Union leaders who were at the beginning the supporters of the Congress gradually drifted away. By 1960 the word famine was dropped and the Mizo National Front (MNF) came into being with the demand for the sovereignty and independence of greater Mizoram.

By 1964 the MNF intensified its activities, made forced exactions from people, recruited volunteers, collected arms and provided training to its cadrets in guerilla warfare. In March 1966, the MNF started an armed uprising and declared Independence. The Mizo Union however was satisfied with the fulfilment of their demand for statehood for Mizo hills and in January 1972 Mizoram came into being as a Union Territory. The MNF continued struggle for a completely independent State. The MNF went underground and organised insurgency. In 1976 after months of protracted negotiations Laldenga signed the Peace Accord. However, he went back on it. Soon after there was a new development in Mizo politics with the rise of Brigadier Sailo and his newly formed Peoples Conference Party. When the elections were held Sailo came to power with an overhelming majority. The traditional politicians were alienated from Sailo as he refused to grant them undue favours. Some of his own partymen joined hands with the opposition to pull down his Governmemt. There was political instability in Mizoram even after the mid-term poll in 1979. Underground movement of the MNF continued and Laldenga was taken into custody in July 1979. MNF was declared unlawful. With the change of Government in Delhi in January 1980 all the cases against Laldenga were withdrawn and the stage was set for resumption of peace talks and settlement in Mizoram. The peace talk continued and ultimately an accord was signed between the Government and Laldenga in June 1986. He became the Chief Minister when the Congress incumbent stepped down in his favour. In February 1987 Mizoram State came into being. However, the January 1989 elections brought the Congress (I) back to power.

Arunachal

The large horseshoe shaped territory sprawling from the borders of Bhutan on the west to the Burma on the east is the new State Arunachal. At the time of Independence it consisted of four frontier tracks, which were incharge of the Governor of Assam. These areas were lightly administered. They were constituted into North East Frontier Agency in 1954 and the control of the area was transferred from the External Affairs Ministry to the Home Ministry of the Government of India. Efforts were made to extend regular administration in the entire region. The area is populated by nearly 80 different tribal communities and the density of population is very low. The bulk of the people make a living by shifting cultivation. Permanent cultivation is confined to very small area.

"Till 1965 except the village council which existed from time immemorial there was no representative institution in Arunachal" (Rao, 1976). As an outcome of the recommendation of the Ering Commission a four tier set up with an Agency. Council at the apex was created. The Agency Council came into being in 1969. It was only in January 1971 that union territory status was given to the area and it came to be known as Arunachal Pradesh. It was at this time that adult franchise was introduced for the first time and all the panchayat bodies including Gram Panchayats were made elective. In 1975 the Pradesh Council was converted into a provisional legislature. Elections were held in February 1978 and the two parties contested the elections. Only in two out of thirty constituencies candidates were declared elected unopposed. In twelve constituencies female voters outnumbered male voters. The first ministry lasted barely two years. The Chief Minister had to give up office due to defections from his party. From 1980, however, the Congress has been in power in Arunachal Pradesh. The opposition is not very strong. In February 1987 Arunachal became a full-fledged State of the Indian Union. Two remarkable features of the political process in Arunachal Pradesh have been the absence of Christian missionary influence and insurgency of any kind. This has led to speedy socio-economic development of the region. Inspite of the hilly terrain, the infrastructure for development has been built up with great effort. This has promoted fast progress in all walks of life.

Nowhere else has the tribal society undergone such lightning upheaval as in north eastern India. Tribal societies based on shifting cultivation and very simple community life have been catapulated to grapple with 20th century ideas, technologies and ways of life. Such a change has not been gradual but sudden. The flood gates of change have blasted the bastions of isolation, neglect and repression. Thus a series of explosions have occurred and placed the tribal societies in a state of ferment and turmoil (Sarin, 1980 : VIII). The situation has been complicated by the impact of Christianity which was instrumental in creating a barrier between the bulk of the tribals in this region and the Indian mainstream. Many of the tribes in this region were encouraged to think in terms of sovereignty, independence and secession from the Indian Union. The sinister interest taken by certain countries on account of the geo-political importance of the region, further aggravated the situation and promoted insurgency. This naturally prevented democratic institutions from taking firm roots. The political processes set in by the Consitution were slowed down.

With people realising the fruits of peace and development, gradually the political processes did begin to produce an impact. People enthusiastically participated in the elections and there was a very high turn out of voters. However, local parties mushroomed. These were not so much based on principles or ideologies but were largely leader centred. This led to frequent defections and fall of Governments, in the various States and Union territories. However, with the passing of the anti-defection law this tendency has much been curbed. Another noticeable feature of the politics of the area is the simmering insurgent activity in many States. This is a constant irritant to the State Governments. It disturbs peace and reduces the pace of development. With the passage of time, however, such activity may gradually disappear. The north-east is well on the road to stable political integration with India. Although economic integration with the rest of the country is proceeding a space, with the opening up of the area by speedy means of communication for social and emotional integration we have still a long way to go.

Reference

Aram, M. 1972 : Emerging Situation in Nagaland-*Tribal Situation in India,* (Ed.) K.S. Singh, Indian Institute of Advanced Studies, Simla.

Dube, S.C. 1972 : Inaugural Address in*Tribal Situation in India* (Ed.) K.S. Singh, Indian Institute of Advanced Studies, Simla.

Goswami, B.B. 1979 : *Mizo Unrest,* Aalekh Publishers, Jaipur.

Rao.V. Venkat 1976 : *A Century of Tribal Politics in North East India,* 1874-1974.

Sachchidananda — *The Tana Bhagat Movement.*

1968 : *The Tribal Village in Bihar,* Munshiram Manoharlal, New Delhi.

1972 : 'Tribal Situation in Bihar' in *Tribal Situation in India* (Ed) K.S. Singh, Indian Institute of Advanced Studies, Simla.

1976 : *The Tribal Voter in Bihar,* National, New Delhi.

Sarin, V.K. 1980 : *India's North-East In Flames,* Vikas Publishers, New Delhi.

Singh, K.S. 1963 : Hari Baba Movement in Chotanagpur,*Journal of Bihar Research Society,* Jan-Dec.

1983 : *Birsa Munda and His Movement,* Oxford University Press, Calcutta.

1985 : *Tribal Society in India,* Manohar, New Delhi.

Sinha, A.P. 1972 : Politics and Economic Development in the Hill Districts of Assam in*Tribal Situation in India* (Ed) K.S. Singh, Indian Institute of Advanced Studies, Simla.

Sinha, Surajit S. 1941 : State Formation and Rajput Myth in Central India, *Man in India,* Vol 42, No 2.

Vidyarthi, L.P. 1972 : An Appraisal of Leadership Pattern Among Tribes of Bihar in *Tribal Situation in India,* (Ed)K.S. Singh, Indian Institute of Advanced Studies, Simla.

9

MEGHALAYA : THE POLITICS OF ETHNIC GROUPS

B. PAKEM

The Nature of Politics

In Meghalaya, which is essentially a tribal State, we are witnessing one of the several *Patterns of State Politics in India.* Our conceptual image of State politics is through an understanding of the nature of such politics. Again, in order to understand the nature of such politics, we have to know some of its important determinants which in turn will help us in having a proper perspective of an analytical image of State politics. According to Iqbal Narain, there are some determinants that have exercised an influence towards the building up of a theoretical framework in State politics in India (Narain, 1976 : XVI-XIX).

State politics in India, according to Iqbal Narain, operates within the constitutional framework. The Indian Constitution has provided an almost identical framework for all the States with a pre-eminent position for the Centre. The States are in themselves a whole and a part. They are a whole in that they are individual political persons and a part as a member of a bigger political family of the Centre. Hence, States are faced with the challenge of right ordering of loyalties--to themselves and to the Centre. This does not, however, indicate that we have only two levels of politics in India. In fact, we have a three-tier system with the State standing in between the Central and the local Governments. State politics, therefore, resembles a sort of an inter-growth between the Central and the local tiers; with the Centre "opening into" and the local tier "opens out" to it. In such a system, both the centripetal forces such as planning and one party dominance at the centre and the centrifugal forces like democratic decentralization, regionalism and linguism of the local tier influence the course of State politics. Finally, the panorama of State politics has to be taken and studied as a dynamic phenomenon due to the fact that it operated in a milieu of social and cultural transition. Thus, "the political system of a State in India has got to be viewed as a point of confluence to national, state and local politics; as a system of inter-connections and inter-actions between cultural milieu and politics, between leadership and political institution and process, between tradition and modernity: as a political society in question of a self-identity, through the somewhat self neutralizing process of continuity and change; as a split political person fighting against its own self alienation; and in sum as a miniature replica of State's life in its totality." And now it is in the light of the above conceptual and analytical framework that we are going to study the politics of the State of Meghalaya.

The Conceptual Framework

Institutionally, Meghalaya is the 21st State of the Indian Union. It came into existence on January 21, 1972. Earlier it was an autonomous State since April 2, 1970 to January 20, 1972, excepting the three wards of Shillong Municipality (European Ward, Police Bazar Ward, and Jail Road Ward) and the Cantonment. As an autonomous State, Meghalaya was within the State of Assam. The State is bounded by Assam in the north and east, and Bangladesh in the south and west.

The State had a total population of 10,11,697 in 1971 which rose to 13,35, 819 in 1981 constituting 19 per cent of the national total population. Similarly, the total electorate rose from 4,18,493 in 1971 to 9,38,526 by November 1989.[1]

Originally, Meghalaya consisted of two districts--Garo Hills District and the United Khasi--Jaintia Hills District of the State of Assam. The third district came into existence on February 21, 1972 for the Jaintia Hills Sub-Division of the United Khasi--Jaintia Hills District. On October 22, 1976, the fourth and fifth districts were added to the State by dividing the Garo Hills District and the Khasi Hills District into East and West Garo Hills, and East and West Khasi Hills respectively. The Legislature of the autonomous State of Meghalaya had a total strength of 38 members indirectly elected by the respective members of the three Autonomous District Councils of Meghalaya and three nominated members; and the State

Legislature of the State of Meghalaya has a total strength of 60 elected members.

Except the Shillong Municipality, the whole of Meghalaya is under the jurisdiction of the Sixth Schedule of the Constitution of India. In accordance with the provisions of the Sixth Schedule there are three autonomous district councils, one each for the Garo Hills, Khasi Hills and Jaintia Hills respectively. The first two district councils have a total strength of 30 members each including one nominated member for each district council. The Jaintia Hills Autonomous District Council had a total strength of 19 members including three nominated members. The membership has been recently raised to 25 members including one nominated member.

The capital city of Shillong in the East Khasi Hills District has a municipality since 1876. Till 1971 the municipality consisted of 27 members. Presently, the municipality has been superseded by the State Government. In addition to the municipality, Shillong city has a cantonment board consisting of four elected and two nominated members. The Tura Municipality in the West Garo Hills District was constituted on August 18, 1979 with a strength of 11 members. The Garo Hills Autonomous District Council had also established the Baghmara Town Committee in 1975 with four elected members. Similarly, the Jaintia Hills Autonomous District Council had established the Jowai Town Committee on May 14, 1979 with 12 members including four nominated members. Presently, the Jowai Town Committee consisted of nine elected members and one nominated member.

Next to the institutional determinant, we have the physiological determinant of State politics. In Meghalaya this determinant centred around the dual personality of the State. On the one hand, there is its loyalty to the family of the Indian nation, being one of the units of the Indian Union and where the State administration is run according to the provisions of the Indian Constitution. And on the other, there is its loyalty to self. This is being reinforced by the fact that the population structure in Meghalaya as in some other States in the north-east of India, is predominantly tribal in character. The percentage of distribution of Schedule Tribes in Meghalaya is 80.48 in 1971 and 80.58 in 1981.[2] The heavy concentration of Scheduled Tribes is in the rural areas with a percentage distribution of 86.42 in 1971 and 86.13 in 1981.[3] This naturally leads to the politics of ethnic groups in the State with an ambivalent attitude towards the Centre. As such, the study of Centre-State relations in the case of Meghalaya is as delicate as it is interesting.

Now we come to the inter-active determinant of the politics of the ethnic groups in Meghalaya. This can clearly be seen at all levels of politics in the State from local to State levels. This is being extended to include even at the national level when the independent and separate ethnic groups belonging to regional political parties of North-East India including Meghalaya constituted themselves into the Independent Parliamentary Group in the Lok Sabha during 1979. In the three-tier political system that we have in India, the national-tier politics "opening into" the local tier, while the local tier "opens out" into the national tier. It is the middle tier--the State level which is to act as cushion between the highland thisles of Central interference and the local aspirations of the ethnic groups. The State level of politics in Meghalaya has, therefore, to be on a dual personality--national to the Central local leadership and ethnic to the local opinion leaders and the masses. And more often than not, when viewed negatively, the attitude of political ambivalence amongst the State leaders of Meghalaya is the result. But when a positive view is taken, given the reservoir of goodwill of both the Central and local leaders, there is the hope that the State level of politics in Meghalaya may instead provide an inter-growth between the Central and local tiers of the Indian political system. The State level in Meghalaya can act as a bridge of understanding between two poles of political diversities as it happened in the 1960s during the movement for a separate hill State.

Coming to the socio-economic and political determinant of State politics, we may recall one of the definitions of politics as "who gets what?" This indicates the distribution of "scarce resources" in the State and in the context of the "politics of scarcity" there has always been a competition and bargaining in Indian politics. There has always been a sharpening of the inter-active determinant by centripetal and centrifugal forces in the politics of any Indian State. In India, we have the Planning Commission acting as the centripetal force to bring the State under Central control and direction despite the existence of the National Development Council. The Five-Year Plans including the Annual Plans of the States had to be attuned to Central requirements and objectives. As it is, small States like Meghalaya have sometimes to toe the line of Central direction and control if their total requirements were to be acceded to without any pruning.

This point is further re-inforced by the fact that the North-Eastern States including Meghalaya are members of the North-Eastern Council. The council is a unique institution in the country. Though an advisory body, it has functioned more than a mere recommending body. The Central Government knew it very well in the beginning that economically, small States like Meghalaya would not be viable. But politically, the reorganisation of States in the North-East of India is a necessity. It is against such a background that the North-Eastern Council was brought into existence. The units could have united if they want to put pressure on the Central Government which sometimes try to pull them towards dependence. The North-Eastern Council is asserting its authority over the States of North-East India by becoming the agency to remind its units that the big brother is watching them. (Sharma, 1976;454; Maheswari, 1976 : 465-476).

Finally, we come to king pin of the socio-economic and political determinant which is the elite structure in the State. In Meghalaya the traditional elite is giving way to modern elite. While the role of ascriptive leaders like the *Nokmas* and the *Laskars* of Garo Hills; the *Syiems, Lyngdohs, Wahadadars* and the *Sardars* of Khasi Hill and the *Dollois* of Jaintia Hills[4] has been diminished by their respective autonomous district councils that of modern leaders has increased partly due to their achievement-orientation in the various fields of professions like business, law and teaching. Most of the modern leaders of Meghalaya come mostly from the legal and teaching professions and very few from among the traditional leaders. It is hoped, therefore, that the present political elite of Meghalaya has the capability to cause an interaction between the socio-economic environment and the political institutions prevailing in the State. State leaders have to satisfy the economic aspiration of the local people through various schemes of grants-in-aid, subsidies, concessions, preferences, reservations and the like. The political leaders even take advantage of the buggy of tribalism to convince the Central Government to the extent that borders on the line of illegality as in the case of the small coal-miners of Meghalaya. The small coal-miners of Meghalaya are left to themselves since 1973 when the Coal Mines (Nationalization) Act of the Government of India was made applicable throughout the country. This is possible since the political elite of Meghalaya presents the national image on one side of its face and the tribal image on the other side. But now, they are gradually coming around to realize that to be respected is to stand on one's own leg and to be counted they have to contribute their mite towards the general development of the country. With the beginning of the Sixth Plan period all the States including Meghalaya were asked by the Central Government to raise additional State resources. As a result, during 1980-81, an attempt had been made by the political elite to tap new resources before they could expect a larger plan allocation from the Centre. During the current financial year 1990-91 when the State Government proposed to raise Rs.19 crores from its own resources, the Planning Commission had raised the quantum of annual plan allocation for Meghalaya from Rs. 150 crores in 1989-90 to Rs. 175 crores in 1990-91. The political elites of Meghalaya are beginning to also toe the line of Central Acts and Regulations wherever possible in order to have a bite of the national cake towards further development in all sectors. For example, ever since 1981 the State Government was trying to apply the Coal Mines (Nationalization) Act, 1973 with certain modifications. The Meghalaya Mineral Cess Act, 1989 is a case in point. According to this Act, the State Government has impliedly claimed ownership of minerals like coal, lime-stone, etc. contrary to tribal community, or individual ownership of such minerals in the State.

The above nature of State politics in Meghalaya and its accompanying determinants provide the conceptual framework which will have to be captured in the analytic framework. The analytic framework of Iqbal Narain consisted of three dimensions--contextual, structural and operational. Now we turn our attention to this analytic framework in our study of the politics of ethnic groups in Meghalaya.

In the study of Indian politics, caste has been an important contextual framework. But this is not so in Meghalaya. Here is a departure from or an exception to a general theory of caste in the State politics of India. Contextually, it is the ethnic groups or tribes rather than caste that has been an important framework in the study of State politics in Meghalaya. Historically, Meghalaya is a State predominantly inhabited by various tribal ethnic groups--

the chief among them are the Garos, Khasis, and the Jaintias. Before India's independence, we had in Khasi Hills, the British areas and villages, and the Khasi native States. The integration of the Khasi States to the Indian Union was completed in 1948 after much struggling on how to preserve their identity as a separate ethnic group. It was during that time that the separatist elements caught hold of the British areas also. There was much hope that the States Reorganization Commission of 1956 would recommend a separate State to the hill people of North-East India including the people of Meghalaya. But their hope was belied as all the hill areas had been tagged with Assam as ever before or to Manipur and Tripura respectively. But due to persistent demands for a separate hill State, the Government of India had to accede to some of their demands. The first to gain Statehood was Nagaland in 1963, then other Union Territories like Arunachal Pradesh and Mizoram were separated from Assam. Finally, in 1970, excluding the United Mikir and North Cachar Hills district of Assam, Meghalaya was declared an autonomous State within Assam only to be granted a full-fledged Statehood two years later in 1972.

In the politics of ethnic groups, the early leaders came mostly from the British areas. Leaders like Rev. J.J.M. Nicholos-Roy from Shillong of the Khasi Hills, Rev. L. Gatphoh from Jowai of Jaintia Hills, and Jobang Mark from Tura of Garo Hills came from British areas. All the four Chief Ministers of Meghalaya also came originally from the British areas of Khasi Hills and Garo Hills. This indicates that the British areas provided leaders who used to participate in the representative and democratic institutions since the August Declaration of 1917 of the Government of India. The Khasi States, on the other hand, could not provide prominent leaders during the British period. This fact leads us to think that the traditional political system in which the local traditional rulers operated during the British paramountcy had failed to train up leaders in the parliamentary system of Government. Further, most of the pre-independence leaders from British areas were western educated, cosmopolitan in outlook and comparatively liberal. They came largely from among the urban elite and continued to be at the helm of affairs even after Independence. The British areas also provided men who joined hands in the struggle for India's freedom though their contribution could not be adequately appreciated as they were far away from the main stream of India's struggle for Independence. Presently, political leaders of

Meghalaya came from every nook and corner of the State irrespective of the fact whether they came from the erstwhile British areas or from the erstwhile Khasi States.

The brief historical background mentioned above, gives us an insight into the patterns of political leadership during the pre-Independence period and immediately after Independence. Since the beginning of the 1950, political leadership comes from all over the State as if the State has already had an organic political community. On closer scrutiny, however it is not so. The political integration of the three ethnic groups did not bring the desired result of the idea of one State one ethnic group. A sense of separate identity has always been felt by the smaller ethnic groups, the Jaintias, who are the closest cousins of the Khasis. As a result in 1967 a separate autonomous district council was created for them by the Assam Government with the hope that this would wean them away from the hill State movement under the leadership of the Khasis. But with the attainment of Statehood in Meghalaya, a sense of similar identity with the Khasis is once again felt among the Jaintia leaders. The politics of ethnic groups, however, has not completely died out. It constantly raises it head whenever there is any political crisis in the State as in the 1976 APHLC merger with the Indian National Congress when the prominent leaders from Khasi Hills got themselves estranged from the leadership of Garo Hills and Jaintia Hills over the issue of a merger with the national party.

Then close in the heel of history, geography is another contextual framework. The importance of North-Eastern India need not be overemphasised. Meghalaya, in particular, is very close to the Bangladesh border where a number of tribesmen have spread over on both sides of the international border. The inter-state border of Meghalaya with Assam also contains a number of tribal people in the Assam hill districts of North Cachar and Karbi Anglong and the Assam Plain districts of Cachar, Nowgong, Kamrup and Goalpara. The tribal people of Meghalaya cannot remain complacent if they see that their kith and kin on the other side of the border get better treatment. The politics of the Biates an ethnic group of Meghalaya can be understood in its context. The ethnic Biates of Meghalaya are divided from the ethnic Biates of North Cachar Hills of Assam by the river Kupli. There has been an aspiration for a Biate political unification so that they can stand united against any political step-motherly treatment on the part of any Indian States, be it Assam or Meghalaya. Similarly, the ethnic Jaintias of Karbi Anglong of Assam have expressed their hope and aspiration in uniting themselves with the Jaintias of Jaintia Hills of Meghalaya. Occasionally, there is even an outburst of suppressed feeling that Jaintiapur, the capital of the old Jaintia Kingdom in Bangladesh be restored to Jaintia Hills of Meghalaya. Further, the proximity of Meghalaya with Arunachal Pradesh, Assam, Manipur Mizoram, Nagaland and Tripura has made this area which was at one time a land of peace and tranquility into a land of communal disharmony, violence and disorder. The solution of the problems of the different ethnic groups in the area may help us in ushering in an era of peace and happiness once again.

Next to historical and geographical framework we have the infrastructural framework. This includes among the other things, ethnic, religious, linguistic and regional structure. At the individual level the framework of ethnic groups and religion appear to have lost ground while at the political level their grip is becoming more firm. There has been a feeling that the more advanced Khasis are dominating the less advanced Garos and Jaintias in political as well as in administrative fields. In a House for sixty legislators there are twenty five Khasis, eighteen Garos, eight Jaintias, and nine non-tribal representatives.[5] Similarly, in the administrative field, out of 27 Indian Administrative Officers allotted to Meghalaya as on March 31, 1981 there were thirteen Khasis, one Garo, four other tribal and nine non-tribal officers. Two I.A.S officers who originally belonged to Jaintia Hills had been included among the thirteen Khasis.[6] Then at the religious level, the Protestants (Presbyterians, Baptist, etc.) tend to dominate the Catholics and followers of other religions (Hinduism Islam, Buddhism, Jainism, Sikhism, etc.) and tribal religions (Niam Khasi Niam Tre, Songsrok etc.) In the present Ministry (May 1990) of the State there are eighteen Ministers who belong to the Protestant group, four Catholics, one Hindu, and one Niam Khasi. Religionwise, Meghalaya Christians constitute 52.62, Hindus 18.03, Muslims 3.10 Buddhisto.20, Skihs .13, Jains .04 other religious persuations including tribal religions 25.77, and those who do not state their religion are only .11 per cent.[7]

Linguistically too, the Garos and Jaintias have yet to develop their languages. Khasi language has already been introduced in the post-graduate courses of the North-Eastern Hill University since 1983 and is being considered as one of the Indian languages by the Sahitya Academy. Garo language, on the other hand, is yet to follow the Khasi language in this direction. The case of Jaintia language lies on a different footing altogether. The Jaintias are not united on the issue whether to treat their language as distinct from the Khasi language. During the demand for a seperate district council, they had listed language as one of their points of difference from the Khasi language. Though the Assam Government had accepted the recomendations of the Jarman Commission for seperating the Jaintia areas from the Khasi area in matters of the autonomous district council, it was done on the basis of "administrative convenience" only. In the early 80's there was a group led by the Hynniewtrep National Front for a seperate linguistic State for Khasi and Jantia Hills only; and recently a section of the Garos had raised the issue of a seperate linguistic State for the Garos.

The politics of ethnic groups and language as an infrastructural framework appears also on the question of job reservation on the basis of ethnic group and language. There is a job reservation of 40 per cent for the Garos, 40 per cent for the Khasis and Jaintias. The Jaintias are not satisfied with this arrangement. They keep on demanding for a separate quota for their ethnic group. They feel that by having a combined reservation of jobs with the Khasis, they will not be fully represented in the Government establishments. It is very difficult to find out whether this contention is valid as the Jaintias particularly of Shillong Town, have indicated their ethnic groups either as the Khasis or Jaintias whenever it suits them.

The style of State politics in Meghalaya further depends on the stage of its economic development. The economic growth of the State is tardy due to absence of medium scale industries and not to speak of large scale industries. There is no strong entrepreneural group in Meghalaya to start small scale industries either. Therefore, terms like public sector, private sector or joint sector are almost meaningless in the context of Meghalaya. Added to this, is the peculiar situation prevailing in the State against the entry without licence of non-tribal people into trade, commerce and industry in the Sixth Schedule (tribal) area of Meghalaya. It is a heavy burden upon the leaders of the State to put Meghalaya into the industrial map of India. With such industrial backwardness, the politics of economic bargaining in the North Eastern Council for rapid industrialization in the State. With the presence of adequate raw materials like minerals and forest produces, Meghalaya could have easily raised its bargaining policy not only with the States of the region but also with the Centre. Simultaneously with economic backwardness, the State is yet to witness the coming up of trade unionism and left politics. Such unionism and politics at present is confined mostly to a section of service and students' associations which the establishment had so far effectively dealt with as in the case of the Shillong Electric Supply Unit's strike of 1978-79 or the students' agitations during 1979-80 and 1987.

The stage of economic growth in Meghalaya leads naturally to the politics of regionalism of the ethnic groups. It touches all concerned including political parties. All of them cannot afford to ignore the aspirations of the tribal people to develop their State if not by the local people themselves, at least by the Government. The Government is expected to help the local people in raising their industrial establishments. Given the will, the political leaders of the State can achieve this objective since there is practically no difference in their ideology. The economic plank of all political parties in the State--national or regional-contains similar entry in their election manifestoes to the effect that the State should be developed by the local and tribal people themselves. It is in this sense that regionalism is still relevant to the people of Meghalaya even after attaining Statehood.

Human resource is another contextual framework indicating the other dimension of the politics of ethnic groups. The majority of political leaders being tribal, there is, therefore, predominantly, a traditional orientation of their attitude and behaviour. This is often reflected in their attitude and behaviour in their respective political roles. Even members belonging to national parties had on a number of occasions raised the slogan of the traditional values of the local people. Rev. J.J.M. Nichols-Ray, a moderate leader during and after the British period was one of the makers of the Sixth Schedule to the Constitution which provided among other things, the preservation and promotion of tribal life and culture.

Since Independence, other leaders of Meghalaya have become more progressively regional in outlook so much so that they had been nearer the border line of what may be called provincial nationalism. During the 1950s and 60s, the East India Tribal Union (EITU) leaders and subsequently leaders of the All Party Hill Leaders Conference (APHLC) had tasted bitter experiences in their dealings with the Assam leaders when the latter rejected their demands. To wean them away from provincial nationalism, the Central leaders tried a bit of compromise between the Hill Leaders and the Assam Leaders through an idea of an autonomous State. While the moderate leaders accepted the idea, that of a more militant section of the APHLC under the leadership of Mr. H.S. Lyngdoh, broke away to form the Hill State People's Democratic Party (HSPDP) to fight for a full-fledged State and for the cause of the tribal people. Later on during the 1970s when the full-fledged State came into existence, the State Government under the leadership of the APHLC had been severely attacked by one of its sections for having failed to deliver the goods and to help the poor cultivators, workers, petty traders and businessmen in the State. The result was that the Public Demands Implementation Committee (PDIC) later on renamed the Public Demands Implementation Convention (PDIC) was brought into existence by breaking away from the APHLC.

The above typical leaders in Meghalaya indicate that whatever touches the regional feeling, whatever touches the tribal sentiment, whatever touches the lots of the down-trodden people of the tribal society and whatever semblance of any let down by those in power and authority, the human resource of Meghalaya immediately springs into political activism. It requires the courage of leaders to have a more national and wider outlook by leaving regionalism behind and embracing the national party. But this they did only at the cost of their popularity. Their party, the ruling Congress, was reduced to a minority of twenty in the 1978 General Elections to the Vidhan Sabha and till May 1990 could not obtain a majority in the House.

By and large, political leaders in Meghalaya are qualified educationally. Out of fifty eight members in the present Legislative Assembly (May 1990) there are eleven Post-graduates, thirty Graduates, twelve Under-Graduates, one Matriculate, and four non-Matriculates. The Post-Graduates include two law Graduates, two Graduates in Teaching, two Post Graduates in Science, one Post-Graduate in Arts, and two Doctorates in Philosophy[*]. A majority of the honourable members are teachers at one time or another. Of course it is true that one may be educationally illiterate and yet politically literate. However, the fact remains that literacy is an important factor for political development. Judging from this criterion Meghalaya was doing well with its 1971 literacy rate of 29.49 per cent which was slightly higher than the national figure of 29.45 per cent, and its literacy rate had gone up to 34.08 per cent which was slightly lower than the national average of 36.23 per cent in 1981. However, inspite of the fact that the majority of leaders are educationally qualified, the whole State does not have the climate of political urbanity. Leaders may be urbane yet the State is under-developed due to lack of much economic and industrial development. The result is that more people are leaving the rural areas and flock to the urban areas particularly to Shillong, Tura and Jowai towns. The number of towns in Meghalaya had increased from six in 1971 to twelve in 1981 and the percentage of urban to rural population had increased from 14.55 per cent in 1977 to 18.03 per cent in 1981 with the decennial growth rate during 1971-81 of 25.95 per cent for rural and 62.74 per cent for urban areas.[9] Many political leaders of the State including those representing rural constituencies, can be found in one of the above three towns. Thus, there is always a tussle between the political pragmatism of town and urban areas with that of the political idealism of the rural areas. The political leaders of Meghalaya in such a situation are like men living in two worlds neither enjoying the one nor disregarding the other and thereby tear themselves into pieces.

The Structural Analytical Frame work

So far we have been discussing about the nature and concept of State politics in Meghalaya. We have also discussed about the contextual analytic framework. Now we are looking into the structural analytic framework. This framework will give us an insight into the constitutional functionaries in the State and formation of State ministries. It will further provide an understanding of the role of political institutions and processes, and the role of administrators in Meghalaya.

In terms of functionaries, Meghalaya as an autonomous State was under the Governor of Assam acting as "Governor in relation to Meghalaya".[10] It is here that the difficult position of the Governor of Assam could be appreciated. As a Constitutional head he acted on the advice of the Council of Ministers of Assam, and of Meghalaya respectively. The time was too short for a proper examination of the role of the Governor under the autonomous State of Meghalaya.[11] However, it indicated the future role of the Governor of the full-fledged State of Meghalaya. With the use of the phrase the "Governor of Meghalya" in 1972, the Governor of Assam had ceased to exercise his jurisdiction over Meghalaya. But since the Governor of Assam and the Governor of Meghalaya was, for some time, the same incumbent, he had to act more judiciously while acting on the advice of the respective Councils of Ministers. This was done as in the case of inter-State boundary. Presently, the two States of Assam and Meghalaya have two separate Governors.

Another constitutional functionary in the State is the Chief Minister. The Chief Minister of an autonomous State was like any other Chief Minister excepting that he had limited constitutional powers. In a sense, he resembled the Chief Minister of a Union Territory in that he did not have full constitutional authority in passing laws within his territory. In the autonomous State, there was a single party Government led by the APHLC. The thirty five members of the Legislative Assembly were elected through the system of indirect election by the respective members of the three autonomous district councils. In addition to elected memebers there were also three nominated members. Being a new experiment in constitutional practice and being too short a time for the autonomous State to function properly, it is too difficult to have a proper assessment of its success or otherwise. At present, we have a Chief Minister of a full-fledged State.

The selection of the Chief Minister of the State depends mostly on the politics of ethnic groups. The first Chief Minister,Capt. W. A. Sangma (1972-78) came from Garo Hills. He had a command over the politics of his district since the days of the Hill State Movement. The Khasis too were reluctant just at that time to face the question of leadership. The second Chief Minister, D.D. Pugh (1978-79) was from Khasi Hills. He had the support from Garo Hills and to a certaion extent from Khasi and Jaintia Hills. But soon, there was an open struggle for leadership among the Khasi leaders for the post and the third Chief Minister, B.B. Lyngdoh (1979-81) came from Khasi Hills but with the support from the other political parties and groups. That was why the remaining term (1981-83) had to be shared with the first Chief Minister who was from Garo Hills. Unlike the first Chief Minister, the second and third Chief Ministers had to lead coalition ministries. Compared to the first ministry based solely on the APHLC majority and subsequently on the Congress majority, the coalition ministries were more marked with the politics of ethnic groups. The fourth Chief Minister, Shri P.A. Sangma (1988-90) was again from Garo Hills. After his coalition ministry collapsed, the third Chief Minister took over power since March 1990.

The Jaintias being the smaller ethnic group are yet to come up in the struggle for State leadership. There are only seven members for Jaintia Hills in a House of sixty. Because of the politics of ethnic groups, the Jaintias are yet to aspire even for deputy leadership. It would be almost a truism to say that since they constituted a little over one-eighth of the total membership of the House it always proved safe for them to play a second fiddle in the State. As an ethnic group, they have yet to produce a State leader. At the sametime, Jaintia leaders realised that the ethnic Khasi group is always trying to keep them in secondary role. This naturally leads them to an unexpressed understanding with their distant cousins, the Garos, as it happened during the APHLC merger with the Indian National Congress in 1976.

Excepting the choice of the first Chief Minister, the subsequent choices had been a difficult task in Meghalaya. During 1978 when there was no political party to command a majority the two main political parties of the proposed coalition the APHLC and the HSPDP chose their own respective leaders and the final choice of the Chief Minister was then through a system of lottery between the two leaders. The lottery went in favour of the APHLC. In the second coalition of the APHLC-PDIC in 1979, the same Chief Minister continued in power as the PDIC partner had only two members. In the third coalition, leadership is a shared one between the leader of the APHLC section for the first two years (1979-81) and the leader of the Congress(I) for the last two years until 1983. The HSPDP, a major partner is contented with the role of the Deputy Chief Minister. Again, after the 1983 State General Elections, the APHLC leader from Khasi Hills became the Chief Minister of the coalition Government for about a month only to be replaced by another coalition headed by the Congress(I) leader from Garo Hills till the end of the term (1983-88). The Chief Minister for the next term(1988-90) was more or less imposed by the Congress (I) High Command inspite of the fact that it was a coalition Ministry. The present Chief Minister (March 1990) is acceptable to all the ethnic groups as a matter of necessity rather than by choices.

The relationship between the Meghalaya Chief Minister and the Prime Minister of India is another field where we have yet to have an indepth study. We can only generalize at this stage that much depends on the personality rather than the office of the Chief Minister or the Prime Minister. There was a close working relationship between the Chief Minister of Meghalaya and the Prime Minister during the period from 1976 to 1977 when the Chief Minister belonged to the same political party as at the Centre. Of course, much earlier, during 1970-76 there was a spirit of patience and tolerance on the part of Smt. Indira Gandhi, Prime Minister and of co-operation on the part of the APHLC Chief Minister since the latter owed it to the Prime Minister for ushering in an autonomous State as well as the full-fledged State later on. The Chief Minister and his party men even agreed to have an electoral understanding with the Prime Minister whereby six seats were not contested by the Chief Minister's APHLC in the 1972 General Elections to the Vidhan Sabha against the Indian National Congress.

But things changed very drastically from 1977 to 1980 when Shri Morarji Desai and Shri Charan Singh were then Prime Ministers respectively. The Meghalaya Chief Minister had certain difficulty in pulling on with the Central leaders. The seed of apprehension was sown in the mind of the Chief Minister and his colleagues when Shri Morarji Desai indicated his opposition to the idea of small States and his doubts about the sincerity of the tribal people in imbibing Indian nationalism.[12]

From 1980 onwards, the leaderships of Smt. Indira Gandhi had once again rekindled hope in the people of Meghalaya in getting a fair deal from the Central Government. Despite the unusual move against the "foreign nationals" in the State, the working relationship between the Prime Minister and the Chief Minister was just cordial and a note of concord was struck particularly after the remaining term (1981-83) of shared Chief Ministership (1979-83) went to the Congress (I) leader. In passing, it may be noted that the idea of sharing the office of Chief Minister of Meghalaya is unique in the history of Parliamentary practice in India in that it helps the political opponents who cannot muster an absolute majority in the House to work together in the interest of the State. It also helps in Centre-State relations because of the fact that one of the opponents is like to be in favour of the Central leaders. Further, it helps in cementing the cordial relationship among the various ethnic groups when the shared post is also shared by members belonging to such groups.

Coming to the relationship between the Meghalaya Chief Minister and his colleagues it was not marked by any difference of opinion till November, 1976. It was during the APHLC merger with the Indian National Congress in November, 1976 that four senior Ministers resigned from the Cabinet due to difference of opinion. Since then there appears to be a new experiment in the Cabinet system of Government in Meghalaya. In the formation of United Legislature Party (ULP) coalition Government in March 1978, the relationship between the Chief Minister and his colleagues was quite contrary to the normal practice of the principle of Cabinet joint responsibility. Under the ULP, the three partners had chartered the course of governmental policy and action in a style quite different from the conventional Parliamentary practice. While constitutionally there was one Chief Minister, in fact, the ministry had been led by the three parliamentary groups in the ULP coalition, each leader of the group assuming the role of a Chief Minister for his group. At the time of the distribution of portfolios also, a list had already been prepared so that it could be tied up with the lottery for the post of Chief Ministership. While preparing the list of portfolios, every care had been taken to see that the side getting the Chief Ministership would not have more major portfolios. The result was the failure of the ULP coalition Government to exist even for a year. The coalition broked down just after 11 months in office.

In the third coalition under the United Meghalaya Parliamentary Democratic Forum (UMPDF) of 1979, similar steps had been taken to see that no political group should have a major share in the running of administration. This was when the coalition was just a bare majority of one vote. But when the UMPDF had nearly a two-third majority, a general reshuffling of the portfolios took place in December 1980 in such a way that the UMPDF coalition appeared to have become a single party Government. However, immediately after the general reshuffling, one Cabinet Minister resigned from his post in deference to the Chief Minister without assigning any reason. And as if in setting right the crack, two more Cabinet Ministers, and one Minister of State were inducted into the ministry. Since then the subsequent coalition ministries in the State functioned as any other coalition in India. The fourth coalition after the 1983 General Elections under the Meghalaya United Legislature Party (MULP) existed only for 29 days; the fifth coalition under the Meghalaya Democratic Front (MDF) took over from the MULP on April 2, 1983 and continued till February 8, 1988 when the sixth coalition under the United Meghalaya Parliamentary Front (UMPF) assumed office after the 1988 General Elections for a little more than two years. The seventh coalition under the UMPF (B) and the opposition Regional Democratic Front (RDF) assumed office on March 26, 1990 and remained till date.

Every Government which had been formed so far had strenuously tried to keep the interest of the main ethnic groups. In the first ministry (1970) there were two Khasis, two Garos and one Jaintia. The present Ministry (May 1990), the largest ministry so far, consists of thirteen Khasis, nine Garos, and two Jaintias. It is in the formation of ministries and the allocation of protfolios that Meghalaya reached the apex of the politics of ethnic groups. This politics of ethnic groups also appears in the legislative and administrative role of the political elite. Some key posts both at the party level and at the governmental level have been kept to accommodate the various ethnic groups. In the election to the legislative committee too, care has been taken to see that the committee do not only represent the expertise of a Member but also the party interest as well as the interest of an ethnic group. For example, in the Public Accounts Committee (May 1990) there are three ruling and two opposition members out of whom two are Khasis, two Garos and one non-tribal members.

Another dimension of a structural framework of politics in Meghalaya is the framework of its political institutions and processes. Meghalaya has seen the existence of a number of political parties since its inception. The major political parties are the APHLC, Indian National Congress including Congress (I) and Congress (S), Communist party of India (CPI), Jaintia National Union (JNU), the Janata Party, HSPDP, and PDIC. The national parties like the Indian National Congress, CPI, and the Janata Party do not have much strong appeal to the local people. It will take a long time to completely remove the image of the national parties as non-tribal parties from the minds of the hill people. So far no national party has been able to command an absolute majority in Meghalaya.

The regional political parties have their prospects in Meghalaya up to the extent that they continued helping on narrow and sectional interests of the local people. The APHLC which had spearheaded the Hill State Movement in 1960s, was in the doldrums in 1970s due to the fact that there had been an over-tone of "national outlook" on its assuming power in 1970. The organisation of the Shillong APHLC (English Section for the benefit of the non-tribal people) had added more fuel to the political fire that had engulfed Meghalaya under the leadership of the more militant HSPDP with their "regional outlook". The APHLC was caught in the cobweb of national/regional situation prevailing in Meghalaya politics. While trying to overcome the HSPDP at the political level, the APHLC had overlooked the economic, social and administrative aspects of the issue. This made one of its senior members, to strongly condemn against the leadership of the APHLC which led ultimately to his expulsion from the party. Thereupon he founded his PDIC in July 1973. The thrust of his party is on the economic well-being of the hill people, particularly the down trodden classes, peasants and cultivators. But unlike the HSPDP, the PDIC was silent on the question of national/regional outlook. Its main theme is on the implementation of the 16-Point Programme for the economic development of the State.

An indepth study of the various programmes and policies as reflected through the respective election manifestoes of the regional political parties in Meghalaya, do not indicate any major difference between the APHLC, HSPDP and PDIC. They all claimed to be leading the local people to the promised land of plenty and happiness. All the regional political parties could have combined together had it not been for the consideration of personal qualities attached to various leaders of their respective political parties. These personal qualities also include the ethnic backgrounds. Hence, the politics of ethnic groups in Meghalaya is not so much an ideology-based as it is personality-based. This personality-based politics of the ethnic groups has spread further to smaller ethnic groups of Meghalaya. The Jaintias of Meghalaya constitute a small ethnic group of people in the State. They feel more secured in having their own political leader than being led by any of the major ethnic groups. The outcome was the founding of the JNU in February 1977 out of the splinter group of the Indian National Congress after the APHLC merger with the latter in 1976, and that of the constitution of the new Jaintia Durbar in 1978 which was formerly a constituent of the APHLC.

Meghalaya is yet to have a strong opposition party in the legislature. There was no opposition in the Legislative Assembly of the autonomous State of Meghalaya; and there was practically no opposition party in the first Legislative Assembly of Meghalaya after the 1972 General Elections. Similarly, the Congress(I) as a unit of the Meghalaya United Legislative Front (MULF) could not play its effective role of the opposition when that opportunity came after the 1978 General Elections. In terms of sheer number, the APHLC opposition of 1979 could be more effective than any other opposition parties so far. True, they did play their role during the movement for detection, deletion, and deportation of "foreign nationals," but not so effectively. Of course, it was a "nightmare" for the UMPDF Government during that period. But this "nightmare" was mainly due to public disorder and violence which the opposition parties had taken advantage of. With the failure of the movement to get beyond control, the opposition parties also staged a retreat to the extent that there was again practically no opposition party since the 1980 Winter Assembly Session of the Meghalaya Legislative Assembly. The realignment of political forces after 1983 could produce more or less an effective opposition which could force the resignation of two Ministers on ground of moral responsibility for the scandal in the Public Health Engineering Department of the State. On the other hand, the realignment of forces after the downfall of the UMPF coalition Government in March 1990 is yet to fully crystallise itself.

During the movement against "foreign nationals", another dimension of politics in Meghalaya is the question of finance. Except the national parties which could support their State branches in the form of financial assistance, regional political parties do not have their publicly known sources of income. What appears outside is only the income from the membership fees and donations. But large scale organisation of the movement against "foreign nationals" definitely requires a large amount of money too.

The leaders of the movement, or the pressure groups if you will, were mostly students, women and young people. They could not simply have such unlimited supply of cash. At one stage, the publicity materials from the organisers of the movement were more than what the Government could cope with.

A study of another aspect of the political parties syndicate that factional politics is very much rampant in Meghalaya. The Indian National Congress had its own fractional politics during 1976-77 on the question of the merger issue as well as the question of the Congress split at the Centre. Similarly, there were factional politics in the APHLC since 1968 when one of its leaders was expelled from it. Later on in 1973, another leader was also expelled from the APHLC. The latest expulsion was of a prominent member of the APHLC in 1979. It was factional politics that had raised one of the members to the position of the leader of the APHLC parliamentary group in 1978 which subsequently enabled him to be the leader of the House by lottery. The HSPDP is a party which is strong and united since 1968. But since 1983 it began to show signs of factional politics within its rank and file. The PDIC has no major problem of this nature though the coming back of one of its leaders from his ambassadorial post in 1984 had created such a situation. The best example of factional politics is, however, that of the JNU. The JNU which originally consisted of one MLA and five MDCs had broken in the course of one year during 1979-80 into three pieces.

The administrative framework is another structural framework through which we may peep into the politics of Meghalaya. The inter-action between the bureaucrats, the technocrats and the politicians is another dimension of State politics. Bureaucrats of Meghalaya have still a long way to go from a regulatory bureaucracy into a developmental bureaucracy. In such a situation the inter-action between democracy and bureaucracy is slow and tardy. Similarly, it retards, the inter-action between politics and administration. As a result, there has always been a misunderstanding between the party members, particularly of the ruling party, and the bureaucratic elites. This happens especially with the beginning of the ULP Government in 1978. Before that date, the single party Government of the APHLC and of the Indian National Congress respectively could manage to bring together the bureaucrats and the party elites up to the level of regulatory requirements. With the beginning of coalition Governments ever since 1978, the bureaucrats are having their hey day. And it has become almost a rule that coalition Governments while having a responsible bureaucracy do not generally produce a responsive bureaucracy. The result is the slow progress of development works in the State. This happens because the bureaucracy is taking advantage of the overlapping developmental functions. For example, a particular APHLC Minister incharge of one development department may have to deal with his colleagues the HSPDP Minister and the PDIC Minister incharge of two other connected development departments. This had actually happened during the ULP Government of 1978, when the three coalition partners could not jointly agree on certain development activities as in the case of the development of the Headquarters of the Amlarem Civil Sub-Division. Thus, in the coalition Governments of Meghalaya there is always the possibility that delay may occur in the implementation of various development schemes at the one or the other level.

The Operational Analytic Framework

The study of the operational dynamics of State politics consists of a number of components, the importance of which are the components of role-orientation, political behaviour, and functional dimension. It is with these three components that we shall now engage our attention.

The role-orientation of the actors in Meghalaya politics involves the question of whether the legislators, Ministers and bureaucrats have any image of their role or have thought about it seriously and worked to live up to it. A random perusal of proceedings of the Meghalaya Legislative Assembly will convince us that there has been an earnest attempt on the part of all concerned to view their role-orientation as a necessary concommitant of the responsibilities reposed in them. We also observe that there is a proper decorum in the House and it is efficiently run with the cooperation of all the Members.

The content analysis of the local press on the other hand, gives us a negative view point of the role-orientation of the legislators, Ministers and bureaucrats once they are outside the House. This is particularly true of the press coverage during the period from 1978 to 1980. In the later part of 1978, the Chief Minister and the Revenue Minister had resorted to dialogues in the press through Press Notes which could have easily been thrashed out either at the personal or cabinet level. The issue of the Garrison Ground in Shillong Town is a good example of such controversy.[14] The controversy thus raised by the two colleagues had reached a stage where they had failed to view their role-orientation properly. It simply reflected the political difference between the two colleagues who belonged to two different political parties. It was the politics of coalition carried too far. This kind of episode, also took place (April 1990) between the present Chief Minister and the Home Minister on the question of boundary disputes between Assam and Meghalaya. The Home Minister had strongly opposed the statement of the Chief Minister that there was no dispute between the two States.

The same question may be asked about the role-orientation of the political parties in Meghalaya. So far their role-orientation towards elections is concerned all political parties in Meghalaya have been able to project their image. The only sad aspect of their role is to be found in the election politics where political parties appeal mostly to the politics of ethnic groups. They rarely involve themselves in educative politics. Of course, one may say that educative politics is involved during election politics. But what we mean here is that there is no separate educative politics apart from election politics. In Meghalaya, educative politics after any elections by political parties is non-existent except through their political newspapers and journals which in many cases do not carry the same educative value as it is during the election time.

Another component of the dynamics of operational politics is the political behaviour of the political actors. This is one of the difficult aspects in the study of State politics. It relates to attitudes, values and norms that a functionary brings to bear on his role performance. There is always a difference between profession and practice. Any political actor has to weigh his own utterances. The pattern of behaviour is always different between what is said informally with that of what is formally indicated. Again, the behaviour of a political actor may be different when he speaks on behalf of the institution he represents and when he speaks in his individual capacity.

This behavioural pattern of the political actors can be seen in Meghalaya especially when we study about the electoral politics in the State[15] (Datta Ray, 1978). In the 1972 General Elections, there was an understanding between the APHLC and the Congress in that the former did not contest from the six Congress dominated constituencies. This was done as a mark of appreciation to the Congress on the part of the APHLC for the creation of a full-fledged State of Meghalaya. In 1976, before the Mendipathar Special Conference when the APHLC decided to merge with the Congress, a faction of the APHLC from Khasi Hills who had refused to completely merge with the Congress wanted an adjustment with the HSPDP. But the HSPDP did not find any basis nor any occasion for such an adjustment. They realized that it was only a ploy on the part of the APHLC from Khasi Hills to change their internal leadership. When the 1977 Lok Sabha Elections were announced, both the APHLC and the HSPDP explored the possibilities of finding out a "common candidate" while retaining their separate identities. It was during that time that difference between profession and practice can clearly be seen. Both the groups knew that it was well nigh impossible to have a "common candidate" and yet they still explored the possibilities almost to the final hour when both the political parties set up their respective candidates.

After the 1978 General Elections to the Vidhan Sabha, there were also talks about the unity of the regional political parties through the ULP against the Congress and its MULF. Serious attempts at uniting the regional political parties were further made when the first two coalitions had broken down. The movement against "foreign nationals" made all the regional political parties to profess their laudable intentions to unite but on one pretext or another the talks fell through and there was no unity at all. Of course, the opposition parties, the APHLC and the PDIC, had formed just on the eve of the 1980 Lok Sabha Elections a form of a united regional political party under the name and style of the Hills National Union (HNU) to fight against the UMPDF. The HNU, however, disintegrated just after it was born. Subsequently, during 1983, the two factions of the APHLC were also talking in terms of unity while at the same time, one of the factions was toying with the idea of a broad based and "Federal" political organization to include all the political parties of the State subscribing to the Congress ideal while retaining their separate regional identities. The real attempt to unite the regional political parties was partially successful in 1984 when the APHLC and the HSPDP set up "common candidates" for the Lok Sabha Elections. In 1985 the APHLC and a section of the HSPDP could finally form the Hill People Union (HPU). However, another section of the HSPDP and the PDIC are still outside the HPU.

The behavioural pattern of the political actors could also be gauged from the voting behaviour of their constituents. In the 1972 General Elections because of the popularity of the APHLC arising out of the fact that it had brought about the Meghalaya State a majority of the electorate voted for it. The APHLC secured thirty two seats, Congress nine, HSPDP eight, and Independents 11. The APHLC, however, captured only two out of six seats from the Jaintia Hills and thirteen out of thirty seats in the Khasi Hills. In the Garo Hills, the APHLC secured seventeen out of twenty four seats. The APHLC success in the Gargo Hills was mainly due to the leadership of Capt. W.A. Sangma, the Chief Minister. In addition to this, the Garos fought more on the tickets of the Garo National Council (GNC), a constituent of the APHLC rather than on the APHLC itself. The Upland of the Garo Hills is the traditional home of the GNC with its traditional kin-group bonds, in-group tribal sentiments and traditional authorities of the *Nokmas* (clan chiefs).

This trend in the Garo Hills was repeated in the 1977 Lok Sabha Elections when the hill areas of the Garo Hills went to the APHLC while the plain areas of the Garo Hills and the hill-cum-plain areas of the Garo Hills voted for the Congress. On a community basis, the Garos preferred the APHLC while the Hajongs, Koche and the Rabhas fought for the Congress and strangely the non-tribal voters were divided. Another feature of the political behaviour of the voters in the Garo Hills is the religious groups like the Baptists tend to follow the Baptist candidates and the Catholics to prefer the Catholic candidates. (Datta Ray, 1978).

In the 1978 General Elections again the Congress secured the largest number of seats in the Garo Hills with eleven out of twenty four while the APHLC secured only eight and the Independents five. In the Khasi Hills, unlike in the Garo Hills the Congress had a limited base. On the other hand the APHLC with the Janata support could get the support of the non-tribal voters particularly in urban areas. The PDIC with its associate the JNU secured votes with the personal popularity of one of its leaders in many areas of the Khasi and Jaintia Hills, particularly in the Khyrim Syiemship of the Khasi Hills and in the North Jaintia Hills. The result was that the regionalism and exclusiveness of the HSPDP made its candidates the winners in the West and North Khasi Hills as well as in the East Jaintia Hills. This led to the emergence of the HSPDP as the leading party in the Khasi and Jaintia Hills in the 1978 General Elections to the Vidhan Sabha. It secured fourteen seats out of thirty six seats while the APHLC secured eight seats, Congress nine, PDIC two, JNU one, and Independents two.[16] This trend of the behavioural pattern is that the political preference in the Garo Hills is for the Congress, in the West and North Khasi Hills for the HSPDP, in the East and South Khasi Hills for the APHLC, and in the Jaintia Hills, a mixed preference for regional political parties. All the Congress candidates in the Jaintia Hills were defeated in the 1978 General Elections while the HSPDP secured three, the APHLC two, and the JNU and the Independent one each. With the participation of the Congress (I) in subsequent coalition ministries in the state and the coming of Indira Gandhi to power, the Congress (I) in Meghalaya constituted the single largest party with twenty five members in the 1983 General Elections. The same position was maintained by the Congress (I) after the 1988 General Elections though reduced to twenty two members. However, the Congress (I)'s performance had indicated a change in the behavioural pattern of the voters. The Congress (I) did well in the Jaintia Hills returning five out of seven members, and in the Khasi Hills with ten out of twenty nine seats, but went down in its usual stronghold in Garo Hills by winning only seven out of twenty four seats. Similarly, the HSPDP had gone down to four members only while the PDIC remained constant with two members. This aspect of behavioural pattern is, however, yet to be properly analysed. Suffice it to say for the present, the emergent of the HPU and the change of leadership in the State Congress (I) camp are two important factors for these changes.

Since the consideration of personality rather than principles is the guiding factors in Meghalaya politics, the norms of political behaviour are yet to get crystallized. Presently, these norms are still in an embryonic stage. This can be seen from the profession of patterns of election strategy and campaigning and the practice of politics and administration after the elections. For example, the exclusively regional HSPDP professed during the election campaigns of 1977 and 1978 to strictly remain as the defender of tribal ways of life but in practice did not hesitate to join hands with the Congress (I) in the formation of the UMPDF coalition Government in 1979. Surprisingly, a faction of the APHLC which was very much anti-Congress by resigning from the ministry in 1976, also agreed to join hands with the Congress(I) in the same coalition of 1979. Stranger than fiction, however, is the case of the JNU which was formed in 1977 after splitting from the Congress in 1976, to join hands with the Congress (I) in the UMPDF coalition Government of 1979 along with the HSPDP and the above APHLC faction. Having said this, let us hasten to add that this does not mean that the PDIC and the other faction of the APHLC are free from the politics of personality. In 1979 some political parties worked together in the second coalition Government of Meghalaya with a non-tribal member as one of the members of the ministry irrespective of the fact, that the two political parties professed during the election campaigns and inside the Meghalaya Legislative Assembly to stand for regionalism and tribalism.

This leads us to the question of defection as a political behaviour. The politics of defection is very much rampant in Meghalaya. In 1972, the APHLC went up from thirty two to thirty nine members. Similarly, after the APHLC merger with the Congress in 1976, the Congress members shot up from eight to fourty two and in the first part of 1979, the APHLC rose up from sixteen to thirty one members. All these figures clearly indicated a large scale defection in Meghalaya politics and the process goes on as long as there is the politics of personality and of ethnic groups in the State. The UMPDF Government of 1979 started with thirty one original members in April 1979 and was joined later on by nine other members. Paradoxically, the recent anti-defection Act has failed to curb the politics of defection in Meghalaya. The UMPDF coalition Government of 1988 with forty eight members was reduced to a minority of twenty six members in March 1990. The HPU with nineteen members after the 1988 General Elections was divided into four groups with five HPU, four HPU (B), seven HPU(BC), two HPU(PD), and one HPU member was disqualified by the Speaker in late 1989. The HSPDP too, with six members, was divided into two parts, four HSPDP and two HSPDP(DL). These various factions in the Meghalaya Legislative Assembly came up only to avoid the penalty provisions of the anti-defection Act.

An important determinant of behavioural component of the operational dynamics of State politics is its functional dimension. Functional dimension is a balance sheet of performance based on the behavioural aspects of attitude, values and norms that a functionary brings to bear on his role-performance. It consists of in part qualitative and in part quantitative. Qualitatively, it refers to the study of policy decisions in specific context, and quantitatively, in the study of achievements and failures in terms of policy implementation.

The issue of "foreign nationals" may be taken as a functional dimension of State politics in Meghalaya during 1979-80. It touches all the levels of politics, national, State, local party, semi-Governmental and even autonomous institutions. This issue is one functional aspect giving the total view of State politics in Meghalaya at that time.

With the formation of the UMPDF Government in May 1979, there were rumblings in the State. All forces, opposition parties, youths, students and women joined hands in trying to topple the Government which was alleged to have failed to "detect, detain and deport foreign nationals". Since October 1979 to February 1980, it was a period of "night-mare". Violence broke out, human lives were lost and properties were destroyed. The Government resorted to preventive measures like the Preventive Detention Order (PDO) and armed action was organized to quell down disorders and lawlessness. The whole Governmental set up was completely shaken. The people of Meghalaya had never, in one's living memory, witnessed any such dimension of actions on both sides, the agitators on one side and the police including the Central Reserve Police (CRP), the Border Security Force (BSF), the Assam Rifles, the Assam Regiment and the Army on the other. There were indications that the Government was about to fall when the Budget Session of the Legislative Assembly during March 1980 was prorogued without the budget being passed. A section of the HSPDP was against the PDO, some action of the CRP, the arrogant attitude of some officials of the State government and the arrests of many prominent and peaceful citizens of the State.

The policy of the government was very clear that the movement should be crushed by all constitutional means. The government, however, realized that "rude measures" alone will not solve the problem. Hence in order to secure any achievements in the implementation of its policies, it had also to placate the leaders of the movement by various means including the acceptance of the suggestions that "foreign nationals" be detected, detained and deported. The official machinery was moved and leaders of the movement including the students were also invited to join in the vigilance committees to take up necessary steps against "foreign nationals". Judging in terms of law and order situation, the Government was successful by the winter of 1980 when the whole State celebrated its joyous Christmas in the spirit of peace and happiness once again. But when judged in terms of developmental activities the State had suffered a lot. A number of field officers connected with development works especially non-tribal personnel had to remain absent from their duties for quite sometime. This had retarded the economic and industrial progress of the State, and State Government instead of taking the blame, shifted the same to the "misguided elements". The Government also blamed the opposition parties for fanning out troubles in the State. Curiously, while blaming the opposition parties a number of resolutions coming from the opposition parties were accepted by the UMPDF Government during the resumed budget session of 1980.

It was during that period that the style, vocabulary and language of State politics had reached the highest form of emotional expression compared with all the years since the inception of Statehood in Meghalaya. Phrases like "tribal identity", "sons of the soil", "reservation", "national outlook", "foreign nationals", "autonomy" and the like had become almost worn out due to their being over-used. It was very interesting to note the role of non-tribal members who had not only participated fully but also tried to out-tribalise the tribal members.

A Concluding Review

The above review of State politics in Meghalaya throws some lights on certain issues of contradiction and unique salient features of the politics of ethnicity and of regionalism. Since Meghalaya was created on the basis of ethnic considerations, the tribal people of the hills believed that their social and political leaders could bring about not only their economic prosperity and their general well being but would also further enrich their language, culture and polity. But soon it proved that the politics of ethnic groups alone will not solve the social, political and economic problems of Meghalaya. Some also believed that Meghalaya would entirely belong to the tribal people but the fact remains that 15 per cent, later on reduced to 10 per cent of jobs are reserved for the general population other than the Scheduled Tribes, Scheduled Castes and other backward classes. Further there was a 16 per cent representation of the general population in Meghalaya Legislative Assembly in 1978. Besides that, there is also a sizeable representation of the general population in Government establishments, private establishments, trade and commerce.

Another contradiction is that so far no Government, not even a single party dominance could effectively deliver the promised goods to the people. During the single party dominance of the APHLC since 1970 a sense of complacency prevailed. At that time, it was only the HSPDP and the leadership of the PDIC which had stressed the importance of the common man particularly the tribal people. But with the APHLC split in November 1976 during the APHLC merger with the Congress the leaders seemed to have reliased the importance of the common man and his problems. The result was that all political parties stood by the common man on the eve of the 1978 General Elections to the Vidhan Sabha. However, the common man and his electorate had indicated a change in their voting behaviour through their political choice by giving power to no political party. It was then that the political leaders had to shoulder the responsibility of either forming a coalition Government or facing the President's rule. Of course, they choose the former.

On the question of Centre-State relations, the politics of ethnic groups and of regionalism played a very important role. Ethnic regionalism in the context of North-East India in general and Meghalaya in particular is quite different from the concept of regionalism, say in South India, Jammu and Kashmir or Punjab. It appears that there has been a crisis of relevancy of regionalism in other parts of India. But in North-East India, ethnic regionalism is very much relevant in the context of social, political and economic aspirations of the people. At the third Convention of the Forum of North-Eastern Hill Areas Regional Parties meeting at Shillong on 19 and 20 February, 1981 the question of ethnic regionalism was raised since certain misgivings about ethnic regionalism in North-East India being secessionist and anti-national were expressed in many quarters in the country. A confused idea or call it a contradiction has been created in the minds of the tribal people of North-East India including Meghalaya on the question of what is more national. That Forum was still exercising its mind over this vexed questio when it became dysfunctional. Its finding may also help other parts of India in assessing their relevancy or otherwise of the politics of ethnic regionalism in the country.

The question of State-local relations is yet another contradiction in Meghalaya. Elsewhere the Panchayats may influence State politics but it is State politics which ultimately percolates to the local level. In Meghalaya, the members of the autonomous district councils under the Sixth Schedule to the Constitution of India are as influential as any of the State leaders. Similarly, the village authorities based on traditional hierarchy have generally wider influences over the masses. During Assam's time, State politics rarely percolated to local levels. It was local politics which had reached the height of the State level. The Hill State Movement started with local politics and with the creation of Meghalaya, the politics of ethnic groups of ethnic regionalism while continuing the process of local politics that penetrates into state politics, the latter has also penetrated more into local politics in recent years.

Of late, it has been realised by the social and political leaders that political stability is the pre-condition of social and economic development. For the last twelve years, beginning from March, 1978 Meghalaya did not have a stable Government. Even during the period from January 1970 to November 1976 and from November 1976 to February 1978 it can be said that real political stability did possibly not exist. Apart from political defections that had taken place during the period there are other factors which are responsible for political instability in the State.

First, due to the State being new, political leadership has yet to properly settle down. Secondly, the APHLC was never a homogenous body. It was a regional grand coalition of a number of districts and ethnic political parties like the Garo National council, the Jaintia Durbar, the Khasi and Jaintia National Conference, the Eastern India Tribal Union and others. Thirdly, the politics of ethnic groups whether under the regional APHLC or under the Indian National Congress will not be the type of politics where we can expect the real homogenous political party which can guarantee: a more stable Government. Given the present area and the population structure of the State, political instability in Meghalaya is and will be a salient feature of its political dynamics as it was in the past. Finally, for a small state like Meghalaya, a small margin of one to five votes could set limits to the tenure of any Government that were formed with uncertain support. The first coalition Government (ULP in 1978 consisting of thirty three members was in power for eleven months. The second coalition (APHLC-PDIC) in 1978 with thirty two members remained in power only for two months and the 1979 UMPDF coalition with the original thirty one members at its installation in May 1979 had increased to forty members. The third coalition created a precedent which is unique in Meghalaya and we are yet to find out such a political arrangement anywhere else in the world where political stability is sought to be brought about by such a working arrangement of sharing the office of chief ministership in an otherwise unstable political situation. And it was done with the hope that a period of political stability would bring social and economic upliftment. Perhaps it is in this context that the term "tribal genius" which we invariably, hear in Meghalaya particularly in Shillong Town is to be understood. We hope that this "tribal genius' will be the only alternative to the present and future political instability in the State.

Notes

1. Tabulation from Census Reports, Election Reports and Newspapers.
2. Census Reports of 1971 and 1981.
3. Census Reports of 1971 and 1981.
4. All the above designations refer to traditional leaders of the tribal groups of Meghalaya. Of course the offices of *Laskara* and *Sardars* were created by the British.
5. These figures are for the second Assembly (1978-83).
6. Compiled from the Civil List of I.A.S. Officers for 1981.
7. Census of India 1981.
8. The other two seats are lying vacant due to the passing away of one graduate and another under-graduate disqualified by the Speaker.
9. The figures in this paragraph are from Census of India 1971 and 1981.

10. *Meghalaya Legislative Assembly Proceedings*, Vol. I, April 1970, p.1.

11. The Autonomous State of Meghalaya existed only for one year and nine months, that is between April 2, 1970 and January 1972.

12. *Young India* (Shillong), November 9, 1978.

13. Both the members of the ruling coalition from Jaintia Hills have been inducted to the Ministry. Sometimes there were three Ministers from the area as in 1978 and 1988.

14. *Implanter*, (Shillong), December 17, 1979.

15. Chief Electoral Officer, Meghalaya, *Election Hand Book* Shillong, (1978).

16. *Election Hand Book*, Meghalaya, op. cit.

Reference

Maheswari, S.R. 1976 : The North-Eastern Region, in *State Politics in India* (Ed.) by Iqbal Narayan, New Delhi.

Narain, Iqbal 1976 : *State Politics in India*, New Delhi.

Sharma, M.L. 1976 : Troubled North-East India, in *State Politics In India* (Ed.) by Iqbal Narain, New Delhi.

10

EMERGING PATTERN OF TRIBAL LEADERSHIP IN JAINTIA HILLS OF MEGHALAYA : PERSISTENCE AND CHANGE IN THE POWER STRUCTURE

L.S. GASSAH
J.B. BHATTACHARJEE

The Jaintia Hills District, which lies to the eastern part of the State of Meghalaya covers a land area of about 3819 square kilometers. It is essentially a plateau with steep slopes on the southern border adjoining Bangladesh. The total population of the district, according to the Census 1981, is 1,55,993, out of which the rural and urban segments are 1,43,085 and 12,908 respectively. The percentage of literacy to total population is 23.77 (males = 23.68; females = 23.87).

The district is predominantly inhabited by the Jaintias who belong to the Scheduled Tribe Category. "JAINTIA" is a generic term which covers the Pnars or Syntengs and other sub-groups such as the Mikirs (Karbis), the Bhois, the Biates and the Wars. The district is also called *KA RI KHAD-AR DOLOI* (the land of the twelve *Dolois*) after the twelve administrative units or *Elakas*. Each *Elaka* or division is under the administration and supervision of a *Doloi*. This concept of *Ka Ri Khad-ar* as historical document suggests that the actual number of the *Elakas* or *Doloiships, Sirdarships* and *Patorships* varied from time to time throughout the long history of Jaintia Hills.

Origins of Leadership Pattern

The Jaintias are supposed to have migrated from South-East Asia (Pakem, 1977 : 1). It is also believed that the Amwi people and their allied tribe, namely, the War Syntengs, who inhabit the Southern slopes of Jaintias Hills, formed a parent tribe of the present Khasi Pnars in their earliest period of settlement (Barch, 1967 : 11).

Linguistically, the Khasi-Jaintias belong to the Mon-Khmer family, and the South-East Asian traits are still prominent in the features and culture. They are still in a pre-industrial stage. The greater proportion of the population subsists by cultivation. In the past, besides agriculture, the people depended much on markets for trade and commerce. The people had a long history of trade relations with the other people in the plains, especially with Sylhet (Gassah, 1988 : 485).

The Jaintias, during their migration, moved from one place to another either in search of shelter against onslaught of the enemies or in search of suitable land for cultivation until they found the impenetrable forest areas of the present day Jaintia Hills. They also found their present habitat, its climate, the natural resources and its soil to be more fertile and more suitable for cultivation than the places which they came across on their way. Their prosperous life in the hills inspired several other batches of the Rindreds to join them subsequently. The leadership emerged during the migratory phase. Any senior male member of the family or clan or any male member, generally a priest, having divine knowledge, could become the natural leader of the group (Pakem, 1984). After they had settled down, the families and clans formed the smallest unit of the political society; called *Chnong* or a village. Centering around families and clans was generally a society where leadership fell on the senior most male member called *U Knyi*, literally a maternal uncle of the family or clan. In case where there was no male relative at all, the family and clan concerned had to hire a male member to be a religious leader. The Jaintias called it *Thied Knyi*, which literally means to purchase a maternal uncle. (Pakem 1984 : 50).

The original or founding clan or clans enjoyed special status in the Jaintia political system. This privilege was granted to such clans because they were the first to come, occupied and settled in a particular area, they cleared the forests and became the proprietors of the land. They organized administration within the territory under their control. The late comers had to place themselves at a subordinate position being under the over-all supervision and administrative control of the leading male members of the original clans. The eldest male member of the original clans performed the role of a leader and head of the administration. Thus, the traditional authority structure and leadership among the Jaintias was patterned in a rigid form and based strictly on ascriptive footings at the two higher levels of administration viz, *Syiem*ship and *Doloi*ship. Succession to these office was based on a hereditary basis at the family and clan levels. Further, in the case of the office of the *Syiem* or King, heredity passed from the uncle to the nephew as the Jaintia society adopted a matrilineal system (Gassah, 1984 : 197).

Emergence of State

In the early phase of polity formation, the Jaintias were under the administration and leadership of *U Langdoh* or priest, both at the village and groups of villages or *Raid*. The *Langdoh* combined in himself both the sacred or religious and secular functions. The first incumbent of the office of the priest of the *Raid* was elected from among the priestly families of the villages in the *Raid*. But with the increase in the number of families and clans and the area and size of population, there was also an increase in duties and functions of the *Langdoh*. This called for restructurisation of the administrative set up. As a result, it was necessary to bifurcate the dual functions of sacred and secular nature which were concentrated in the authority of the *Langdoh*. In the process, it was necessary to hand over those functions which were purely sacred in nature to the priest and the administrative functions to the secular chief, *U Doloi*.. The kingship or *Syiemship* came into existence when the *Doloiships* increased in number and the *Dolois* felt the need for mutual co-operation for the purpose of the inter-*elaka* relations, defence and foreign affairs. But the question arose on who would be the leader of the confederation. In the deliberations that followed, the Sutnga *elaka*, the youngest and the least powerful among the then seven *elakas*, was entrusted with the function of leading the confederation. In the process, the institution of a Rajah or *U Syiem* came into existence. In the beginning, however, no one was inclined to shoulder the responsibility of a *Syiem* (Pakem, 1984 : 52). This is because in pre-colonial Jaintia, a *Syiem* or *Rajah* was much despised in the eyes of the people (Singh, 1985 : 1617). However, to fulfil the deterent needs of the society and at the same time to circumbent the spiritual interdiction, the institution of Syiemship was introduced. But once a person had been choosen to be the *Syiem*, religious rites were performed when all the articles symbolic of his office were handed to him--the sword, the spear and the buckle, as the head of the army, the handcuffs, and the iron chains, the rope and the bludgeon, as the execution and judicial executive. This religious installation sanctified or consecrated the *Syiem* and imbued him and his clan with a protective spiritual shield against *Ka Byrsieh* and gave him and his *Kurs* or clans divine powers to relieve others of evil afflictions. His *Kurs* were in no way treated as inferior but as equals and respected because paradoxically the very office of the *Syiem* placed him in a position of honour in the State, as the ultimate protector (Singh,1985 :17). If these are the conditions that have to be faced by an incumbent to the office of a *Syiem* and if no one in the society is willing to take up the office, hence, there must be a way out by which such a leader be found either by forcing somebody to take up the job or to create a miraculous origin myth to convince the people that the Divine had also a hand in the selection of *U Syiem* or a *Rajah*. Such rulers were known as *Ki Syiem Blai*, the Divine Kings. The Jaintias chose the later course of action as the former idea of forcing somebody might not enforce discipline in the society as *U Syiem* or a *Rajah* would then appear merely as a petty servant of the State. In such a situation, the rulers were referred to as *Ki Syiem Mynroo* (the slave kings) (Pakem, 1977 : 1).

We come across some legends which ascribe miraculous origin to *Ki Syiem Sutnga* (the Sutnga Kings). One of them refers to a mermaid, *Ka Li Dakha,* who was captured by a Jaintia, named *U Luh Ryndi* from *Ka Thwai Syiem* (a royal lake) at a distance of about one kilometer west of the present day Sutnga village. Since this incident was supposed to have occurred within the Sutnga *doloiship,* the royal dynasty was then called *Ki Syiem Sutnga* (the Sutnga Kings or dynasty). This dynasty came out of a union of *Ka Li Dakha* and *U Luh Ryndi.*. Their eldest son, U Chyngkhlein-Am was appointed as a King and he ruled the Jaintia Kingdom from Sutnga as its first headquarters. His successors continued to rule the kingdom from Sutnga, and after further territorial expansion into the plains of Nowgong in the north and the Sylhet in the south, they ruled the Jaintia kingdom from Jaintiapur, the seat of the capital in the southern plains during winter and from Nartiang, the headquarters in the hills during summer respectively. They continued to do so until the coming of the British in the 18th century A.D. It was this dynasty which had brought all the political units of Jaintia Hills under one central authority with wider latitude of powers granted to the units called *Raids* or *Elakas.* Such union was a sort of a loose federation where the *doloiships* were completely independent of each other in internal matters (Pakem, 1977 : 55).

According to another legend, popular in the plains, a Garo, Landahvar by name, married a Sutnga mermaid called Mutchodduree. Their son, Bar Gossain or U Bor (or Mar) Kuhain in local usage, was the first ruler of Jaintia State. But U Box (or Mar) Kuhain ruled Jaintia State in 1250 A.D. In any case, the two versions confirmed the divine theory of kingship in Jaintia State, though in fact it was invented only to cover up the choice of the Sutnga people for a couple whose off-springs could take up the much despised office of kingship (Pakem, 1977 : 55).

The final extent of the Jaintia State was the result of the integration of a number of smaller unions. The first phase was the evolution of a State-like territorial organization called *Hima*, or a combination of petty politics (*Raid/Elaka*) in the Jaintia Hills that had emerged from the indigenous egalitarian tribal base through social stratification. With his headquarters at Sutnga, the *Syiem* gradually extended his territory towards the neighbouring plain in Assam (Brahmaputra valley) and Bengal (Surma Valley). In the Assam plains, he imposed his overlordship on petty tribal chieftaincies called *Desh*. In the Surma valley, it covered the territory of the erstwhile kingdom of Jaintia which had disintegrated into a number of small principalities called Raj. It was after Jayantia that the Sutnga *Syiemship* came to be known as Jaintia ever since the capital was shifted to Jaintiapur (Surma Valley) in the 16th century. Each *Elaka* in the hills and *Desh* in the Assam plains enjoyed considerable local autonomy even after the State had reached its final phase when the autonomy of the Raj was greatly curtailed as these formed the vital revenue-yielding areas of the State. The earlier formation in the area, *viz* the ancient Jayantia, provided the required Brahmanical Hindu legends for legitimation of the assumed status of the Hinduised *Syiem* of Sutnga as the Raja of the extended State (Bhattacharjee, 1990 : 47-64).

Pre-Colonial Hill Polity

The Office of *Syiem* or *Rajah* came into existence at the last stage of Polity formation among the Jaintias. Although this office came into existence at such a late stage, it occupied the apex position in the administrative hierarchy and leadership before its abolition in 1835 by the British. With regard to internal organisation and administration in the hill portions of the Jaintia Kingdom, it was split into several administrative units which consisted particularly of the *Elakas* and villlages.

The Jaintia kingdom extended over both the hills and plain areas. However, the same uniform power and functions of the Jaintia *Syiem* did not apply over both these areas. This state of affairs was bound to take place on the basis that the position of the hill people of the kingdom was distinct from that the conquered subjects or *Ryots* of the Jaintia kings in the plains.

In the hill areas of the kingdom, the *Syiem* was only a titular head. The *Syiem* reigns but the ultimate source of legitimate authorities lies with the people. Moreover, as the hill section of the kingdom was left entirely in the hands of the *Dolois*, therefore, the King had only a nominal authority over them. The *Dolois* could allow the King to handle only matters of common interests (Pakem, 1977 : 2). The only symbol of allegiance and the semblance of power which the *Syiem* had enjoyed over the *Dolois* from the hills was an annual tribute of one he-goat from each *Elaka* under their administration. But this was more ceremonial or religious than political though technically, a tribute system is symbolic of a basic power structure. The *Syiem*, to his people in the hills, was no more than a symbol of their unity; and if his activities threatened that unity, the later would strongly oppose him (Pakem, 1972 : 353). The he-goats received by the *Syiem* from the *Dolois* were used for religious sacrifices at Rajbari in Jaintiapur.

When the office of the *Syiem* was in existence, the Jaintia *Syiems* considered the *Dolois* as important administrators or ministers of the hill areas of the kingdom since it were the latter who actually ran the administration in the hills. The *Dolois* being powerful heads of the hills administrative units, served the *Syiem* in those days in the capacity of military commanders, as well as ministers and even as ambassadors to foreign courts, especially that of the Ahom court. Whenever engaged in exercising their functions as ministers, they stayed at Jaintiapur, the capital of the kingdom (Baseh, 1967 : 267-279). Moreover, the *Dolois* used to spend six months in a year at Jaintiapur to assist the *Syiem* in his administration. During their absence, the *Dolois* entrusted to Pators or Deputy-Governors, the management of their respective *Elakas*. The *Syiem* used to convene the *Dolois* to his court where State Councils were held for settling problems arising out of inter-*Elaka* relations

(Baseh, 1967 : 267). As far as the administration of hill areas of the kingdom was concerned, the *Dolois* wielded much power over their respective *Elakas*. Further, in the *Syiem-Doloi* relationship, there were a number of cases which proved that the *Dolois* and their people from the hills could even take a decision to do away with a *Syiem* if he so incurred displeasure or acted in a ruthless manner against them.

Unlike that of the status and position of the *Syiem* as the hill areas were concerned, in the plains he was an absolute ruler where no one could question his authority as these areas were his personal domains. The *Rajah* (as addressed to him by his subjects in the plains) was the supreme administrative head and the fountain head of justice. He also owned all the land in the plains areas (Pakem, 1977 : 1). In the plains, no class of persons had any right in the land as against the State. The land was parcelled in small plots to the cultivators who paid revenue partly in labour and partly in kind. The class above the tenants, *Shikdars* and *Choudhuries* were also removable at pleasure of the *Rajah* (Ali, 1954 : 86). It is stated that, the revenue was received by the *Rajah* partly in produce and partly in labour, and all tenures were voidable at his Will. No class of persons had any recognized rights in the land (Hunter, 1975 : 261). Added to this, the power and authority of the *Rajah* over his *ryots* in the plains ranged from calling upon them to supply all his requirements, to pay him land revenue, and to furnish him with persons who would be offered annually as sacrifices to goddess *Kali* at *Yale* falls on the Kupli river (Pakem 1977 : 1-2). With regard to the *Rajah's* control over his ryots in the plains, Hunter, pointed out that 'the native Government is described as a pure despotism. (Hunter, 1975 : 261).

On the basis of the background stated above, we find that the actual personal power and control of the *Syiem* or *Rajah* prevailed only over the conquered territories of his subjects, both in the northern and southern plains of the kingdom. On this account, the *de facto* power and functions of the Jaintia *Syiem* could be said to have existed only over his ryots in the plains.

The office of the Jaintia *Syiem* was abolished by the British in 1835 following their taking over the entire administration of the area, both in the hills and plains. Though the British abolished the *Syiem*'s office, they, however, retained the offices of the other traditional institutions of the *Doloi Pator* and the village headman to assist them in running the administration. Traditionally, during the British period and even after that, the *Dolois* played an important role in providing leadership in the society. Against this background, we now discuss in detail about the *Doloi,* his administration and the leadership role provided by this traditional institution among the Jaintias.

Evolution of Doloiship

The *Doloiship* is the most significant institution in Jaintia political system. At a certain stage of social development when the other institutions at the grassroot level could not properly deliver the goods on account of the increase of population and size of the territory coupled with the ever increasing functions of the social leaders, the Jaintias had decided to create an institution which would gather to the general needs of families, clans and villages. As the highest institution of an autonomous political unit, it was to cater to the needs of the unit and bring together the different groups of families and clans and villages within the unit under one central authority. The process was initiated when the groups of migrants to the Jaintia Hills came to lead a more settled way of life. After they had permanently settled in the land, further development in the organization of their traditional polity also took place. They had initially established villages for their respective small groups or clan-clusters under the leadership of *Waheh Chhong* or village headman. There had been conflicts and war when the groups of the immigrants intruded into the settlements, besides inter-villages disputes and clashes. To avoid these wars and conflicts, the groups of adjoining villages formed larger units, called *Raid,* under the leadership of a *Langdoh* each.

At the next stage, the groups of each adjoining *Raids* formed *Elaka* under a *Doloi.* The rise of *Elaka* as an autonomous territorial organization was indeed crucial in polity formation processes in the Jaintia Hills long before the Jaintia stage formation. For example, the Jowai *Elaka* was formed by combining the four *Raids,* viz. *Chrymang,* Jowai, Tuber and Yalong. Occasionally, an extra tier between the *Elaka* and the *Raid* was instituted wherever the *Elaka* was too large to be managed by one *Doloi.* Such an extra tier was usually placed under a *Pator.* A *Doloi* could either function directly or through his deputy, *U Pator* with the assistance of *Ki*

Tymmen Ki San or simply *Ki Wasan* (elders) who were the representatives of their respective clans. Once a *Doloi* took up his office, he normally held it for the rest of his life. But he could be punished, expelled or stripped of his office, should he develop sufficient hostility with his people (Pakem, 1984 : 52-53).

A *Doloi* was the administrative head of an *Elaka*. The number of *Elakas* in Jaintia Hills did not remain constant, especially in the pre-independence period. At a particular point of time, it seems, the whole of Jaintia Hills was divided into 12 (Twelve) *Elakas* because the Jaintia Hills is sometimes referred to as *Ka Ri Khad-ar Doloi* or the Land of the Twelve *Dolois*. However, after the British annexation of the whole of Jaintia Hills, they created more number of *Elakas*, so that at another point of time, there were as many as 25 (Twenty five) such administrative units including the *Sirdarships* created by the British. Coming to the period after independence, the United Khasi-Jaintia Hills Autonomous District Act, 1953 mentioned that there were 18 (eighteen) *Doloiships* or *Elakas* and 1 (one) *Sirdarship*. One *Patorship* that of Suner, was not mentioned in the Act. In the list now available with the Jaintia Hills Autonomous District Council, there are 18 (eighteen) *Doloiships*, 1 (one) *Sirdarship* and 1 (one) Patorship (Gassah, 1986 : 1010).

Methods of Election

A *Doloi* was usually elected from among the adult male members of the original or founding clans (Kurs) of the *Elaka*. Further, even from among the original clan (s), the candidate (s) for the post of the *Doloi* were chosen mostly on ascriptive criteria rather than on grounds of achievements (Pakem, 1977 : 2). However, as far as 'election' is concerned, it was mostly on achievement basis. In course of time, the choice of candidates remained limited to the members of the original clans(s), but in the actual election process, all the adult male members of the *Elaka* were involved. In other words, the electorate consisted of all adult male members of all clans in the *Elaka*.

The original or founding clans, however, enjoyed special status in the political structure. These clans were regarded as such because it was they who were the first or earliest settlers in a village or *Elaka*. They also became the proprietor of the land. The landownership decided political power and authority. The original clans also became the legitimate ruling clans within the area under their jurisdiction and extended their protection to new or latecomers who joined and settled within their fold. Such clans are regarded as *Ki Khian Kur,* literally small clans or outsiders. The *Khian Kurs* are deprived of the right and privileges to set up candidate for the office of *Doloi,* which is exclusively meant for the *Kmai Kur* or big or original clans. Against this background, only the *Kmai Kur* could produce leaders who could aspire for any office of political significance in the *Raid*. The *Khian Kur* would not have any say in the running of the political affairs of the *Raid,* except of course, the right to vote in the election of the *Doloi* or *Pator*. The original clans or *Kmai Kur* are usually referred to by the total number of clans as *Ki Soo Kpoh* (four clans) of Jowai, or *Ki Ynniaw Kur* (seven clans) or Sumer, or *Ki La Poh* (three clans) from the villages of Lamin, Nongtalang and *Nongbareh* and who are the descendants of *Ka Iaw Shibia* or *Ka Iaw Shibidi,* their ancestress (Gassah, 1987).

As stated above, exclusive right and privileges were granted only to the members of the original clans for setting up of candidates for the office of *Doloi*. For example, in the Jowai *Elaka,* the *Doloi* was nominated by the members of the *Soo Kpohh* and later on by the other clans as well and elected by all the adult male members of the *Elaka.* Likewise, in the Nongtalang *Elaka,* the *Doloi* was nominated by the members of the *La Poh* and accordingly elected by all the adult male members of the *Elaka.* Against this background, it may be noted that no one could be nominated or appointed as a *Doloi* unless he belonged to one of the original clans of the *Elaka.* Other clans could not aspire to an elective post or participate in the decision-making process of an *Elaka,* except the right to vote in the election of a *Doloi* or a *Pator*. However, there had been attempts by the members of the non-original clans in the past and in recent times too, to put forward their claims to office of a *Doloi* or a *Pator*. In the British period, members of non-original clans were sometimes elected to the office of a *Doloi*. But that was only a temporary arrangement. The Jaintia society as a whole has not yet accepted such principle to bring in drastic change in their traditional customary practices or to introduce the modern concept of democratisation for election of a *Doloi*. Even when such occasional deviations took place it proved to be a total failure.

Once a *Doloi* was elected, he normally held the office for the rest of his life. Traditionally, and till the advent of the British, the tenure of office was for life. However, a *Doloi* could be expelled or asked to resign. If a *Doloi* showed some kind of hostility towards the people by inflicting unduly harsh punishments or irrationally suppressed them against the norms of the society, and the people felt collectively that such inflictions were not according to the law, customs and usages of the land, they had the right and authority to strip the *Doloi* of his office. The *Dolois* could not, therefore, misbehave towards their people. The people could appeal to their *Langdohs* if the *Dolois* had acted in any way contrary to the social norms. And if the *Dolois* were found guilty, they were removed accordingly (Pakem, 1977 : 52). The British Government also upheld this principle. In 1907-08, the Deputy Commissioner, Khasi and Jaintia Hills, dismissed *U Shan, Doloi* of Shagpung, as unsuitable to continue in his office on the basis of the unfavourable report and several complaints filed against him by the people of his *Elaka.* In another case, U Manik, *Doloi* of Darang *Elaka,* had to resign from office in 1892, as he did not find favour with his people. After the election, the *Doloi* used to be ceremonially installed in the office. Some of the rites pertaining to the investiture of the doloiship are still followed. In the pre-Colonial period, the newly appointed *Doloi* used to receive a *tola* of gold from the *Syiem* as an act of confirmation to office by his people (Laloo, 1908: 256; Laloo, 1893).

Colonial Transition

In the pre-British period, the *Raids* or *Elakas* were little republics. Like the *Syiem,* the *Dolois* also had to rule according to the popular opinion. This is clearly noticed from the fact that all actions initiated or taken by a *Doloi* had to be approved by all the citizens of the *Elaka,* through the general durbar (*Durbar Raid* or *Elaka*). The people appointed their rulers to supervise their activities. The people, therefore, elected their chiefs in order to supervise the administration and not to suppress or oppress them. For sometime even after the British Political Agent was appointed to look after and conduct the affairs of administration of Jaintia Hills, he granted permission to the people of the area to elect, retain and remove the *Dolois* according to their own traditional customary practices (Pakem, 1961 : 29).

The *Dolois* had certain executive, political, judicial and religious functions to perform within their respective jurisdiction. In the past, they also performed military functions. Besides extending their hands in assisting the *Syiem* in his administration, the *Dolois* on their part executed and exercised important decisions in matters relating to the administration and welfare of the people in their respective *Elakas*. In running the administration of his *Elaka*, the *Doloi* was and is still assisted and guided by the *Durbar Elaka* or *Durbar Raid* and an executive council consisting of leading persons like the *Pator*, the *Wasan* , the *Dan* (collector), the *Duhalia* (musician), the *Sangot* (village crier or announcer), and others. The *Doloi* could either function directly or through his deputy, the *Pator*, with the assistance of *Ki Wasan*, the latter acting as representatives of their respective clans. The *Doloi* although being the chief of the *Elaka* cannot act or decide things all by himself. Any decision concerning the *Elaka* has to be approved by the *Durbar Elaka* (Pakem, 1977 : 53).

Certain new changes were brought by the British in the administration of Jaintia Hills after the area was taken over by them. After the abolition of the *Syiem's* office, the *Dolois* and other traditional chiefs were retained and allowed to continue as heads of their autonomous *Elakas* and villages. But many of their powers and functions were stripped off in the subsequent years following the British decision to get themselves totally involved in the administrative affairs of Jaintia Hills.

One of the effects of the British administration on the institution of *Doloiship* was the change made on his tenure of office. Traditionally, once a *Doloi* takes up his office, he normally holds it for the rest of his life. Of course, for quite sometime the British did not interfere in the matter of election, appointment and removal of *Dolois*, but subsequently the British Political Agent in his own analysis found it not suitable and convenient to allow this traditional practice of the people to continue any further. The reason given by the Political Agent was because of a perpetual struggle between the influential inhabitants of many of the *Elakas* to procure the dismissal of the *Doloi* in office, and to replace him by some other candidates of an opposite faction. This led to constant turmoil and discontent among the people without any corresponding advantage. The Political Agent wanted to stop this and in November 1850, passed an order that, for the future, persons elected and appointed as the *Dolois* were to hold their offices for *three years* (emphasis ours) provided they conducted their duties efficiently; at the end of every three years a new election was to take place, but the former *Doloi* might be re-elected as often as the people chose to elect him. This surely created a big chasm between the traditional practice and the British innovative plans. Moreover, the British authorities changed the traditional practice of 'election' to that of 'nomination' by the people in respect of appointing a new *Doloi* of an *Elaka* and such a *Doloi* was to be confirmed by the Principal Assistant Commissioner, otherwise his election to the office will not be a valid one. Such changes made by the British were not without overlooking the objection and criticism of the *Dolois*. For example, the *Doloi* of Jowai, objected to the system of election for a period of three years only and asserted that the bulk of the population disliked it.

Not satisfied with the change in the tenure of office of the *Dolois*, the British authorities went further to the extent of not even allowing the *Dolois* to absent themselves from their *Elakas* for more than six months in a year without the permission of the Principal Assistant Commissioner. In this respect, an order in the form of warning was issued to the effect that if a *Doloi* be compelled to be absent from his post for any length of time, the villagers with the sanction of the Principal Assistant Commissioner, should proceed to elect a *locum tenens*, who should possess and exercise the full powers of the absent *Doloi*. In order to put more stringent control over the powers and functions of the *Dolois*, on many occasions, the British Government on some flimsy grounds asked the *Dolois* to tender their resignation. Similarly, in some other cases, the *Dolois* were either fined or dismissed from their offices on similar flimsy grounds (Allen, 1975 ; 69-72).

The British administration also imposed several restrictions on the civil and criminal powers of the *Dolois*. In 1841, the *Dolois'* jurisdiction in civil suits was made limited to the value of Rs. 50 (Rupees fifty) and they were prohibited from trying criminal cases in which they, their relatives and dependents, and other chiefs were in any way concerned. Appeals from all orders and decisions of the *Dolois* and *Sirdars* in civil and criminal cases, were decided by the Political Agent and the parties who chose to prefer their complaints, civil or criminal direct to the Political Agent, were permitted to do so (Allen,1975 : 66; Mills,1853 : 4).

Some of these changes and restrictions were drastic in nature which had far reaching effects on the civil and criminal as well as other administrative and executive powers and functions of the *Dolois* and other traditional chiefs. Besides this, in 1860, when a house tax was imposed on the Jaintias, its collection was to be exclusively through the agency of the traditional chiefs, especially the *Dolois.* They were to receive a 'Commission' of 20 per cent on their total collections. The status of the traditional chiefs in this respect was thus reduced to that of "Commission Agents" of the British Government.

Post-Independence Pattern

Soon after India's independence, the tribal leaders of North-East India had demanded political autonomy and the introduction of administrative measures to enable the tribal people to run the administration of their respective tribal regions according to their own genius. Inspite of the opposition of two members from Assam, the Constituent Assembly incorporated the Sixth Schedule to the Constitution of India which provided for District and Regional Councils in the hill districts of the then composite State of Assam. A District Council for the Khasi and Jaintia Hills was inaugurated in 1952. The immediate effect was that the powers and functions of the pristine institutions of the Khasis and the Jaintias were placed under the control and supervision of the District Council. This was another blow to the traditional leadership which had actually started during the British period. Although majority of the traditional institutions, with the exception of the office of the Jaintia *Syiem,* were retained by the British authorities, their powers and functions were greatly reduced. These were further curtailed by the District Council as per the provisions of the Sixth Schedule. In the case of the village *Durbars* (Councils), the Census Report of 1961 (United Khasi-Jaintia Hills) observed that the present powers of the *Durbar* under the District Council has greatly been reduced in comparison with its powers under the chiefs (Census, 1961 : 46). If the District council could interfere in the village affairs, it was more so in the case of the *Durbar Raids* (Councils at the Commune level) (Pakem, 1977 : 355). The same Report was very clear on this point when it stated that, the part of the *DurbarRaid* is played by the District Council (Census, 1961 : 47). Precisely because of this fact, the *Dolois* in Jaintia Hills were under the control of the District Council. But most of the *Dolois* did not like to part with the power which they had enjoyed under the British, and some even treated the District Council with Disdain (Pakem, 1977 : 1).

Evidently, the powers of the traditional chiefs in Khasis and Jaintia Hills had been threatened by the new administrative set up since India's Independence. The stepping of the District Council into the shoes of either the traditional institutions or the British and post-Independence constitutional authorities, did not bring any improvement in the power position of the traditional chiefs. On the contrary, the new power structure has radically reduced the powers of the chiefs. (Pakem, 1977 : 3). Moreover, on many occasions, there have been tussels between the traditional elite represented by the chiefs and the modern political elite (popular elected representatives). On one pretext or another, the chiefs might be suspended or even dismissed by the District Council on charges like insubordination, mal-practices and disobedience (Pakem, 1978 : 236). This tussel is a continuing affair.

The traditional chiefs are now treated by the District Council as its subordinate officials. The chiefs and headmen are completely under the control and supervision of the District Council. Under the provision of paragraph 3(i) (g) of the Sixth Schedule, the Indian Constitution has empowered it to make laws with respect to the appointment or succession of chiefs or headmen. The United Khasi-Jaintia Hills Autonomous District (Appointment and Succession of Chiefs and Headmen) Act, 1959, made provision not only for its authority to appoint the chiefs and headmen, but also the removal and suspension of the same by the Executive Committee of the District Council if in its opinion these incumbents violated the terms and conditions of their appointment. This Act not only brought radical changes in the pattern and procedure of the election and appointment of chiefs, but reduced their position and status, and the District Council even treated them as its 'administrative heads'. At one point of time, the District Council even suggested to the State Government not to correspond with the traditional chiefs directly. It is, therefore, obvious that such actions taken by the District Council had created resentment between the traditional and modern institutions. Thus the relationship between the traditional chiefs and that of the District Council was all along under strains. The Honourable Supreme Court in 1960 in the case of T. Cajee, Chief Executive Member of the United Khasi-Jaintia Hills Autonomous District Council versus U Jormanik Syiem, the *Syiem* of Mylliem, observed that "the position, after the coming into force of the Constitution was that the chiefs lost whatever ruling or administrative powers they had with the merger of these twenty five States (*Khasi States*) in Assam and the governance of these States was to be carried on according to the provisions of the Sixth Schedule." Paradoxically, these new situations during the transitional period are a threat to the traditional institutions and democratic practices of the people. It may even be said that with the dawn of Independence and especially with the setting up of the District Council, the period of an 'erosion of democracy' in the area begins. Such new political institutions which were created after Independence were in fact eroding the powers and functions of traditional councils instead of improving upon them (Pakem, 1986 : 35).

The District Council appears not only to be alien to the traditional institutions, but the powers and functions of the traditional chiefs have been threatened due to its existence in the area. Because of this reason, the District Council was never welcomed by the traditional Chiefs. The stepping of the District Council into the shoes of either the Jaintia *Rajah* or the British and Indian authorities did not bring any improvement in the power position of the chiefs. On the contrary, the new power structure had radically reduced their powers (Pakem, 1977 : 3). For example, the United *Khasi-Jaintia* Hills Autonomous District (Appointment and Succession of Chiefs and Headmen) Act, 1959 (herein after referred to as the Principal Act), introduced two fundamental changes from the traditional customary practices of the people as per Sections 10 and 11 which relate to the appointment of Deputy Chief (Section 10) and an Acting Chief (Section 11). The Jaintia Hills Autonomous District Council which was established in 1964, adopted the Principal Act as it is during its initial years of existence. In the subsequent years, this District Council made certain amendments to the Principal Act. For example, the Jaintia Hills Autonomous District Council passed an amendment Act in 1973 which deleted the entire Section 10 of the Principal Act relating to the appointment of Deputy Chief. The District Council realized the uselessness and inapplicability of such a provision of the act and more importantly it shows the complete deviation from the traditional customary practices of the people. However, the Executive Committee of the Jaintia Hills District Council still retained Section 11 of the Principal Act relating to the appointment of an Acting Chief. Armed with this constitutional power, the Executive Committee of the said Council appointed a number of Acting *Dolois* from time to time, either after the death, removal or suspension of the regular *Doloi* in an *Elaka.* Such appointment of an Acting Chief has been criticized as it tantamounts to complete deviation from the traditional customary practice of the people. The critics are of the opinion that there was never a customary practice of appointing an Acting Chief. A chief once appointed, held the office for life, unless removed for very strong reasons, like moral turpitude or commission of heinous crimes. Moreover, according to the traditional customary practices, a chief must be a person belonging to the particular clan or clans chosen from time immemorial. No other clans in the society which do not enjoy this particular privilege, have the right to setting up of candidates for the office of *Doloi*. But according to the aforesaid Section (Section 11) of the Principal Act, it mentioned very specifically that the Executive Committee of the District Council may appoint "any person" who could be from any clan to act as an Acting Chief and exercise all the powers and functions of the chief. This step taken by the District Council is sure to create confusion in the minds of the people. It also shows a complete deviation from the traditional practices and against the norms of the society.

The traditional chiefs being treated by the District Council as its subordinate officials, are accountable for their actions to it. They have been directed to desist from criticism of the functioning of the Executive Committee of the District Council in any form. The chiefs are also debarred to participate in any demonstration or resort to any form of strike in connection with any matter pertaining to their condition of service. These conditions laid down by the District Council gave rise to suspicion and mistrust between the two institutions. Likewise, the various Acts enforced from time to time by the District Council under the Sixth Schedule to the Constitution brought radical changes in the pattern and procedure of election and appointment or succession of Chiefs and Headmen in Jaintia Hills District of Meghalaya.

Thus, under the new Constitutional set up, the chiefs are pushed behind the line of leadership. They are to keep themselves content with whatever power and functions left to them by the District Council though the District Council granted certain unofficial pickings to the chiefs, it however reduced them to a much lesser status. In the District Council's dealing with the chiefs, there is a strong feeling that it has not fully appreciated their continuance as institutions of the best in their traditions and has therefore been dealing with them as personalities or individuals of their respective Elakas and villages. This naturally leads to different or discriminatory treatments of *ad hoc* nature without a firm and definite policy of preserving the institutions in their pristine purity. This has also caused a sense of confusion among the people in general, a feeling of uncertainty, if not of mistrust or suspicion among the chiefs of the motive of the District Council as to their continuance as custodians and trustees of the customs and traditions of the people. As of now, the absence of any association or union among the *Dolois* or other village authorities in Jaintia Hills to act as pressure group or lobby in order to assert their grievances or even their feelings about the functioning of the District Council, makes their position very weak and ineffective. They have, therefore, to accept whatever policy decisions taken by the District Council in their relationship with it. On the other hand, the District Council took advantage of the situation and passed many such Acts as well as framed the rules in its favour which are at the same time binding on the chiefs to act in accordance with the Council's prerogatives. The District Council has thus become an authority to control the *Dolois*; and at the same time, an integrative agency for the different *Doloiships*. In a sense, it is not far away from becoming a centralised authority. The *Dolois* are now completely under the control of the District Council, though they were not so much used to the system of control when they were nominally under the Jaintia *Rajahs* (Pakem, 1978 : 234-35).

The relationship between the traditional institutions and the District Council is all along under strains. Paradoxically, the present situation is a threat to the traditional institutions as well as to the democratic practices of the Jaintia people. This has, drastic effects on the power, functions and leadership role of the traditional chiefs with the coming into existence of the District Council. The frontal leadership in the area or for that matter in the whole State of Meghalaya has passed into the hands of the emerging elitist middle class. The prevailing condition appears to be more in favour of such elites of the society than the old guards of tradition.

A Summing-up

The leadership pattern in the Jaintia society has undergone changes under stresses and strains of time and circumstances. The glimpses of early structure preserved in oral traditions suggest that the egalitarian social base gave way to pristine notables who led the groups in course of their migration to Jaintia Hills. The settlements that developed in this land of adoption continued to adhere to the leadership of those individuals on the basis of their qualities and contributions. The concept of territory at the clan and village level grew along side the development of area councils and leadership as the total spatial expanse of the hills became limited to the jurisdictions of such settlements in the form of *Chnong* or villages. The social stratification processes were accelerated by the growth of population when the immigrants new comer accepted the leadership of the original clans and by the spontaneous privatisation of land and resources at the differentiated clan and individual levels by degrees. The development of the *Raid, Elaka* and *Hima* (Sutnga) by stages through integration of the groups of *Chnong, Raid* and *Elaka* respectively till the early medievial period witnessed the parallel growth of the leadership of *Waheh Chnong, Langoh, Doloi, Wasan, Pator* and *Syiem* at various levels, besides a *durbar* or council at every level, while the customary sanctions ensured the legitimation of the assumed secular and ritual status of the chiefs as well as the democratic functioning of the society. The territorial expansion of the State in the mediaeval period by integration of the Hindu villages in the neighbouring plains accomplished perfection of the extended State formation in Pan-Indian Brahmanical Hindu model. The Jaintia society in the hills, however, by and large was unaffected by these changes because the *Chnong, Raid* and *Elaka* survived as autonomous organizations under indigenous leadership governed by traditional customs and practices. The British administration and the District Council, established under the Sixth Schedule to the Constitution of India, tempered with the autonomy of the institutions and the leadership of the society has by now definitely passed into the hands of the emerging elitist middle class which is a creation of the British administration and modern education.

Notes

1. *Selection of Records of the Government of Bengal,* Vol. XVII, Rowlatt to Secretary, Government of Bengal, 9 April, 1862.

2. *Report of the Land Reforms Commission for Khasi Hills,* Shillong 1974, p. 8.

Reference

Allen, W. J. 1858 : *Report on the Administration of the Cossyah and Jynteah Hill Territory,* Shillong 1975 (Reprint).

Ali, S.M. 1954 : *History of Jaintia,* Dacca.

Bareh, Hamlet 1967 : *"The History and Culture of the Khasi People,"* Shillong.

Bhattacharjee, J.B. 1990 : "Brahmanical Myths, Royal Legitimation and the Jaintia State Formation," *The North- Eastern Hill University Journal of Social Sciences and Humanities,* 8 : 1.

Gassah, L.S. 1984 : "Emerging Political Elite in Jaintia Hills" *NEIHA*, Fifth Session, Aizawl.

1986 : "The Concept of Ka Ri Khadar Doloi (Jaintia Hills); A Critical Assessment", *NEIHA* ? Seventh Session, Pasighat, 1986.

1987 : "Founding clans: Their Role in Jainitia Traditional Polity Formation," Paper presented in the XVIII Sociological Conference, Indian Sociological Society, Deptt of Sociology, NEHU,

1988 : "Trade Routes and Trade Relations Between Jaintia Hills and the Sylhet District in the Pre-Indepedence Period," *Proceedings of North-East India History Association* (hereafter *NEIHA*), Ninth Session, Guwahati.

Govt. of India 1961 : *Census Report of India,* III ; VI: B

Hunter, W.W. 1975 : *A Statistical Account of Assam* Vol. II (1879) B.R.Publishing Corporation, Delhi. (Reprint).

Laloo, S.S.	1908	:	*Ka Behdienkhlam* Annual Report on the Administration of Khasi and Jaintia Hills for the Year 1907-08, No. 484, Shillong, 3 April 1908; Jackson to the Commissioner Surma Valley and Hill Districts.
	1893	:	*Political Report of the Khasi and Jaintia Hills* for 1899 - 93, Assam Secretariat, Forgn. A., Progs., July 1893, Nos. 22-23; Gray to the Secreatry to the Chief Commissioner of Assam, No. 902, Shillong, 11 April 1893.
Mills, A. J. M.	1901	:	*Report on the Khasi and Jaintia Hills*, 1853 Shillong (Reprint).
Pakem, B.	1972	:	"The Socio-Political System of the Jaintia Tribe of Assam: An Analysis of Continuity and Change in K. Suresh Singh (ed.) *Tribal Situation in India*, IIAS.
	1977	:	"The Changing Power Structure of the Political Institution of Jaintia Chieftainship," *The Journal of North East India Council for Social Science Research*, I : I.
	1978	:	"Meghalaya : Some Aspects of Political Development", in S. M. Dubey (ed.) North East India: *A Sociological Study*, Concept Publishing Co., Delhi.
	1984	:	"State Formation in Pre-colonial Jaintia," *The North Eastern Hill University Journal of Social Science and Humanities*, II : 3
	1986	:	"Political Development and Change in North East India," In A.P. Sinha (ed.), *Changing North East India*, Gagan Publishers, Ludhiana.
Singh, Kynpham	1985	:	"*Syiem* and *Durbars*" in *Khasi* Polity, in S.K. Chattopadhyay (ed.) *Tribal Institutions of Meghalaya*, Spectrum Publications, Guwahati.

11

POWER AND PRIVILEGE OF THE CHIEFS IN THE MANIPUR HILLS

B. B. GOSWAMI

Almost every village in the hills of Manipur was first established by a single person at his own and others initiative joined him subsequently. The founder became the head of the village and others who joined him recognised him as village chief. In some of the villages particularly, in the Kuki village, the chief is still regarded as the owner of the entire village.

In hill areas, particularly among the Nagas, the village lands are generally divided into two categories,namely holdings of individual villagers and common lands of the village. The practice, however, varies according to the customs and there may as well be some non-kuki villages where the village lands are regarded as the property of the chief. The ownership rights of the chief or individual villagers are not derived from any statutory law but seem to have the sanction of custom which varies from village to village and from tribe to tribe.

There has been no survey and settlement of the village lands, except in small areas of Churachandpur and Tengnoupal Districts where survey of terraced land or land under permanent orchard has been done. No land revenue is generally levied in the hills. Hence, there are no regular revenue records which can be relied upon to establish the ownership of these lands. However, the boundaries of the village have been fairly well settled among the people more by usage than by administrative acts. In some cases, such settlements have taken place through court decrees in boundary disputes between the villages. The enjoyment and possession of the lands in the villages for cultivation, hunting, putting up huts, etc. by the villagers is a matter left for internal settlement between the chief and the villagers, and there is no record of the dues payable by the villagers to the chiefs. For the first time, an attempt was made under the Hill Regulation Act, 1947 to list out the villages and recognize their existence statutorily. Under the same law, the right of the village chief and his Council of Elders to settle by compromise land disputes within the village was recognized. However, according to the decisions of the Court of Judicial Commissioner, this law is no longer in force. The Government, following the practice introduced by the British Government however, levies a house-tax in the hills. The tax is collected through the chief and credited to the Government. But, for this, there is practically no interterence in the enjoyment of the lands by the villagers according to custom. This, in brief, is the position in the Hill Areas so far as the village lands are concerned.

Among the Kukis, as already stated that the entire village belongs to the chief and everything found on the village land is regarded as belonging to him. A villager who has been given land for cultivation in a Kuki village, therefore, pays a part of the harvest to the chief as well. When any villager migrates, the chief, according to the traditional custom can take away the crop harvested by the villager and also can prevent him from disposing of his house on the ground that it belongs to the chief. On the other hand, in the Naga villages of Manipur where the village lands are generally divided into village common lands, and individual holdings, individuals can dispose of their holdings but the common land remains the property of the village community and cannot be alienated. The villagers do not pay any rent for their holdings, and therefore, enjoy full proprietary rights in respect of such lands. Similarly, no rent is paid by individual villagers for the use of common lands. However, among Tangkhuls in Ukhrul area, the practice of paying *lousal* (rent) to the village chief and his elders for enjoying natural products from the common land is in vogue. The amount of *lousal* is nominal and is more in the nature of payment to the village community than to the chief.

This differing conception about the chief's rights over the village lands is often inter-linked with the right of succession of chiefship. Among the Nagas, chiefship is not regarded as hereditary although the son of a chief often succeeds his father if there has been no estrangement between him and the villagers. On the other hand, among the Kukis, the chiefship is regarded as hereditary with the result that succession goes even to persons who may not be residents of the same village. It is also customary for chiefs to receive a variety of gifts or tributes from the villagers such as head or leg of an animal (killed by hunting), a basket of rice from each household at the end of the harvest and so on. These are merely customary payments relatable more to the social status of the chief than to his economic rights over the village lands.

The introduction of the system of election for the Village Authority according to the Village Authority Act, 1956 (Chief is ex-officio Chairman of the Authority) coupled with the lack of any statutory recognition of the chief as the owner of the village lands, seems to have given rise to a somewhat unusual situation in the Kuki villages. The village chief who dominated the scene with the help of the village elders, can no longer derive any assistance from them in managing the affairs of the village and, particularly, in recovering his dues from the villagers. In the village authority, he has to sit with the elected members and cannot have his say because the village authority takes its decisions by majority. His position is worse in villages having mixed tribal population. For instance, in a Kuki village having *Hmar* population, the *Hmars* sometimes refuse to recognize the chief and do not pay his dues. This in the past has led to migration of the minority tribes to other villages. It has been reported that in some villages the villagers have stopped paying the dues for the last twenty years or so i.e. even before the system of elected village authorities came into existence. Due to the lack of statutory recognition of the rights of the chiefs, they have also become powerless to recover the dues. It seems that this tendency on the part of the villagers to refuse payment of the customary dues has considerably increased with the introduction of the system of elections to the village authorities. Representations have been received by the Manipur Government from the chiefs from time to time requesting that either their ownership of the village lands should be recognized by statutory law to enable them to realize their dues in the shape of rent or Government should acquire their present customary rights on payment of compensation as was done in the Mizo Hills of Assam.

Under the Law, 'Chief means a chief recognized by the Government. There is, however, no statutory law in Manipur under which the chiefs are recognized. The tribal custom however recognises the chief. As mentioned earlier the chief is also the ex-officio Chairman of the village authority. The ownership of village lands is not vested in the village authority. The village authority is mainly concerned with maintenance of law and order in the village.

The important principle underlying the implementation of the land reforms is that ownership right should be conferred on the actual tillers. Unless it is made compulsory by law to register/record the tillers, tenants, sub-tenants, share croppers etc. the objective of conferring ownership right to the actual tillers of the soil cannot be attained. With this object in view, the Manipur Land Revenue and Land Reforms (Amendment) Bill, 1975, as passed by the Assembly, provided the State Government by notification to extend the whole or any part or section of the Act to any of the hill areas of Mainpur specified in the notification.

Fear of Land Alienation

As regards the fear of alienation of land many administrators view that the possibility of alienation may be greater when individual ownership comes. As such the remedy should lie in making such alienation difficult even after individual ownership has been created. Section 158 of the Manipur Land Revenue and Land Reforms Act, 1960 prevents transfer of the tribal land to a non-tribal, except with the previous permission of the Deputy Commissioner concerned. The text of this Section runs as follows:

> "158. Special provision regarding STs:
>
> No transfer of land by a person who is a member of the Scheduled Tribes shall be valid unless--
>
> (a) The transfer is to another member of the Scheduled Tribes;
>
> or
>
> (b) Where the transfer is to a person who is not a member of any such tribes, it is made with the previous permission in writing of the Deputy Commissioner;
>
> or
>
> (c) The transfer is by way of mortgage to cooperative society.

To make the provision still more stringent a further amendment was made to the effect that the previous permission of not only the Deputy Commissioner but also the District Council will be necessary for transferring any land to a non-tribal. The hill people appreciate such a perspective and desire for its strict application.

12

TRIBAL POLITY IN WEST BENGAL : AN OVERVIEW

AMAL KUMAR DAS

It is intended to present in this paper a profile in brief of the existing political organisations and functions thereof, of the tribal communities of the State. It is proposed at the first state to present some basic demographic characteristics as well as migration history and settlements of the tribals in different parts of the State. The existing structure and functions of the indigenous tribal political institution would be discussed thereafter in the backdrop of the above information. Side by side, the role of traditional leadership vis-a-vis statutory panchayat system would be presented very briefly.

There are at present thirtyeight communities in the list of Scheduled Tribe (S.T.) of West Bengal. They constitute 5.63 per cent (30, 70, 672 persons) of the total population of the State (5, 45, 80, 647) as per 1981 Census. These communities may be grouped under three broad linguistic categories (1) Austric Family; (2) Dravidian Family and (3) Tibeto-Chinese Family of languages.

In the true sense, in this State there are no exclusive pockets of tribal concentrations as are found in the neighbouring States of Bihar, Orissa, Andhra Pradesh, Madhya Pradesh etc. In West Bengal the characteristic feature of the tribal settlements is that these are interspered in nature with general population. Out of 38, 036 inhabited villages of the State, the tribals have more than 50 per cent of the population in 5,000 villages. In the plains of West Bengal the tribal settlements are mainly found in the Western Region (Midnapore, Bankura, Purulia and parts of Burdwan and Birbhum districts) adjacent to the neighbouring States of Bihar and Orissa whereas in North Bengal these are spread over in the districts of Darjeeling, Jalpaiguri and Cooch-Bihar quite adjacent to the States of Sikkim and Assam. Thus, it reveals that in the historic past majority of the tribal population settled in the border districts of the State of West Bengal, migrated from their traditional homeland in the neighbouring States. In this context their migration history may be examined.

It is a known fact the tribals were mainly forest dwellers and their socio-economic, political and cultural life took shape and developed in accordance with the forest life. The forest was like mother to them. It provided them with food, shelter, materials for their domestic life and also formed the very core or essence of their culture. But this symbolic relationship was gradually destroyed with the advent of the British Colonial Administration since the later half of eighteenth century. The forest was considered as the source of earning revenues instead of maintenance of ecological equilibrium. The tribal folk were compelled to migrate from their forest abodes in search of new avocations and settlements due to imposition of several restrictions upon them by the alien rulers. Ousted from forests, they started settling in fixed villages by making unfertile land cultivable by their hard labour. But here also they could not live in peace. As in the case of forest law which curtailed their rights over forest, permanent settlement on land tenure also very adversely affected their land holding position. The unscrupulous money lenders, zamindars, jotedars and mahajans got entry into their areas and started exploiting these simple folk by adopting various unlawful means which resulted in large scale alienation of their vast fertile tract of land and throwing them in utter distress and poverty. When the situation was like this, many of them were taken to work as labourers in the tea gardens of Darjeeling and Jalpaiguri Districts of West Bengal in the middle of last century as well as in the tea gardens of Assam. These uprooted people from a number of villages having diverse ethnic affiliations, started a new pattern of life in this new agro-based industrial area. A new society emerged there with new value system with blending of their traditional heritage to varied extent. But in a new set up their old norms, values and behaviour changed to a perceptible extent. As in the case of tea gardens, a large number of tribals were also brought to work in colliery areas of the State. Here they started living in labour barracks leaving many of the traits of their traditional culture. The colliery labourers regularly coming from villages however are in better position in the maintenance of their traditional way of life in comparison to others. However, a good deal of changes have taken place in the life of their tribal folk due to the impact of collieries. The tribal population from Chotanagpur plateau of Bihar and also Mayurbhanj area of Orissa (namely the Oraon, Munda, Bhumij, Santal and others) were also brought to Sundarban area towards the end of eighteenth century for reclamation of forest land and making it cultivable. These migrant population settled here after becoming totally cut-off from their congeners in Chotanagpur. Here in the new set up due to the constant interactions with the neighbouring communities they could build a new social order after having integrated much with the regional cultures. The colonial administration also brought tribal labourers from neighbouring States to work in the indigo plantation of Bengal. These people also got settled in the districts of 24-Parganas, Nadia, Murshidabad, Midnapore and in many districts of present day Bangladesh being totally cut-off from their original homeland. After independence due to installation of heavy industries, irrigation canals/dams, thermal projects etc, many tribal people were displaced from their original homeland. Many of them were provided with compensations (cash/land/service etc.) but these were not adequate and not in consonance with their traditional way of life and culture. Deviations and changes took place in the tribal life due to displacements as well as installations of industries etc. in their areas. The seasonal migration of the tribal population from the districts of Purulia, Bankura and Midnapore to the areas of Burdwan, Hooghly and Howrah districts during the sowing and harvesting seasons as well as in the brick fields also adversely affected their normal way of life. All these have also brought changes in their mode of living. A trend has recently developed to employ a good number of the tribal labourers by the contractors in Calcutta and other big cities in the construction works connected with different development projects. This type of seasonal migration by some members (both males and females) from individual tribal families poses a serious problem for the smooth and effective functioning of their family as well as normal village and social life. At present due to spread of modern education as well as job reservation a good number of educated tribal males and females with or without their families live in Calcutta and other cities and towns in messes, quarters, hostels etc. Changes have taken place in their mode of living and thinking.

The above facts and figures concerning demography, migration and settlement history unravel some significant characteristics which are summarised below:

(1) Above 90 per cent of the tribal population of the State are covered by a very few tribal communities numbering eight only. Of them the Santals constitute more than half of the (54.28 per cent) total tribal population of the State. The Mongoloid tribal groups numbering nine cover only 3.50 per cent. Nowhere there exists any particular area of tribal dominance as in the other parts of the country. In the State of West Bengal, the tribals are generally interspersed with the non-tribal population and they are mainly concentrated in the border districts of western part of Bengal (Midnapore, Purulia, Bankura) and in the northern districts of the State (Darjeeling, Jalpaiguri and Cooch-Bihar) adjacent to the States of Sikkim and Assam. In the pre-colonial period due to the forest act and permanent settlement of lands, the tribals mostly lost their traditional right over forest and land and became landless peasantry and were forced to migrate to different parts of the country as well as outside. In the State of West Bengal, they emigrated as tea garden labourers, colliery labourers, as labourers for reclaiming forest land in Sunderban area and as workers in indigo plantation, brick fields and to different fertile areas to work as agricultural labourers. Changes have also taken place in the tribal way of life and thinking due to imposition of different laws, acts and orders and also colonial administration and judiciary system in India. During post-Independence period due to installation of heavy industries, irrigation canals, construction of dams, thermal power stations etc. in the tribal areas displacement took place and compensations made were also meagre in nature. The tribal labourers are also brought to different urban centres by the contractors to work in various types of construction jobs. Due to all these factors changes gradually took place in their life from historic past and their traditional institutions were also exposed to different forces of changes leading to modifications or realignments and readjustment. Due to different protective and ameliorative measures in the Constitution of India and also for different development activities, spread of education among tribal folk took place at a rapid pace and also for measures adopted for economic betterment, their living condition also improved to certain extent. All these factors brought changes in the life and activities, institutions and outlook of the tribal people. These trends of devlopment in pre and post colonial periods would be helpful in understanding the present day condition of the indigenous tribal political organisation vis-a-vis their mind and outlook.

II

Nowadays among majority of the tribal groups of West Bengal a rudiment of traditional *'panch'* still exists; the functions whereof are mainly restricted to the settlement of minor socio-political disputes. The traditional *panch* mainly exercises its power in socio-religious and moral matters only to regulate the spirit and moral life of the village community. Any breach of social and religious customs by any villager is dealt with by the village *panch.* The secular and criminal cases are under the jurisdiction of the State Police and Court. The *panch* mainly consists of the elderly members of the society.

Though structurally and functionally the panch among different tribal communities of the State present somewhat uniform pattern, still the existing picture of *panch* from each of the linguistic groups would be described. That is the Santals will represent Austric speech Family; the Oraons, Dravidian Speech Family, the Lepchas and the Totos, Tibeto-Himalayan group of Tibeto-Chinese Family and the Rabhas, Assam Branch of Assam Burmese group of Tibeto-Chinese Family of languages. They are expected to provide an overall picture of the existing pattern of tribal political organisation of the State.

Santal

The present village or political organisation of the Santals, a vestigeal form of the past traditional political system, involves four distinct instrumentalities related to each other: the village Assembly made up of village elders; the village Council composed of several office bearers; the *pargana* Assembly with its chief officer, the *parganait* and the Hunt Council.

The village Assembly is the legislative as well as the judicial organ of the village community. It is made up of elders, generally male members. The village council (*More Hor*) has a number of officers, each with distinct functions. The *Manjhi,* village headman, is assisted by a *Paranik* (the deputy headman), a Jog *Manjhi* (entrusted with guarding the morals of the villagers), a *Jog-Paranik* (Deputy) a *Naeke or* a *to-Naeke* (village priest), *Kudam Naeke* (assistant priest), *Godet* (messenger) and *Bhogdar* or *Bhoddor* (advisor). All these officials may not be found in every village. But the following five officers are, generally found in every Santal village of West Bengal, *Jog Manjhi, Paranik, Jog Paranik, Naeke* and *Gorait*. The succession to these posts are generally hereditary unless the village elders think otherwise due to some moral corruption, physical inability, incompetency, selfishness etc. on the part of an official when they elect a new one from among the members of the community. Earlier authors have reported that the village officials are customarily elected at the time of the foundation of a village. Later on succession to these offices become *hereditary*, the eldest son succeeds the father. In the absence of a son the office passes on to a brother or near relative on the paternal side. In this connection it may be mentioned here that after the Santal Insurrection of 1855, the British Government established a new district known as Santal Parganas and the Government by the Police Rules of 1856 made the post of the Headman to be appointed by the Deputy Commissioner. To make the British Government more acceptable to the tribal people, the Headman as an agent of their rule was appointed following traditional customary rule of the community. Outside Santal Parganas, this system of appointment was generally not introduced. The role of the *Manjhi* of fixing the rent of law with the proprietor and distribution of the land to the villagers became obsolete with the introduction of new system of relationship between the *Raiyat* and the *Zamindar*/Government direct. Apart from his economic role the *Manjhi* used to play vital role in settling disputes (land, inheritance etc.) among the villagers with the assistance of the *panch*. In day to day social and community life (birth, initiation, name giving, marriage, death, rituals, festivals, recreations etc.) the *manjhi* and his*panch* played dominant role. This helped in maintaining discipline, harmony, integrity in their life and activities. But this traditional system gradually lost its hold due to the internal and external forces giving rise to strains and stresses and the wider political system engulfed the indigenous system. Nowadays the minor disputes are generally decided by the village *panch* though it lost its past glory and influence on the society.

The *Manjhi Than* is the usual place for talks and council meetings. Previously, the tribal polity did not end with the village. It was a part and parcel of the larger political unit, the *pargana*. The Pargana Council stood over the village council which had its jurisdiction over a number of villages. The Santals used to divide various parts of the country, where their villages were located, into *parganas* with distinctive names. The Head of *pargana* was known as

Parganait who was generally selected from the Headmen (*Manjhis*) of the constituent villages and assisted by *Desh Manjhi*. With the advent of the British Administration, the *Parganait* system gradually lost its hold and started disappearing. However, during the first half of this century the British Administration in some districts of West Bengal particularly in Maldah district, appointed some *Parganaits* for assisting the administration in the management of the tribal officers, more particularly in relation to disputes concerning *Bitlah* (Social Ostracism), witch hunting, inter and intra-community feuds etc. These *Paraganaits* acted as contact men or liaison personnel between the administration and the Santals. This system continued upto the middle of this century and gradually abandoned by the local administration. At present there are some hereditary *Parganaits* and a *Dihui* for each larger district which is responsible for calling the Annual Hunts. The *Parganait* presides over the *Lobir* or *Lobir-durup* or *Sendra durup* which is the Supreme Council of the Santals. This council sits on the night which intervenes between the two days of hunting for hearing and giving verdict. This ceremonial hunting is generally held now a days in this State in two districts, purulia (in large scale) and Bankura (in small scale) in the month of April. All sorts of disputes are placed before this highest council for judgment and these are followed strictly. Due to enactment of Forest Laws and imposition of several restrictions and many other associated factors, the annual hunting of the tribals has lost its past glamour and glory and their participation is also gradually becoming limited (Ray, Das & Basu, 1982 : 3-33).

There is no doubt that 'change' started taking place in the traditional socio-political life of the Santals prior to the advent of the British Administration in the State. But that type of 'change' was not so abrupt or destructive in character as in the case of the British Administration. Prior to that the Santal polity was rather stable in character and there was no serious threatening from outside agency. But with the advent of British Rule the tribals including the Santals became the part of the exploitation of colonial capitalist net work. The process of land alienation threw them into the wider labour market to act as manual labourers. Exploitations, oppressions, tortures etc. led to protests, revolts on different times and the most important of them is the Santal Rebellion of 1855. To keep the region in permanent peace the British Administration found it profitable to turn the village headman as their agent and therefore they recognised in the village headmanship and issued *pattas.* (in some places *parganait* also). This change introduced by the Government led to peace and contentment to the Santals as well as monetary gain to the rulers (De, 1988 : 1-15).

During the post- Independence era Statutory Panchayat system has been introduced as per provisions in the Constitution. With the introduction of this system in the villages the traditional institution is getting lesser and lesser important day by day. At the initial stage conflict was noticed between the old traditional system and the newly introduced Statutory Panchayati system. But because of the official recognition of the Statutory Panchayat the old system is fading away. Further, at the *Gram Panchayat* and *Anchal Samiti* levels, even in some districts of the State in *Zilla Parishad* level, the tribal people got entries in all the tiers of the Panchayat System though that may not be quite adequate in cases of all the districts of the State. But in tribal concentrated districts of the State the representation of the tribal people in Panchayat is not negligible. On an enquiry it is found that the opinion of the tribal people are given due weightage in Panchayat bodies in relation to the development and other activities. This is a healthy sign. Further, our field study reveals that the young tribal members of the *Gram Panchayat* quite often consult and seek the advice of the traditional leaders prior to introduction or adoption of new measures through Panchayat. This healthy and cooperative attitude is acting as a fillip and helping in neutralising the zone of conflict and tension. The Santals, being the largest tribe of the State with sufficient exposures are taking a leading role in this respect.

The Santal society was subjected to many social movements mainly of reformistic type. Very recently a reversal trend is noticeable in which the splinter groups formed in the past, are trying to get into the core element of the society. In doing so political instruments are being used to establish their lost identity. In certain pockets of Santal concentration in West Bengal, Bihar and Orissa peasant movements started and crystallysed and peasant unions were formed. In the process of these movements some elements of violence were observed which challenged the age-old authority. The neo-literates among them started taking leadership in different socio-cultural and political movements to overcome their identity crises.

Oraon

As stated earlier the Oraon is the second largest tribal community of West Bengal. They were brought to Sunderban area of deltaic Bengal to reclaim forest land and the tea garden areas of North Bengal to work as labourers from Chotanagpur plateau during the middle of last century. In both the areas they now speak in *Sadri* dialect. As in the case of many facets of their life, changes have also taken place in their socio-political institutions. Each Oraon village has its own *Gram Panchayat* (village council) which is now-a-days mainly concerned with settling minor socio-religious disputes. The *Parha Panchayat* (inter-village council) does not exist at present. Previously, traditional Panchayat used to play a dominant role in settling disputes in all matters of public as well as private life of the Oraons, but at present it plays a very insignificant role. Many of the Oraons are found to approach law courts or police when the judgment of the village council goes against them. The Oraon traditional *Panch* of Sunderban area generally consists of a *Rajmoral* (Headman), a *Mantri* (Assistant and Advisor to *Rajmoral*), Members (village elders membership not fixed), a*Chowkidar* (messenger). The post of the *Rajmoral* (Headman) in hereditary. But on number of occasions it is found that the hereditary leadership is overthrown by the personal efficiency and influence. The *Rajmoral* selects the Assistant Headman known as the *Mantri* considering his status, influence over the people etc. The members are selected from the village elders considering the above characteristcs by the *Rajmoral* in consultation with the *Mantri*, and other village influentials. The *Chowkidar* or the messenger is selected by the Panchayat. The office bearers alongwith the members have to administer an oath, in the name of *Dharma* or *Bhagwan* after their selection, in front of the assembled villagers, that they will be loyal to their purpose and refrain from any sort of injustice while taking a decision or making any judgement. Non regular members of the Panchayat may take part in the discussions as and when required or called for (Das & Raha, 1963 : 227-234).

With the introduction of the new Panchayat Raj System (village self Government) the traditional Panch has almost lost its hold over the community. Under the natural law changes started taking place in the Oraon life in their homeland of Chotanagpur Plateau as a normal phenomenon. But in spite of this, the Oraons maintained equilibrium in their life through their socio-political institution of Panchayat (village organisation) and *Parha* (inter-village organisation) and *Parha* Federations (inter-*Parha* organisations). To crush their inner-strength the British Administration took some measures and imposed certain restrictions which directly or indirectly affected in the effective functioning of the village and intervillage organisations as well as the institutions nurtured by the Oraons through generations. A new element *Mahato* (selected by British Administration) as secular Head of the village council, responsible for collecting revenues, was introduced. Thus changes took place in the traditional *Panch* of the Oraons in their original homeland. That process of change accelerated when they were uprooted and brought over to Sunderban and tea garden areas of Bengal as labourers, where they started new settlements in new socio-economic, cultural and physical environment. Further, with the introduction of Statutory Panchayat and other legal, development and administrative measures during the post-Independence era, the traditional *Panch* lost whatever hold it had on the community. The statutory Panchayat at the village, as well as Anchal (Block) and Zilla (District) levels has been well accepted by the Oraons because they were once accustomed with such structure of Panchayat at different organizational levels in their own traditional way, which however, had no legal status, but the organisation of the present set-up enjoys better position because of its official recognition. In many of the Oraon concentrated areas the Oraon youths got entry in the statutory Panchayat bodies and they have a say in their affairs of development. The traditional community *Panch* exerts its influence to a very limited extent and that too in some socio-religious affairs of importance. In tea plantation areas the traditional Oraon *Panch* started loosing its hold since long. Now-a-days it is almost defunct.

Lepchas

The Lepchas are a Mongoloid tribal group concentrated mainly in the Darjeeling District of West Bengal. Their language is *Rong*. It is believed that the Lepchas settled in Sikkim sometimes between ninth and thirteenth century, and it became a political entity in the fifth decade of the seventeenth century when the Lama of Lhasa, with the aid of two other Lamas, converted the people of Sikkim into the Buddhism and appointed Phuntsog Namgyal to be the first King. Since then a number of Kings came into power in Sikkim. In 1835, the King of Sikkim 'presented' the Hills of Darjeeling to the East India Company 'out of friendship' for the Governor General of India, Lord William Bentinck. At present Sikkim is one of the States of India. Darjeeling is one of the Seventeen districts of the State of West Bengal.

Though the Lepchas were the original inhabitants of this area they were gradually outnumbered and over dominated by the alien rulers and people like the Tibetans, Bhutanese, Nepalese and others from the historic past in their original homeland. Contact with these people brought several changes in the structure and functioning of their society and culture. With the advent of the British rule over this part of the country rapid changes started taking place with the introduction of tea gardens etc. The area as a health resort and tourist spot attracted people from different parts of the country. The Nepalese were encouraged to settle in this area in large numbers to make the hilly land cultivable with their hard labour as well as for different infrastructures. The Nepali speaking communities exerted great influence on their life and activities. At present almost all the Lepchas are well converted in Nepali language. During post-Independence era several development measures brought further changes in their socio-economic life and outlook. The Lepchas mainly profess Christianity and Buddhism or Lamaism, the religions which they adopted from their British and Tibetan rulers. Their indigenous beliefs and practices still play a significant role at the submerged level. Keeping these facts in the background the role of traditional Panchayat in their present day life is mentioned below in brief.

Previously the village council of the lepchas was present in each village, but now-a-days in many of the villages these do not exist. In those villages where the ethnic councils still exists these are found in vestigeal form. At present these are more or less functionless, only internal disputes of minor nature are settled and dates, times etc. of important socio-religious festivals are fixed by the traditional village councils. The village council among the Lepchas was more popularly known as *Tyang Gang Sa Achiran Matbu*. Which means council of seven for administering justice. The head of the council was known as Lachren and assistant to the headmen as *Tyangsa Aring Matbu*. Under them were the village elders who acted as council members. In the past the village council used to impose heavy fines and inflict severe punishments to the person who dared to violate the society's norms and customs. The village headman (who was also known as *Tassa* or *Patnyom* or *Mondal*) used to collect the land revenue and even used to fix the land revenue in consultation with the village council. Revenue was usually paid from the farm produce.

The Lepchas are numerically a less dominant community. They are dominated by the Nepali communities in every sphere of activities. They suffer from a psychological complex of a loosing race. Their representations in the Statutory Panchayat at all the three tiers starting from village to district levels (Gram Sabha, Anchal Samities and Zila Parishad) are negligible, though the presence of 'literates' among them is quite high in comparison to other non-Mongoloid tribal groups. A considerable section of educated persons among them belong to Christian section who are mainly urban dwellers. Population strength alongwith political consciousness, organisational ability, leadership, extent of exposures and education are some of the key factors which have helped the Nepali population to take the leading role in the instrument of decision making in this area. In that context the Lepchas are no match to the Nepali speaking population (Das, 1978 : 125).

Toto

'Totopara', a cluster of three small hillocks at the foot-hills of the Himalayas, the only tract of land where a small tribal group of about nine hundred people known as the Totos live, is a small village situated in the Madarihat Police Station of Alipurduar, sub-division of Jalpaiguri District. The Totos are Mongoloid tribal group included within the schedule under the broad term 'Bhutia'. Previously, the place was under the control of the Bhutia. The Totos were sent to this village by the Bhutias about eight generations ago and they settled down here by expelling the Rabhas towards eastern direction. In the sixties of the last century it came under the domination of the British. It was the British Policy to keep Totopara as a sort of reserve of the Totos--allowing no other people to settle there. The whole area of *mouza* (village) comprising about 3.12 sq. miles was recorded in the name of *Toto Mandal* or chief on behalf of the whole community during the first settlement operation conducted by Sunders in 1889-94. Due to some malpractice by the Toto chief, portion of the community land went to the possession of the outsiders. Noticing this lapse on the part of the chief, the State Government took steps in 1970's to vest rights of land to individual (Totos). The ethnic environment of the Totos was completely different about two generations ago when the inhabitants were solely Totos. At present there are good number of the Nepali families living in different hamlets of Totopara. The Totos do not lead a secluded life at present as in the past. Due to several developmental activities during the post-Independence era the area is no more isolated from the rest of the country. All these have resulted in bringing changes in their mode of living and thinking.

The traditional Toto council comprises the *Kali Mondal, Panchayat*, Messengers and the*Chowkidar*. Previously, the office of the *Kaji* and the *Mondal* were held by the same person. The office of the *Mondal* was separated to cope with the growing complications of work when the territory was transferred to the jurisdiction of British from that of the Bhutia. The *Kaji* is generally regarded as the religious head of the Totos. The post is hereditary, the *Kaji* is to settle in consultation with village elders, any question connected with the manner and social customs. The *Mondal* is the secular chief of the village. The post is hereditary. The *Mondal* settles, in consultation with village elders, any dispute of land etc. among the villagers. The main duty of the Panchayat in the past was to assess *Chowkidari* tax and realise it. But at present all matters with regard to breach of law and order in the village *e.g.* quarrel between two Totos etc. are settled within the village by the Panchyat in consultation with the village elders. The 'Messengers' are to carry the *Kaji's* as well as the *Mondal's* summons to villagers. The *Chowkidar* works under the general supervision of the Panchayat.

During the *Puja* of Kaleswar (*Mahakali*) it is customary to hold meeting of the Panchayat. Cases are tried and the judgment is obeyed as it is pronounced within the holy compound. The court is known as *Dem-sha*. About ten or twelve village elders form the *Panchayat*. The offences tried are of very simple nature connected with socio-religious affairs. The Panchayat sits for a day or two in the evening and all the cases are disposed of. Day to day arbitration is done by the *Mondal* with the assistance of the*Chowkidar* and other elders (Das, 1969 : 101-104).

There are a few Toto members in the statutory *Gram Panchayat* but the Nepalese dominate there. The Toto members are the influential members of their society and they often found to exploit their position for their own benefit. The young Toto generation is gradually becoming politically conscious. There remains ample scopes to utilise profitably this generation in the development of their own community.

Rabha

The Rabhas are mainly the inhabitants of Cooch Bihar and Jalpaiguri Districts of West Bengal. They may be divided into two distinct groups from the ecological point of view--(i) those living in the villages having agriculture as their major subsistence activity and (ii) those living in the Reserve Forest *Bastees* being employed as forest labourers by the Department of Forest of the State Government. They are passing through a phase of matripatri culture complex. The cultural pattern of the village Rabhas is quite akin to the dominant neighbouring Rajbanshi community whereas forest dwellers have still retained many of the traditional socio-religious beliefs, custom and practice (Das & Raha, 1967 : 1-2).

The activities of modern political parties are very much restricted in the case of the Forest Rabhas whereas ideologies of various political parties have exerted a great influence on the Village Rabhas.

The village council among the Forest Rabhas is known as *Marab Sen* i.e. "Council of Elders" consisting of the elderly and able persons of the *Bastees*. The officials Headman is known by the term *Mondal* (selected by the Forest Department) who at present in majority of cases happens to be the traditional Headman i.e.*Pare*. The*Mondal* as the official Headman enjoys more power vested upon him by the Forest Department in comparison to the *Pare,* the traditional Headman whose power is very much restricted. A *Mondal* enjoys more acreage of land and some other facilities which the Pare does not get. The selection of a member in the village council depends on the decision of the council itself. The *Deosi* and the *Dhami* (the priests) also act as the members of the council by virtue of their traditional position. Disputes of socio-religious nature are generally attended by the council, but it has no jurisdiction over disputes of criminal nature which are taken care of by the Forest authority. In the case of inter-*Bastees* disputes the meeting of the joint council of the different *Bastees* is convened. The *Pares* of different Bastees along with some important members attend such meetings.

The post of *Pare* as also that of the *Mondal* among the Forest Rabhas at present is not hereditary. The daughter's husband (heiress) used to succeed such office previously. Now the selection is made on the basis of efficiency, and that is done by the Forest authority. As a *Mondal* now enjoys more economic power than the *Pare*, the Rabhas are found inclined to select *Mondal* as the *Pare*, there the office of the traditional headman (*Pare*) has been merged with the newly created headman of the administration (Mondal).

As in the case of Forest Rabha the Village Rabhas had also their own full fledged village council i.e. *Marab Sen.* All types of socio-religious matters of the community were looked after by this council. At present the village council has a very limited function that too concerning socio-religious affairs. Due to the influence of neighbouring communities and political ideologies, the Village Rabhas in general, are less concerned with happenings around them i.e. concerning their fellow villagers. This is not the case with the Forest Rabhas where a social or religious offence affects the whole *Bastee* as they lead a comparatively secluded life under the control of Forest authority. The village Rabhas are well acquainted with the present day statutory Panchayat system and have accepted it whereas this is not the case with the Forest Rabhas (Das, Raha & Dey, 1990 : 219-227).

III

As in other parts of India changes took place in the structure and function of the socio-political institutions of the tribal people to varied extent, in the State of West Bengal also mainly due to the following major factors-normal process of acculturation, introduction of new administrative system along with different laws and orders and legal system during the British Administration and also utilisation of the indigenous political institutions of the tribals with slight modifications in the structure and function mainly for collection of revenues and maintenance of liaison between the tribal and the local administration; during the post Independence period on account of several constitutional safeguards, protective and ameliorative measures and also intensive development activities changes started taking place in every facets of their life including their institutions and they have gradually been brought to the main fold of national life and activities; emergence of new elite class due to spread of modern education gave rise to conflicting position between the traditional leaders and neo-literates in relation to the decision making affair.

Article 40 of the Constitution of India contained under the Directive Principles of State Policy lays down that the State shall take steps to organise village Panchayats and endow them with such powers and authority as may be necessary to enable them to function as units of self-Government. This resulted in the introduction of Statutory Panchayat system in different States of India. Thus, the West Bengal Panchayat Act 1957 and the West Bengal Zilla Parishads 1963 and later on for reorganisation of Panchayats in rural areas of West Bengal an enactment of the West Bengal Panchayat Act, 1973 were introduced. Direct elections on a political party basis to the three-tiers of *Gram Panchayats,* Panchyat samities and Zilla Parishads are held after every four year cycle. Under Section 210 of West Bengal Panchayat Act, 1973 the State Government has been vested with the power of appointing two members of Schedule Castes or Schedule. Tribes and two women to be members of any *Gram Panchayat,* Panchayat Samiti and Zilla Parishad to represent their interests if such representation could not be secured through direct elections.

The impact of statutory Panchayat has been profound on the life of the rural folk including the tribals of the State. As the Panchayat is primarily responsible for planning and implementation of development programmes from village level upwards, it automatically gets importance and weightage from the people. All these factors are directly or indirectly responsible for making the tribal people politically conscious and bringing them under the fold of one or the other political party. There are twelve I.T.D.P. areas constituting 33 units covering 5,823 mouzas of the State where half of the tribal pupulation (50.60 per cent) live. In this tribal concentrated area, the tribal people play to a certain extent a positive role in relation to the management of their own affair. It is found that their representations in the *Gram Panchayat* are not negligible though it is not encouraging at the Anchal Samiti level. At the initial stage i.e., during 1958's representations of the tribal folk in the Statutory Panchayat was almost nil but later on their representations in the Panchayat bodies are found gradually improving and that is due to their political consciousness and impact of the welfare and development programmes implemented at the grass root level.

At present attempt is being made to examine the practicability and feasibility of blending suitably the traditional leadership with the statutory Panchayat bodies for making this peoples' insititution more effective, meaningful and purposive for them.

References

Das, A.K. and M.K. Raha. 1963 : *The Oraon of Sunderban*, Spl. Sr. No. 3 of the Bull. of C.R.I., Calcutta.

Das, A.K. and Raha, M.K. 1967 : *The Rabhas of West Bengal*, Spl. Sr. No. 9 of the Bull. of C.R.I., Calcutta.

Das, A.K. 1969 : *The Totos*, Spl. Sr. No. 11 of the Bull. of C.R.I., Calcutta.

1978 : *The Lepchas of West Bengal*, Editions Indian, Calcutta.

Das, A.K., Raha, M.K. *and S.K.De* 1990 : *Tribal Situation in West Bengall* Firma K. L. Mukhoopadhyay, Ltd., Calcutta.

De, R. 1988 : Santal Tribal Polity : *An Enquiry* in *Asian Studies* 6(2).

Government of West Bengal, n.d. : *Panchayat in West Bengal*, Calcutta.

Ray, U.K., Das A.K. and Bisu, S.K. 1967 : *To be with Santals*, Spl. Sr. No 9 of the Bull. of C.R.I., Calcutta.

13

CULTURE AND POLITICS IN TRIBAL BIHAR

R. M. SARKAR

I

The political behaviour in human communities takes a particular pattern in the background of the socio-cultural situation. The Political conciousness and its various perspectives have got their fullest development within the framework of the social structure of the community concerned, conditioned by economic development, mental situation as well as historical factors. Thus the political organization of a community is essentially based on variegated traditional concepts of the way of life relation to the concerned people. Culture of a group or community has got its specific role in the stopping of the value pattern of these people concerned which do a great deal in formulating the group behaviour-patterns. The political organisation of any human community is characterized by "a common membership and loyalty, shared traditions and welfare, and a system of external relation" (Kessings, 1958 : 287). All these basic elements of behaviour are the outcome of the group actions conditioned by cultural traditions.

Society is regarded as the end product of the culturally shaped human populations. The organization of any kind in this society is consciously based on learned and well-established patterns of conduct, or, in other words, on culture. Culture works on different perspectives and it responds to different settings. Human nature and behaviour get their shape through the complicated interactions of genetic, environmental and socio-cultural features. Thus the political behaviour of the human communities can best be understood in the background of their development in varied eco-cultural settings. The leadership patterns are seen to be specifically oriented by the interactions with various components of the environment.

Bihar is a land of diversities. This particular landmass is characterized by glorious and inspiring cultural heritage. It is witnessed by the unfolding of human genius which spread its "manifold petals from the days of remote antiquity adding to the splendid stock of "India's magnificent culture" (Datta, 1967 : 4). The tribal areas in Bihar are interspersed with forests, hills and rivers with fertile valleys. Chotanagpur and Santal Parganas regions of Bihar are the homeland of the tribal people who represent different levels of socio-cultural development. These two tribal concentrated regions are rich in natural wealth--the underground part is impregnated with varied mineral resources where the land surface in covered by forest wealth. It is said that in these regions history and pre-history move hand in hand. Throughout Chotanagpur region one can see a gradual process of change through time in respect of its socio-economic character. The tribal villages had developed into urban settings which in turn got the shape of industrial horizons. These changing situations have brought effective attraction in life-history of the people.

Chotanagpur and Santal Paraganas regions of Bihar are the abodes of variegated tribal people who depict all levels of cultural developments starting from nomadic food gathering stage upto the conspicuous patterns of industrialization in the strict sense of the term. The Birhors of Chotanagpur are still continuing the age-old food gathering stage of subsistence. There are Malers in the Santal Parganas region who practice shifting-hill cultivation known as the *Khallu*. The Munda, Oraon, Santal and the Ho are successful settled agriculturists and whose agricultural operations go parallel with those of peasant societies in rural areas of Bihar. The members of a section of these tribes have made their entries into the industrialized spheres of the State. The mining and industrial centres of the region have offered varied jobs to the tribal groups specially to the Ho, Munda, Oraon and the Santals. The Chotanagpur plateau is characterized by having multiple veins of different kinds of minerals known to the indigenous communities from long time past. There were some tribal communities like the Asurs, the Lohra and others who could exploit the local minerals and could extract these in an indigenous way. In Chotanagpur region "mining and quarrying activities have taken place at large scale in several areas and pockets, providing ample opportunity to register employment under these activities" (Singh, 1986 : 1960).

As per their economic levels the tribal people of Bihar can be divided into four distinct categories viz. the forest-hunting type like the Birhors and the Korwas; the hill-cultivation type exemplified by the Malers of the Santal Parganas; the Plains-agricultural type like the Mundas, Oraons, Hos and the Santals; and the Simple-artisan type which includes the Asurs, Lohras, Chik-Baraiks and the Mehalis. The typology of the tribal Bihar has been made by Vidyarthi (1968: 129-30), and it has been developed in the context of the phenomena like ecology, economy and modes of behaviour. The tribal people of Chotanagpur and Santal Parganas were originally the migrated population from other regions of India. The Mundas were the first settlers in the Chotanagpur region. They reached Chotanagpur from north-western India and started clearing the forests and valleys which provided them lands for cultivation. Through a continuous process of clearing the forests, the Munda families together constituted here *Khuntkatti hatu* or the village of the original settlers. As time went on, they were able to develop union of several villages, called by the name of *patti*. The chief of the *patti* was known as *manki*, The Mundas thus settled themselves in the midst of hills and forests of Chotanagpur and "in this way, in the heart of the deep dense forests where hitherto the rays of the sun had hardly penetrated, smiling villages grew up, and went on steadily multiplying" (Roy, 1912 : 114).

The Oraons represent the second biggest tribal group of Chotanagpur who reached this country in the remote past but later than the Mundas. The Oraons by virtue of their better knowledge in agriculture and better types of equipments, multiplied rapidly and become predominant tribal group in the north-western part of Ranchi plateau" (Singh, 1986 : 115). They engaged themselves in the extensive clearance of forests and by means of this the Mundas were pushed towards the southern and eastern parts of the country. These people were followed by the Hos, the Kharias, the Bhuinyas, and similar other major tribal groups. Besides this the small tribal communities like the Birhors, the Korwas, the Karmali, the Asur, the Lohra and others. entered the region at different times and gradually they were assimilated with the soil and water of the locality.

The Santal Pargana region was totally covered by dense forests and inaccessible hilly tracts. The Paharias were the original settlers of their region. They took shelter in the midst of jungle and passed their life as primitive hunting-gathering community. Their extreme primitiveness are still reflected in many features of their way of life. The Santals were the new comers to that area and they, during the second half of the 18th century and the early 19th century started migrating to the *Damin-i-koh* or skirts of the hills of Rajmahal from various parts of the country. *Damin-i-koh* was an area formed in 1832-33 by the British administrators and which was distributed among the districts of Bhagalpur, Murshidabad and Birbhum. On reaching there the Santals brought the whole region under cultivation by virtue of their hard labour and profound seriousness. In due course there developed picturesque villages which became the peaceful abodes of these simple-minded and art loving tribal people. Thus the Santal Pargana region was the outcome of the integrated activities of the Santals who proved themselves as befitting groups of people in the midst of nature.

II

The tribal people with their diversities have tried their level best to adjust themselves with the surroundings. Their way of life has taken particular shape conditioned by its interactions with the ecological settings. The tribe of Bihar are forest-economy oriented people. These people have developed not only a friendly with the vest natural surroundings but also a sort of reverential attitude in course of their living. This attitude has witnessed deep penetration in the broad-based cultural life of the tribes of Bihar. In order to understand the patterns of cultural traditions of the tribes of Bihar, an attempt to analyse the basic features of the way of life of a few important tribes would be highly effective in this issue. The life of the Birhors, the best representative of the forest-hunting type, is inextricably interwoven with the forest. The whole economy of the Birhors tribe revolves round hunting in the jungle and collection of chop fibres (Bauhenia scanden) for making ropes. The nomadic nature of the Birhors is the direct reflection of their mode of existence. The migration of the Birhors is thus conditioned by the availability of these materials in the particular region. Their movement, most of the time is effected in a cyclical order the *tandas* which is composed of eight to ten leaf huts or *kumbas* are manifestations of the organized life of the Birhors, on the other hand, the Birhors need closeness to the market and human localities for the easy disposal of the forest products on which they live.

In consequence of their rigid connection with and total dependence on the forest, the Birhors have developed an overall attitude of submission on the forest environment and they very naturally try to get their problems solved in the midst of forest. The very nature around them has made these people staunch believers in the supernatural world and "the most important among these are the spirits of their original native hills or forests whom they call Buru-Bongas or Ora Bonga" (Roy 1987 : 138). Of late, forest-based culture of Birhors has faced a challenge due to the implementation of the enactment centreing round the National Forest Policy which bars the Birhors from random utilization of the forest hunting in the jungle and cutting down trees for making *Kumbas*. The Birhors are now being resettled by the Govt. of Bihar through well-organized scheme for development. But in spite of all the facilities provided by the Government the Birhors are far from being sedentarized with the agricultural lands allotted to them and also the brick-built permanent house constructed for them. The clash between the present situation and the traditional culture is the root cause of the failure of the Birhors Rehabilitation scheme. These people are originally freedom-loving which has developed and accelerated with the boundless and free forest atmosphere and they are always reluctant to surrender this unfathered freedom for any worldly pleasure." (Sarkar, 1986).

The Malers of the Rajmahal Hills in the Santal Parganas practise slash and burn cultivation known by the name *Khallu*. The forest is the provider of the principal economic base for life. Being the original settlers of the virgin Santal Pargana forest region these people had established intimate connection, from the very earliest times, with the vast nature. This vastness of nature is the creator of many supernatural beliefs and practices in the life of these people. The Malers of the Rajmahal Hills are highly dependent on nature in the maintenance of their organic and super-organic life. Their total culture is specifically characterized by the nature and spirit. The spirit world is the resultant of their close interactions with the vast and colourful nature. The rehabilitation programme launched by the Govt. of Bihar, since 1954 meant to bring them from the hilly tracts and to settle on the plains, has cut a sorry figure. This geographical rehabilitation is against their cultural traditions and many a time the Paharias go "to the extent of stating that it compelled by the government to go down on the plains, they would prefer to face bullets and die on the hills rather then lead a comfortable life on the plains" (Vidyarthi; 1963:177). Like the Malers, the life of the Korwas of Palamau is centred round shifting hill cultivation known by the name of *beora.* In addition to this they collect a kind of creeper from the jungle for making ropes for selling these in the local markets. The well-knit forested region of Palamau had been supplying necessary requirements for their living.

But the life of the tribal people living on the undulating plains or plateau is out and out influenced by settled cultivation. These people follow a different pattern of life in the well-developed villages characterized by mixed population which include both the tribals as well as the non-tribals. They have got an economy based agriculture though there are good many problems faced by them in consequence of the factors like land alienation and land fragmentation. The agricultural technology is ill-developed and there is no scope for irrigational facilities. But the agrarian people exemplified by the Mundas, Oraons, Santals, Hos, Bhumijes and the Kisans, are highly kin-oriented. A close co-operation between different kin groups are to be seen amongst them. Within the families there is always a distinct division of labour and a very good understanding prevails amongst the different family members. The Chotanagpur tribals are specifically cooperating in native and in this social system one feels for the other. There are instances of exchange of labour in house building in agricultural activities and in family level ceremonies. The propitiation to nature is the traditional feature of the way of life of these people. The village sacred grove of these tribal people is always represented by the large trees of the forest and it is believed that in this natural set up the village tutelary deity resides in a heavenly pleasure. Various other deities in the tribal pantheons are believed to reside and roam about in the forested regions.

The life of the tribals belonging to the simple artisan type is very much related to the natural phenomenon as these people collect various raw materials direct from the nature to prepare different objects of arts and crafts. The Asurs of Ranchi and Palamou district were one time famous for their iron smelting profession. They used to practise slash and burn cultivation on the hilly tracts also. In spite of their continuous source of natural wealth they could not compete with the factories which sprang up in the neighbouring region. As a natural consequences the Asurs have lost their traditional occupation and have undergone drastic disorganization. The situation has made them to face economic crisis and thereby cultural upset. The section of the Asurs such as the Birjihas is also dependent on the natural resources of the forest for their livelihood and., therefore, they are more closely associated with the forested regions. The Birjihas are the good collectors of lac, wax, honey and various roots and tubers. The Lohras of Chotanagpur live on blacksmithy and manufacture axe, sickle, arrowheads and plough shares. These are regularly sold in the market to the tribal people. The Lohras collect raw materials from the natural surroundings through personal collection or through purchase from other communities. The *Mahlis* are traditional basket makers. They make baskets from bamboo slits. These bamboos are collected from the forests through the payment of taxes to the forest authorities or purchased from the local owners. The Mahli crafts is of special importance to the tribal people of this locality because they require various bamboo containers, traps etc. for their daily requirements. The Chikbaraiks are weavers who engage themselves in the weaving of clothes. These clothes are sold in the weekly markets and the tribal people are dependent on these clothes. Thus the artisans tribes as mentioned above are involved in their traditional crafts, and to maintain this practice they are to depend on various natural resources and thus their relation with the nature is intimate and amicable. But the recent changing situations, resulted due to the starting of large scale factories, enactment of the forest policy and the introductions of powerloom etc. have brought a thorough alteration in the very philosophy of life of these people. Most of the craftsmen in the region under reference have been transformed into daily wage labourers and naturally their indigenous cultural perspective is in the process of rapid change.

The case of the industrialized tribal people is somewhat different. This tribal region especially the Chotanagpur belt is now in a rapid process of industrialization. A large number of tribal people belonging to the Santal and Ho communities enrolled themselves in these industrial units as wage earners. The industrialized tribal groups do not find any interest to follow the traditional culture of the tribal people. Thus changed tribal people cannot respond to the call of the vast and free nature from the core of their hearts. A special value attitude system has therefore come into force especially amongst the younger generation of the people concerned.

III

The traditional tribal political system of Bihar is highly characterized by the close co-operation of the people, mutual understanding amongst themselves, respect to elderly persons, dependence on spiritual powers, adherence to the natural perspectives, as well as supernaturalism. Both the sacred and profane spheres are similarly consulted in the matter of running of active administration of a village community. Thus among the Oraons the village is administered by two principal officers--the *pahan* and the *mahato*. The former is the religious head and the later is secular head. These two posts have ritualistic status and officials always come from aristocratic lineages. The selection of these officers are done through supernatural aid-by the performance of magic *sup* or winnowing fan. There is a strong belief amongst the people that the appointment of these two important officers are laid in the hands of the supernatural powers and, therefore, they have got concrete supernatural background. The *pahan* tries to maintain amicable relationship between the people and the spirit world which, according to them, is a must in retaining peace and order in the village society. The *mahato*, on the other hand, is responsible for the protection of the village community from external disturbances. He always keeps constant watch to maintain good relationship with the outside world. As a chief organizer of all the essential public works in the village the *mahato* pledges to honour the public opinion all through the time. But the *pahan* and the *mahato* have got their limitation. They are not in a position to exercise jural authority. They must perform the judicial functions with the help of the traditional village *panchayat* which is a regular council formed by the elderly members belonging to all the lineages. The Oraons believe that the Dharmes--the Supreme God--is the highest authority to administer justice and after whom comes the *panchayat*. At the time of taking any oath, an Oraon swears in the name of Dharmes as well as in the name of *panch* i.e. *panchayat*. Thus *panchayat* runs in the line with celestial authority like the Dharmes.

The *hatu-panchayat* and the *parha panchayat* of the Mundas are the two important political institutions. The *hatu panchayat* is provided with an age-long tradition as well as indigenous norms and behaviour patterns. It is organized by three officers like the *munda, mahato* and the *pahan*. It deals with the settlement of disputes that are connected with the village concerned. When the matters go outside the boundary of the village, it is the responsibility of the *parha panchayat* to settle these. The *panchayats* are formed by the influential and elderly persons of the village. The *parha* is the characteristic indigenous political institutions in tribal Bihar. A number of villages unite to form this institution. Among the Santals, it is known by the name of *pargana,* which is administered by a *parganait*. The *parganait* functions as a custodian of all social functions of his area. His council settles the disputes. The Santal village organization is a well-knit affair. The *manjhi* is the headman and he looks after all the village affairs. He is assisted by other officers like the *paramanik,* the *jogmanjhi* and others. The *naike* or *priest* is the religious specialist. He is assisted by the *kudam naike.* There is one village messenger who is known as *gorait*. Among the Ho the *Parha* is known as the *pir,* which is administered by a *manki* or divisional headman. Each village is controlled by a headman known the *munda.* Generally the *manki* and the *munda* are selected from the dominant *killi* or clan. The *munda* is assisted by the *dakua;* the *dihuri* officiates in the religious domain. The *parha panchayat* among the *Kharias* is known as the *Kutumba Sabha.* The village is administered by the headman who is known as the *Pradhan.* Sometimes, village panchayat is seen to be presided over by the *Dihuri* who is the religious head. The Mal Paharia village is similarly administered by the *manjhi* who is assisted by the *Paramanik* and the *Gorait.* In this way the tribes of Chotanagpur and Santal Parganas have made organized attempts to give proper and healthy shape to the political institutions. Even the nomadic Birhors maintain the administrative head--the *Naya* who works as priest as well as secular headman of the *tanda.* The *Mati* is the medicine man who is the sole incharge in the treatment and cure of diseases which are caused by varied natural and supernatural agencies.

Different instances of the tribal political institutions their composition and their working principles among the tribes of Bihar indicate that they are patterned in a more or less similar fashion which is principally characterized by group consciousness, specific regard to the original settlers and maintenance of the hereditary transference of the office. These political institutions of the Bihar tribes are exclusively constituted and organized on the basis of their philosophy of friendliness with the surrounding people, their ultimate desire to live peacefully in the midst of the jungle infested region guided by the pantheon of deities and spirits. Their political units as well as working procedures are specifically influenced by divine assistance and this is why the political organizations of the tradition-bound Bihar tribes are free from misunderstandings in, irregular affairs and clashes. Because of this fact the tribal people have got profound love and respect for these indigenous political units and their deep faith in these has gradually been increased due to some sorts of supernatural sanctions behind these. This phenomenon is the result of a specific cultural pattern, and at times it is so great that even after drastic changes in the socio-political system, during the present period, the traditional "offices persist even in those villages which have been completely absorbed in the urban environment of Ranchi City" (Vidyarthi, 1965 : 180).

IV

Being developed and nurtured within the vast nature characterized by the green vegetation, hills and dales as well as the rivers and water-falls, these tribal people in Chotanagpur and Santal Pargana regions have specifically become peaceloving and adjustable. But there were occasions in the past when these tribal people could not maintain their philosophy of peaceloving attitude, and circumstances compelled them to put direct resistance to the unjust activities of other people. It led to serious disturbances and bloodshed. The tribes of Bihar are characteristically freedom loving to a great extent. The deep and green forest as well as the vast open sky provided them this freedom consciousness, and when it was in danger, they rose up to fight for that situation. Thus amongst the Birhor tribes we meet with a number of uprisings which have resulted due to the clash between cultural values and the new policies of the then Government. There were many occasions in the past when these simple minded tribals were exploited in a number of ways by some unscrupulous people. That continuous exploitation enraged the tribal people who ultimately raised their voices against such evil doers. The tribal people of Bihar are basically honest in nature and they believe in establishing amicable relationship with their neighbours. It is the basic pattern of their culture. But when, in the past, such philosophy of them was crumbled down by the local non-tribal groups, the tribal people could not tolerate it. Thus they followed their own course to solve grievances in their own way.

The tribal people in Chotanagpur and the Santal Parganas started their life in the midst of more or less in accessible hilly tracts and jungle-infested regions when they developed a solitary and peaceful existence of them. They could establish their traditional polity in accordance with their own socio-economic perspective of life. But certain socio-economic and political changes in the country as a whole caused a great deal of disturbances in the indigenous thinking pattern of the tribals of Chotanagpur region--the heart of tribal Bihar. The tribals of Bihar experienced a broad-based political movements and revolts during different periods of the 19th century. When in the early part of this century Chotanagpur was brought under the direct administration of the East India Company, it resulted a clash in the cultural values of the indigenous people. The alien administrative system developed a particular situation by the creation of Zamindars and for which the traditional *Bhuinhari* or *Khuntkatti* system of land tenure of the tribal people was very much affected. The tribal people inhabiting this region could not tolerate the intervention of the alien rulers and the Zamindars to dominate in their traditional homeland. The land tenure system devised by the Mundas and the Oraons was influenced by their own traditional thinking. Land is always regarded by these people as the symbol of authority which is believed to have integrated into the way of life of people. It is never thought of only a means for economic basis--it is the spiritual shelter so carefully devised by their ancestors. Thus besides economic linkage there are close linked association of social, cultural and ritualistic values with lands. It was only for that mentality the tribal people lodged their categorical protests in very strong nature when there was a threat to undermine their traditional land tenure system initiated by the original settlers of the country. This land tenure system worked through conspicuous geneological framework governed by the social structure of the tribe concerned. There was a close linkage between the lineage and the land, the lineages had an exclusive right over the land and in no circumstances that right could be waived. The landed properties were all along secured through ritualistic procedures and traditional norms which are handed down through generations without any interruptions. The introduction of the alien administrative system based on different sets of ideas and values in these tribal villages exerted a dead blow to the traditional *parha panchayat* system structured on the principle of engaging the representatives from the original settlers' families and old persons of the society. These two specific machineries for running village administration went under the control of the alien rulers and the Zamindars of the land created under the patronage of the British Raj. The repercussion of the tribal people concerned was far reaching. The tribal people of the region felt that the introduction of the new system was nothing but to neglect their age-old cultural traditions. Thus it was the question of sharing their own stand as human being--it was the delicate problematic situation to keep their cultural heritage alive; and their tradition-bound institutions for honourable life and living, needed their whole hearted patronage at the cost of anything. On going through the causes of breakout of all the small-scale and large-scale movements and uprisings amongst these tribal groups we can understand that all were rooted to the efforts to save and to continue the cultural traditions-based life-situation planned and organized by the indigenous tribal orientation.

The Kot insurrection to Chotanagpur got its root in 1820 when the tribal people rose upto make a sound protest against the foreign interference into the indigenous world of them. But in 1831-32 the revolt became widespread. Their principal grudge was against the *suds* and *dikus* or the outsiders like tax collectors and police officers. The migration of *thinkandars* of lessees in their territory enraged the tribal people as it was planned to neglect the traditional tribal system. The revolt was brought under control by the Britishers, and a year after Chotanagpur and other adjoining areas were brought under the jurisdiction of non-regulation area termed South-west Frontier Agency which after twenty years was renamed as Chotanagpur Division. The movement was thus a type of "protest against the inequalities resulting from the replacement of their traditional system of administration by the rapidly growing authority of their British rulers" (Datta, 1979 : 42).

The Santal insurrection of 1855-57 was a protest against large scale exploitation done on them by their non-tribal neighbours. This great insurrection "had its origin in the economic grievances of the Santals, due to the oppression of frauds committed on those simple-minded people..." (Datta : 1970 : 46). The newly formed *Damin-i-koh* locally was turned by the industrious tribal people into very fertile landmass. Various crops were raised abundantly, and within a very short period the Santals proved their ability in making the *Damin-i-Koh* a prosperous locality which attracted many outsiders to come and settle in *Damin-i-koh*. Their trade and money lending business brought them in close contact with the Santals. Shortly they could understand the nature and extent of simple-mindedness and sincerity of the Santals which they utilized mercilessly for fulfilling their evil designs. The Santals raised their voices against it and approached the administration for justice. But the alien administrative authority not only remained silent over the issue but also gave support to the traders and money lenders for obvious reasons. When the ill-treatment and oppressions reached their peak, the Santals under the guidance of their indigenous leaders Sidhu, Kanhu, Chand and Bhairab--became insurgents and challenged the oppressors. The British government had to face a great trouble in coping with the troublesome situation. This insurrection of the Santals brought some abrupt change in the outlook of the alien rulers on the Santals and a separate non-regulation district known as the Santal Parganas was formed.

The Sardar movement in Chotanagpur was the direct outcome of the improper and unsuccessful working of the Chotanagpur Tenure Act. Started in 1859 it was actually the agitators of the converted tribals (Christian) against the landlords. They refused to pay rent and wanted to stop system of forced labour and other means of exploitations. To drive away the intermediaries and exploiters, the Sardars appealed to alien rulers. But the British officers concerned did not understand the very mentality of the tribals in relation to their emotional connection with their ancestral lands as well as their nature of degradation from the prestigious *Bhuinnar* to the ordinary *raiyat*. Thus their appeal to bring their villages under the direct administrative touch of the Government after rejecting the intermediaries was not entertained by the alien rulers.

The Birsa movement of 1885-90 was the result of continuous discontent of the tribals of Chotanagpur through the ages. Birsa--the Munda young man--proved himself as a spiritual leader in fighting against all the misbehaviours done by the foreigners. The British rulers as well as the non-tribal immigrants to the Munda country. Chotanagpur became the land or exploitation during the closing phase of the 19th century by the non-tribal fortune-seekers; they came in large numbers as Zamindars and their agents, traders and money-lenders. As a result of this the integrity of the Munda villages got disturbed, the *Khuntkatti* tenure of ancestral land was largely damaged by the activities of the Zamindars. At that time the Christian missionaries were very active in planting an alien culture in the Munda villages causing dissensions in the traditional village life of the tribals. Birsa believed to have assisted by the supernatural powers, came out at the crucial period of Munda life, with a strong protest against the exploitation of those people. Birsait movement in Chotanagpur was rooted to the agrarian struggle and to save the indigenous culture of the tribals by establishing Birsa Raj, and in due course it became political in nature. But the British rulers soon arrested Birsa and his followers. After a long turmoil the movement was suppressed. Birsa met death in the prison of the British rulers; many of his followers were sentenced. In consequence of Birsa Movement the detailed survey and settlement operations were made during the period from 1902 to 1919 as a positive measure to minimise the discontent of the suffering Mundas. It followed the passing of the Chotanagpur Tenancy Act.

Then came the Tana Bhagat Movement which was the result of continuous exploitation faced by the tribals due to the oppressions of the *Zamindars* and negligence of the alien rulers. The movement was launched through the attempt of reformation of certain old patterns of life of the tribal communities by inflicting some new ideas. The Tana Bhagats made it a point to bring forth new faith based on certain effective measures for changed behaviour patterns for fighting out the exploiters and oppressors. They stopped the propitiation of many indigenous spirits in which animal sacrifice was essential, and gave up taking of animal food as well as liquor. The ploughing with bullocks was considered by them as cruelty to animals and consequently the practice was stopped. They refused in a body to work any more under the Zamindars, and payment of rent was subsequently stopped. Though this movement had a religious substratum, yet, in course of time, it became oriented in a political perspective. But, on the whole, it could not bring any positive effect to the problems faced by the tribal people for a long time. The Government took strong action to suppress the uprising and some provisions were made to give some reliefs to the tribals though the basic problems remained far from any effective solution.

The continuous discontent amongst the tribals of Chotanagpur and Santal Parganas ultimately gave rise to a situation which led to the formation of regional movement based on the trends of ethnicity and development. The integrated changes through the impact of Christianity amongst the Chotanagpur tribes caused the emergence of a new elite (Sachchidananda, 1979 : 240). The section of the enlightened tribals wanted permanent relief of the tribal people as a whole from age-long exploitation as well as over all development of the tribal life in their indigenous line of thinking. They came forward to launch a broad-based political movement characterized by regional autonomy. The educated section of the tribal people formed a political party known as the Jharkhand Party under the leadership of Jaipal Singh, a Munda leader, in the year 1938. It was formed with a specific intention to help exploited tribals in getting democratic political rights. The Jharkhand Party has got conspicuous speciality of its own and in comparison to the other movements it is considered as an organized and systematic tool for joint struggle to ameliorate the hazards and anxieties in the life of the tribals. The Jharkhand Party was rooted to a movement of the Christian students' organization in the year 1911-12. The main intention of that organization was to awaken the tribals to protect their own land and culture from the attack of the intruders. Efforts were made to raise their voices against all sorts of economic exploitation. With the march of time the character and activities of this political organization experienced changes. The Jharkhand movement became effective to a considerable extent because of the fact that it was always organized by educated persons with some experience in political situations of the country. There is a regional sentiment in Jharkhand, and the tracts inhabited by the tribals in parts of West Bangal, Orissa and Madhya Pradesh were included along with Chotanagpur landmass. Despite Christian domination of the party it was extensively influenced by the ideas and beliefs of the indigenous tribal background. There have always been specific demands for "more dominant role for the tribals and Chotanagpuris in regional administration and better educational facilities and more employment opportunities" (Singh, 1977: 324). The party concerned also has raised voice in the matter of restoration of alienated land and in taking practical measures for getting the unfortunate tribals free from age-long economic and social exploitations. But the Jharkhand party has to face factionalism owing to the separation of the Santals from the Munda-Oraon group. In the later part of the sixties, the emergence of the Bihar Prant Hul Jharkhand Party was the result of the withdrawals of the Santals from the parent body. In addition to all other problems of tribal exploitations, as experienced earlier, this faction of the Jharkhand Party puts forward a few localized demands like creation of a separate Santal Paragana Division and the utilization of Roman scripts for the Santali language. In due course another faction was resulted from it in the Santal Parganas which was called as the Progressive Hul Jharkhand Party. But owing to certain inevitable circumstances there was an alliance amongst the different factions forming the Jharkhand Mukti Morcha in the year 1973 with a basic intention for a separate Jharkhand State. During the recent period the activities of the Jharkhand Mukti Morcha have become heavily integrated and very much effective in the way of establishment of their basic claims. Thus through a process of transformation this political party has exposed itself as a regional organization from a mere ethnic movement during the past period.

Political organization and political movements as well as varied activities in the socio-political spheres amongst the tribal people of Bihar are thus principally oriented by their cultural traditions. Tribal people here are always alert in the maintenance of their indigenous patterns of life at any cost. They are, of course, not against the change but they do not like to create or support such situation that may endanger the patterns of their traditional values so far designed and nurtured by their ancestors. The forefathers are highly respected in tribal tradition and it is believed that until and unless they are blessed by them, the society of the descendants will not run in a proper way. The tribal culture in Bihar is characterized by the love of nature, friendliness with the surroundings, efforts for establishing amicable relation with the spirit world. These specific features in the world view of the Bihar tribes have given rise to a sort of "penetrating network of mutual interactions and an intimate inter-relation of nature, man and spirit" (Vidyarthi, 1963 : 175). For the depiction of tribal culture the integrating forces of Nature, Man and Spirit, in the daily life of the tribals are to be understood in an analytical perspective. This specific attitude is seen to be highly reflected in the formation and functioning of the traditional political institutions of the tribes of Bihar. We have seen from the above discussions that supernatural beliefs exert a positive influence in the selection of the religious heads of the tribal villages. In the administration of justice also manspirit relation exert some positive influences. The traditional Panchayats-both *hatu* and *parha* panchyat--work basically centreing round cultural traditions as well as supernatural sanction. Thus when the statutory panchayats have appeared in the villages owing to the implementations of *Panchayati raj*, a clash of sentiments has become conspicuous.

The immigration to the tribal belt by large mass of non-tribal people brought a lot of change over the general socio-cultural setting. There were clash of values--more often traditional patterns of behaviour of the tribes were not respected, and it was evidenced by the land policy adopted by the British rulers. The indigenous and prestige oriented *Khuntkatti* and *Bhuinhari* land tenure not only came to a standstill but also exerted a deep blow to the very philosophy of life. The number of tribal uprisings and movements which took place through the time were principally directed to a particular motive for saving the cultural traditions as these people always raised their voices against the infliction of foreign traits on their patterns of thinking in social and economical dealings.

The tribal uprisings and movements are all the time rooted to the frustration of the people arising out of outsiders' direct attack on their cultural factors constituting the whole socio-politico-economic system of the community. There were occasions when factions were developed within the tribal groups themselves, and these were resulted through cultural conflicts. When it was seen that basic interest of life of a particular tribe was being dominated by the other, there was a necessity to splitting of the original institution.

The tribal culture in this region has been in a rapid process of change specially due to the integrated impact of Christianity, urbanization, industrialization and many development programmes. These waves of changes have now brought forth emerging patterns of new political thinkings conditioned by the large-scale alterations of the cultural values. The traditional leaders with indigenous belief patterns were replaced by the western educated leaders. The rural society oriented leadership was transformed into the modern society influenced leadership. Thus, after the demise of Birsa Bhagwan, the leadership went into the hands of the Christian tribals. The indigenous culture was overpowered by the alien culture dominated Christian people. It led to the active politicization of the movements. But, in course of time, the influence of the people oriented with Western education and Christian beliefs started declining and a number of local non-tribal people especially Hindu leaders could make an entry into the political unit and thereby gave it a regional stand. The impact of large-scale industrialization and urbanization of Chotanagpur region has moulded the very life-pattern of the past period, and with the broad-based influence of education and outside contact largely effected through the increase in communication a new and thoroughly changing perspective of leadership and political movements have recently been started in the tribal belt of Bihar. The total outlook of the workers in these political units has thoroughly been changed--they are not in favour of lifting the social status of the tribal people by imitating some elements of the way of life of the Hindus. They are also not in a specific mentality to create pressures in keeping the traditional culture intact by not disturbing it by the imposition of outside influence. But their attraction has been drawn to the efforts for improving the material life of the tribals--prosperity in their economic standard caused by availing of job facilities and financial assistance.

References

Datta, K.K.	1970	:	*Anti British Plots and Movements Before 1857*, Meenakshi Prakashan, Meerut.
Dhan, R.O.	1977	:	Tribal Movements in Chotanagpur, in *Dissent, Protest and Reform in Indian Civilization*. Ed. by S. C. Malik, Indian Institute of Advanced Study, Simla.
Jha, J.C.	1964	:	*Kol Insurrection in Chotanagpur*, Thacker, Spink & Co. Pvt. Ltd. Calcutta.
Kessing, K.M.	1958	:	*Cultural Anthropology*.
Ponette, P.	1978	:	*The Munda World*, Hoffman Commemoration volume, Catholic Press, Ranchi.
Roy, S.C.	1912	:	*The Mundas and their country*, Ranchi.
	1978	:	*The Birhors:: A little-known Jungle Tribe of Chotanagpur*, Man in India Office, Ranchi.

Sachchidananda	1965	:	*Profiles of Tribal Culture in Bihar*, Punthi Pustak, Calcutta.
	1979	:	*The Changing Munda*, Concept Publishing Company, New Delhi.
Sahay, K.N.	1986	:	*Christianity and Culture Change in India*, Inter-India Publications New Delhi.
Sarker, R.M.	1971	:	The Santal Insurrection through Ballads, in *Bihar in Folklore Study*, Ed. by L.P. Vidyarthi and G. Choubey, Calcutta.
	1986	:	Sedentarization of the Nomadic Birhors *Vanyajati*, 34 : 1 New Delhi.
Sinha, D.P.	1960	:	Portrait of a Birhor Chief Journal of Social Research, 3 : 2 Ranchi.
Singh, K.S.	n.d.	:	From Ethnicity to Regionalism: A study in Tribal Politicies and Movements in Chotanagpur from 1900 to 1975., in *Dissent, Protest and Reform in Indian Civilization*, Ed. By S.C. Malik, Indian Institute of Advanced Study, Simla.
Singh, R.S.	n.d.	:	*Changing Occupational Structure of Scheduled Tribes*, Inter-India Publication, New Delhi.
Vidyarthi, L.P.	1963	:	*The Maler*, Bookland Pvt. Ltd., Calcutta.
	1967	:	*Leadership in India*, Asia Publishing House, Bombay.
	1973	:	*The Dynamics of Tribal Leadership in Bihar*, Kitabmahal, Allahabad.

1980 : Cultural Factors in Development Process; Case Studies from Tribal Bihar, *Man in India*, 60 : 3-4 Ranchi.

Vidyarthi, L.P. & Rai, B.K. 1976 : *The Tribal Culture of India*, Concept Publishing Company, New Delhi.

14

TRADITIONAL POLITICAL ORGANISATION OF THE MUNDA OF CHOTANAGPUR AND ITS CHANGES

LYDIA ICKE-SCHWALBE

Within the contemporary known tribal communities of India, the Mundas in their main settlement area of Chotanagpur play an active part not only with the economic demands for the needs of the people but also in the political life. Being classified as the Scheduled tribes in some States and different districts of States of India and in others not, the state denotified consideration of the Mundas as a primitive society at one side, or their total incorporation in the developing capitalist class society at the other side, give the head-lines for approaching them. For many centuries they have been living in areas that were almost cut off or aside of the general development of the Indian class society. Despite the external socio-political environment with its changing systems of Government and repeated intrusions into the lives of the tribal communities living in gentile societies, the Mundas have maintained their ethnic independence and authority. Since the 19th Century an incomparable strong impact by the economic and political development of India at all came to all tribal people, especially to those living in Chotanagpur, which became a centre of the necessary economic and industrial development on the basement of the rich natural resources of coal, iron and many other ores. Now-a-days the Mundas as well as others, like the Oraon, Kharia, Santal, Ho and others live in relatively close proximity with each other but also with the people and demands of the class society. There is an extensive exchange and growing similarity in their material culture, since the same implements and tools are used by all the similar economic conditions. All traditional socio-economic systems are equally affected by the impact of the capitalist production methods resulting from the encroachments of industries on their soils. But at the same time it became evident, that there are very different traditional ways and stages of the socio-economic development within the tribal communities, which are not at all a block in itself, but living societies with an own history and different ethnic consciousness, naturally also with an own socio-political control system and organisation. Very often this fact and the socio-political value system have been neglected. The introduction of outside systems, foreign for the people and often headed by foreigners, resulted in disorder, uncapability and revolts in the past.

Traditional Organisation of the Mundas

The traditional political organisation system of the Mundas is deeply rooted in the original socio-economic development and combined with oral tales from their history. The folklore of the Mundas states, that their ancestors came to the virgin lands of Chotanagpur after a long migration. The tribal community was led by Risa Munda, the first chief of the 21000 Munda people who migrated to Chotanagpur (Roy, 1912 : 329ff). It is told that they settled down at Muruma village, which is supposed to be not far from the present town Ranchi, since there were no signs of earlier cultivation done by men, and the oracle was auspicious.

Till this century a relatively well-knit clan system characterises the Mundas as an essentially gentile society with a basic economy of developed agriculture with plough cultivation. In the main settlement areas, which are now-a-days mostly in the district of Ranchi in Southern Bihar, with a high concentration in the Tamaria and Khunti blocks, the clan bonds from the basic relations and the clan organisation is accepted by the members of the society, bearing the same name and sharing the common property of their ancestors, which they inherited through the patrilineal descent. We are very well informed by Father Hoffman in his fundamental "Encyclopaedia Mundarica" about the clan organisation and its political leadership among the Mundas at the turn of this century. All patrilineal members of a clan have an undispersable claim for the common ownership of the main production instruments, particularly the soil and cultivable land. Traditionally the members of a clan settled in a common territory and formed a common settlement. The clan as well as this a *priori* right is represented by the eldest male in the recorded patrilineage to the founder of the clan as the social head and the political representative of the economic and social unit. The Munda call their first representative as "*pahar*" (in the Naguri dialect of mundari) or *para* (in Hazada dialect). According to tradition the office of the *pahar* was given from the founder the clan to his eldest son, and accordingly it is followed within the direct patriline. But in case of incapability of the descendant it was necessary and traditionally accepted to choose the next male relative within the lineage of the eldest son of the clan-ancestor. As Hoffman could get: A man "is *pahan* because he is the real social elder, or head, or patriarch, of the village family. This headship came to him either by virtue of his being the original founder" of a new community or the oldest representative of the original founder (1930-38: 2393,3210.). His first duty was to protect and ensure the existence and forthcoming of the communtiy by his magical virtue, which he inherited directly from the ancestor, who first succeeded to occupy the natural sources and use the forces of the nature for his community. The *pahar* (*pahan*) was the most important political representative of his kin-community and basically responsible for it. His social function was mainly connected with ritual practice and acting as a priest, based on the magical power of the ancestors and the spirits of the nature and territory. His important cult places were the *sasan*--the traditional burial ground of the ancestors and all patrilineal kinsmen--and the *sarna*--the sacred grove. This place and his function there were also the certificate for his office and duty in accordance with the tradition and original ownership of the land gained by the ancestor. The *pahan* was responsible to carry out all necessary sacrifices and ritual ceremonies connecting with agricultural periods as well as social events, as birth, marriage relations, death and burial. He had to watch on the traditional norms and orders of the clan within the *Munda* society and he was also accepted as judge in case of social or political conflicts within his society. The *pahan* was traditionally sided by a second representative called as the *munda*. The mundari language uses a special term for the leadership of the clan, "*munda-pahar*" or the "*munda-para*", which means "the village chief and the public sacrificer", according to Hoffman (1930-38 : 2882). It shows the very close relation of both functions, which are almost taken as one. The office of the *munda* was traditionally inherited within the lineage of the second son of the clan ancestor. It is recorded that the original founder of the settlement community divided his leadership between his eldest and second son. Therefore the *munda* sided the *pahan* as the second eldest representatives of a *Munda-clan*. The

Munda people in the Tamaria and Khunti area explained "The *pahan* is the chief and the *munda* means under him"[1]. The duty of the *munda* mainly was to support the *pahan* in all secular matters, especially to manage the outside contacts with other clans of the *Mundas* but also with outsiders within the territory. He acted as the representative of the *Munda* clan to the outsiders. His office became necessary in contacts with the outside world and officials of the class society within the Indian territory. For them he even seemed to be the only representative of the *Munda* community. But for the *Mundas* themselves he was mainly the helper of the *pahan.*

Within the traditionally Munda--society neither the *pahan* nor the *munda* had special privileges due to their offices. Nobody could rule in an autocrazic way, nor could he get any advantages in kind of extra land, payment or other goods. All had to follow the same clan rules and norms with respect to gain or distribution of the economic wealth and social values. All socio-political decisions had to be released in accordance with the council of elders of the clan, the panchayat. There the *pahan* and the *munda* were taken as *primi inter pares,* but in any case they were accepted by all kinsmen as leaders due to their patrilineal descent from the ancestor.

The two patrilineages are the most important inter-related sections of the mundaic clan system, called the *Khunt* (*khut*), which exist in each separate *Munda-clan.* S.C. ROY did not recognize this division into *khunts* within a clan, but he also designed a *Munda* as *"Khunt-kattidar"*, means being by birth a member of a clan and having property rights in the soil and land inherited from the clan ancestors (Roy, 1912). J.Hoffman very clearly analysed the importance and significance of the specific clan organisation as the basic of the *Munda* society. The *Khunts* are organising parts of a *Munda* clan, called as *kili.* Basically two *Khunts* are existing, representing the line of descents of the eldest and second eldest sons of the founder of the clan. The *Mundas* in the Naguri area deliver also a third and sometimes a fourth *khunt* following the third and fourth sons of the founder of the clan (Hoffman, 1930-38 : 2380 ff). But there is nowhere a concerning tradition in the clan organisation and no importance is given to such family lines. Whereas the *pahan* as well as the *Munda-Khunt* are essential within the social organisation and relations of the kinsmen. Especially in the customs and rules of marriage relations the *Khunts* play an important role. Basically marriage relations take place outside of ones own clan

(clan exogamy). But Hoffmann recorded additional rules, which can be assured even from younger field records (Icke-Schwalba, 1983 : 89). Hoffmann states,

> "Let us suppose that a marriage has taken place between the munda khunt of one village and the munda khunt of another (belonging to a different clan). In the same generation further unions may be arranged between them, but the next generations are debarred from intermarrying as long as members of the set of the people who contracted relationship through these marriages, are alive, and even after the extinction of that first generation, as long as the two *khunts* remain on visiting terms. Meanwhile the *pahan khunt* of one of these villages may freely intermarry with both khunts of other.

Similarly if a marriage has taken place between the *pahan khunt* of one village and the *munda khunt* of another, in the next generation these two khunts are not allowed to intermarry but unions may freely be contracted either between the two *pahan khunts* or between the *munda khunts* (Hoffmann, 1930-38; 2380-81). The strong determination of the clan and the basic role of the kinship for the social and political representatives of the Munda society, the *pahan* and the *munda,* who cannot be separated from their respected patri-clans and lineages.

Another political representative is the *manki* (*Marki*), who acts as the chief of a cluster of settlements within a certain terriotry, called as the *pati* by the more traditional Tamaria Mundas, or as the *Parha* in Naguri dialect of the Mundari language. Again Hoffmann points out, that originally all settlements of a *Pati* belonged to the same clan. That states that the growth of population forced the expansion of the original clan village boundaries following the establishment of daughter settlements within the traditional clan territory. Traditionally, the *Pati* denominates the original territory which a Munda clan inherited from his ancestor, who first occupied a living territory and cultivated the soil, including later mundaic settlers. A Pati now generally comprises several villages and hamlets grouped around the original clan-settlement, and also groups of later settlers (Op. cit : 3311), the raiyats and different craftsmen-castes, so that it is no longer a homogenous area.

Regarding common territorial affairs and matters between the villages and hamlets within such a *pati* or *parha* the soical heads of the village, of the clans and clan splits, elect one head among themselves, called the *manki*. He acts as the head of the common panchayat, which consists of the social representatives of the villages. But his responsibility is confined only to intervillage affairs, he has nothing to decide within single clan or village communities. Hoffmann remarks,

> "There is.... ample evidence to show, that the *manki* is an essential factor in the original political organisation of the Kolarian races, and as such has existed everywhere among them."
>
> (op. cit : 2398).

The *Manki* is the highest political representative within the Munda community. There is no common tribal chief of the Mundas recorded or existing except in the tales about the original migration of the people to Chotanagpur led at that times by Risa Munda.

Transformations and changes by outside Political Systems and Economic Forces

The *manki* as well as the munda became much important to the outside Munda world, when the Britishers introduced their land tenancy acts and demanded the payment of land rent by the rural people at all. The *munda* within the village and the *manki* within a territory got inscribed as the land-holders and made responsible for the collecting of rent from their relatives and the villagers within their territory. In so far an essential transformation of the posts took place, because they were mainly made to be the collector of land-rents or the long arms of the landowner and his special interests, instead of being the representatives of their own people and their interests. Very often these headmen got also corrupted by the foreign power, since they got privileges for their outside duty in kind of rent free plots of land or similar advantages. So, naturally a separation got evident between the traditional function of the ritually and ideologically sanctioned representation of the original law and order, and the secular headship, which had to follow foreign rules to some extent and got more political power than it was possible traditionally.

Again it was Father Hoffmann, who directed everybody's attention to the deep conflicts and social as well as political problems, which would arise and actually followed the foreign land policy introduced by the British Government[2]. In some cases the secular head, the *munda,* who acted traditionally as the second hand of the *pahan,* gtestranged from his own community and tried to increase his political and social power. On the other hand, as soon as such supremacy got evident in a village, the *pahan,* the real eldest chief, tried to insist on his right and duty and to correct the outsiders' view, having his own *khuntkattikins* behind himself. In that way, the *pahans* became at the same time the fighters for tradition and tribal rights to recognize the ancestral property and defend it against the foreign law. This is almost their position until today.

In many cases another person, the so-called *mahato,* took the political power given from outside to rule to some extent on his relatives. Traditionally, the mahato played no significant role. The term is not even related to the Mundari language, but obviously a new introduction due to the necessities.[3] Nevertheless, his post is recorded in some villages and clan-traditions as being the representative of the lineage of the third son of the clan-founder and a social helper for the *munda,* the secular head beside the *pahan.* But mostly the *mahato* was not accepted by the Munda-relatives as a head or chief beside the *pahan* and the *munda.* In many cases he and his family got isolated since his power and interest came only from outside.

Even in present day conflicts between the Munda tribal people and government officials, it is the *pahan,* who understands his responsibility for the continuation of his community from his office, having come down from their forefathers. Mostly it becomes evident during the traditional *melas,* which are social, ritual but also political functions. A *mela* has to be initiated by the *pahan* of the respective village or settlement compound in the tradition-oriented areas like the Naguri or Tamaria and Hazada area in Southern Ranchi district. There, recently, the *pahans* also more and more represent a political function as the most conscious heads of the Munda-community with a clear ethnic responsibility. To some extent the *pahans* have become representatives in the political party organisation of Jharkhand and very selfconscious fighters for the rights and norms of their community up to the demand for political autonomy of the Mundas in their ancestral lands of Chotanagpur. The conflict between the Mundas and Government officials mostly arose, because the last did not accept the actual and traditionally grown headship and representation of the tribal people. There are many cases of the still functioning clan-organisation and strong position of their representatives for instance in the Khunti-area. One case became evident in the early eighties, when the Bihar Government did not recognize the political organisation of the Mundas along with their sacred places, which are important to the Munda community and quasi certificates of the their existence and ancestral heritage. With official order a TV-station should be placed on the top of a very sacred hill (*Sukhuan buru*). The protest and purification of the polluted place was not only a ritual function by all surrounding *pahans* and clan-villages, but also a political demonstration with long lasting effects.

Under the influence of the Hindu-society and in order to adopt modern colloquial terms, now-a-days the social and political heads in the area with main concentration of the Mundas are also called as "rajas" and further reaching political organisations were established. As I have been told recently by the president of the Adivasi Bhumij Rakha and Vikas Samiti of the Hazada territory, the 22 traditional clans or *kili* of the Munda are each represented by a "raja" who very often is identical with the eldest *pahan* of the original patriline of the founder of the clan. The *kilis* are spread presently over several village units, forming a *pati* or *parha* on the traditional soil, handed over the first cultivator. These rajas elect among themselves one head, called as "maharaja" who acts for 10 years as the highest political representative of the *Munda* tribe, after his election has also been accepted by the community itself. Besides such indigenous political organisations the Government of the State of Bihar has spread all over the country the modern political organisation of the village panchayats with elected members of every community living in the territory. It is the interest, that the traditional heads of the communities should be members of such panchayats. But traditional heads never participate in such panchayats, since they may never act together with the outsiders for their purpose, naturally. Other elected members of the community may act within such panchayats. But very often it is visible, as long as they act independently from the traditional representatives that they mostly are less accepted within their community. Lastly they are not only bad representatives of their people but they also do not know the problems and actual conflicts within their villages which are based on traditional norms. This in fact, could be realized in the well-organised blocks of the Netarhat plateau of Ranchi and Palamau districts. The territory houses a mixed population of the Mundas, Oraons, Asurs, Birjias, Korwas and other caste groups, christians and non-christians. The village panchayas are constituted by 4 (four) members, elected by the whole population of the area, and 4 (four) nominated christian and non-christian members, who elect or accept one head among themselves as the *mukhia* (in a village) or *sarpanch* (in a sub-block territory). The mukhia was the responsible person for the development and welfare within the village community irrespective of their ethnic identity. At the time, when I could stay there for studies, a non-christian Asur functioned as the *Sarpanch,* and the *Mukhia* of the mixed village of mostly the Mundas and the Oraons was a non-christian Oraon. Neither the members of the panchayat nor the heads were accepted as representatives of their ethnic communities, but they embodied the administrative organisation of the State in the territory (Icke-Schwalsbe, 1983). They did not know about the traditional structure of their communities and had nothing to say for the socio-political way of life within the ethnic groups themselves. This was left to the parish priest in case of the christian Mundas and to the traditional heads in case of the non-christian Sarna-Mundas.

In the Munda-territory of Chotanagpur in the present time a double political and social organisation can be met mostly; one administrative, introduced by the State Government according to the law and Constitution of the Government of India, and the other traditional bound to the ethnic groups and their indigenous socio-political system. Unfortunately, as long as the administrators cannot succeed to co-ordinate both, which presupposes, that one knows about each other and the Government officials do accept the traditional heads as legal representatives, the double administration is less effective, at least not be able to work progressively, but creates a lot of avoidable conflicts. It should be the aim and task to work with the traditional political structures as long as they represent really their communities, and to include the traditional heads fully-responsible into the government adminstration with their own interest and responsibility for the people and the territory.

Notes

1. Field research results by the author in 1979.

2. He wrote a "Special Memorandum on the Land System of the Munda Country", which got published in his "Encylopaedia Mundarica", pp. 2388-2404.

3. IN HOFFMANN'S Encyclopaedia no special term is recorded. He only uses the term in connection with recent developments within the Naguri area, see p. 2381.

References

Hoffman, J. and A. Van 1930-38 : *Encyclopaedia Mundarica*, Emelen. Vol. S 1-12, Patna.

Icke-Schwalbe, Lydia 1983a : *Die Munda and Oraon in Chotanagpur. Geschichte Wirtschaft and Gesellschaft.* (Mundas and Oraons of Chotanagpur, History, Economy and Society). Berlin.

Icke-Schwalbe, Lydia 1983b : Village studies among Christian and non-Christian Munda in Chotanagpur. *Journal of Social Research* Vol. XXVI, No.1, Ranchi.

Roy, S.C. 1912 : *The Mundas and their Country, London.* (reprinted, Calcutta, 1970).

15

TRADITIONAL POLITY OF THE JATAPU : CONTINUITY AND CHANGE

IAR ALI KHAN

This article attempts to reveal some of the political processes in rural India by depicting the traditional polity of the Jatapu of Koraput in terms of its structure, functionaries, continuity and change therein. The aim of this study is to see and seek functional connections, 'eternal verities' of political action and how village politics, so to speak, at the grass root level are vitally affected by national politics.

The Jatapus are a Telegu speaking tribe mainly concentrated in the 'buffer' region of Koraput district of Orissa and Srikakulam district of Andhra Pradesh. They are endogenous and practise lineage (Banstriya) exogamy. Consanguineous (uncle-niece i.e. MoBr=SiDa) marriages are practised by the tribe. The people are patrilineal, patrilocal and succession is primogeniture. The people are mostly engaged in agriculture and agriculture-labour.

Traditional polity of the Jatapu is of two tier systems one at the village level is known as *Gram Panchayati* (Village Council); and the other at regional as well as ethnic level which is referred to as *mandali panchayati* (regional council).

Gram Panchayati

This council consists of a *saonta* a *jani* and adult knowledgeable persons of their community. The *saonta* is the head of the council, and he is assisted by the *jani*. The posts of the *saonta* and the *jani* are hereditary and the succession is primogeniture. Women in any case are not considered for the post of the *saonta* and the *jani*. In such cases where the *saonta* and the *jani* have no male issues, there the succession is found out one from their relatively nearer consanguineal kins by the consensus of the adult knowledgeable persons of the village. At this point it may also be mentioned that if suitable consanguineal kins are not available there again the consensus of the adult knowledgeable persons are required to select the *saonta* or the *jani*. But, according to them the chances of the last category of selection hardly occurs and it is beyond their repertoire of knowledge and memory.

The *saonta* is the head of the customary village polity. When a dispute is brought to the notice of the *saonta,* he convenes a meeting of the adult knowledgeable persons in which the complainant and the accused are informed to be present. Both the parties are allowed to put their statement or witness as the case may be and after hearing thoroughly the *saonta* in consultation with the *jani* and other knowledgeable persons points out the persons found guilty and at the same time he announces the nature of punishment imposed on the persons. The verdict of the *saonta* is final. At this juncture, it may be mentioned that the meeting of the council is called upon either through the *jani* or a person of the village. It is rather unwritten rule that when any person of the village is asked by the *saonta* to convey the message of the sitting of the council, he gladly obeys the order of the *saonta.* The post of the *saonta* is purely honorary.

The *jani* is a ritual specialist and messenger of the customary polity. He is included in the council by virtue of his special knowledge of rituals and mode of their observances. As the customary polity functions on the basis of norms, traditional customs and usages and the *jani* being the sacred specialist, his advice is highly considered when a verdict on a dispute is announced. And it is in case of breach of taboo the *jani's* decision is final though it is announced by the *saonta.* Actually, in such cases the *jani* is the *de facto* head of the council. In this context a brief reference of a case of lineage endogamy may be mentioned. As a rule lineage endogamy is tabooed among the Jatapu. The case cited here took place at the village Bhakhorguda under Kothapeta Panchayat of Rayagada Tahsil in the district of Koraput. The boy and the girl belonged to *himrika* lineage (bansiya) and were also consanquineal kins. The girl was the Fa Br Da of the boy. Both were literates, and the boy was working in the State Government. Somehow, they developed some sort of affairs and wanted to marry each other. The villagers came to know their plan and strongly objected to it as this type of intralineage marriage was treated as incest taboo and the village deity would be displeased and certainly would bring disasters to the villagers. But the boy and the girl were not willing to deviate from their understanding and so they left the village and got married. The news of their marriage reached the villagers who became very much afraid of this circumvention and consulted the *jani* to get rid of the calamities. The *jani* performed a ritual to appease the *jhakiri*, the village deity, as this action was against the norm and strongly condemned. The family members of the respective spouses had to undergo expiation and bore the expenditure incurred in connection with the ritual for expiation.

Nature of Punishment

The traditional polity is authorised to impose fine to an offender in terms of cash or kind. But frequency of imposing fine in kind is more prevalent and it is a common practice to ask the persons found guilty to purchase local-made liquor to entertain the villagers who attend the meeting. The quantity is fixed up by the council. In case of homicide they certainly refer the case to the police. Similar treatment is followed in case of heavy bloodshed. In case of stealing and minor bloodshed the council try to tackle the case for settlement. In such cases if the verdict of the council is not obeyed then they refer the case to the police authority.

Besides, when an offender does not carry out the verdict of the Panchayat and if it is not a case of stealing or bloodshed then the offender is excommunicated by the villagers. He is forced to lead the life in isolation. In this matter, if necessary, they also take the help of adjoining villagers to give more pressure on the excommunicated person. Thus a situation is created in such a manner so that the guilty person under force--*majeure,* finds no other way but to surrender to the villagers. Thus, surrender means, he will have to obey the verdict of the Panchayat and then only the villagers will lend their helping hands to him and renew all sorts of social intercourses.

There is no inter village Panchayat. However, disputes in which the other village is involved are undertaken by the *saonta* and elderly knowledgeable person of the respective villages. In this connection a case is mentioned herewith

A girl of the village Adapatiguda was married to a boy of village Bhakhorguda under Kothapeta Panchayat of Rayagada Tahsil in the district of Koraput. The boy paid *oli* i.e. bride-price as customary norm of the society. After some months due to incompatibility of temperament they failed to adjust with each other and the girl left her husband's house and went to her parents. So long she was with her parents there was no problem. But as soon as the girl started to live with a boy of her parents' village as husband and wife, then the first husband of the girl claimed *oli* from the second husband of the girl. And according to custom the second husband of the girl was bound to pay the *oli* claimed by the first husband of the girl. But the second husband of the girl showing utter disregard to the convention and usage of the society, refused to pay the *oli*. Then the matter was brought to the notice of the *Panchayat* by the second husband of the girl by her first husband. But the said Panchayat did not pay any attention to the complain lodged by the first husband. Then he appealed to the *saonta* of his own village to settle the dispute by exercising his power. Then the *saonta* discussed about the matter with the *saonta* of the village of the second husband of the girl and categorically told him if he did not take interest to settle the dispute then in future they would not cooperate in any matter with them and this would not lead to chaos and disorder in the society. Then the *saonta* of the accused village realized the importance of the traditional norms and agreed to settle the matter. And ultimately the dispute was settled in which the *saonta* and some elderly knowledgeable persons of the complainant's village were invited, and the second husband of the girl was asked to pay the *oli*. And the accused obeyed the order of the Panchayat. Further enquiry in this line revealed that the accused was the Fa Br of the *saonta*. And that was the reason not to settle the dispute at its initial stage.

Other Activities

Customary polity is also convened on the eve of the ritual observances of the village deity *Jhakiri*. The *Jhakiri* is the supreme deity of the Jatapu and worshipped by the *jani* once a year in the month of Baisak (April-May). They have to sacrifice goat and there are also other expenditure in connection with the ritual. Thus, the meeting of the council is convened to discuss the matter and also the date and rate of subscription are fixed up to make the worship a successful one.

The meeting of the council is also convened to settle the disputes related to *podu* cultivation, inheritance of movable and immovable properties, adultery, illicit love, marriage and divorce.

Social Offence

However, frequency of social offences in the Jatapu society is not alarming. This is manifested in their number of sittings of traditional council for tackling such offences. Stealing is one such offence which is dealt with by the Council either traditionally or statutory; cases of extra marital or pre-marital sexual indulgence are hardly taken up by the council. This is not because of the fact that it is overlooked by the society, but this is because of the fact that occurrence of such phenomena is very rare due to the freedom and status enjoyed by the women. A woman leaves her husband if she is not satisfied with him. Even then, some cases are brought to the notice of the council, very rarely. In such cases the man involved is imposed fine in cash and then liquor is purchased with that amount and consumed by the persons attending the society. Further, if the husband of the woman does not like to take back his wife, then the man involved in it, is forced to marry the woman, and the council asks the man to pay back the oli to her previous husband. In such cases the women do not generally get any punishment.

Mandali Panchayat

Regional as well as ethnic level customary polity is known as *Mandali Panchayati*. The head of the *mandali* panchayati is known as *Mandali Naidu*. The area of jurisdiction of the *mandali naidu* varies from ten to twelve villages. The Council members of the *Mandali Naidu* consisted of the *saontas* of these villages. This post is also hereditary and honorary, and the succession is primogeniture through the males only. It deals with the disputes exclusively of the ethnic group i.e. the Jatapus. Generally, the complicated cases or disputes which the *saonta* fails to tackle, are referred to the *Mandali Naidu*.

The *Mandali Naidu* and its council and knowledgeable persons deal with the cases of intra-ethnic disputes, and look after the interest and prestige of the community. This body of council also keep strict vigilance so that the norms, customs, taboos and usages are maintained properly. Whenever they find out any violation of customary laws, they immediately convene the meeting of the council. For breaking the taboo one has to undergo expiation to get readmittance in their society as per the decision of the *Mandali Panchayati*. Disobeying of this verdict means excommunication and readmission is granted only when the verdict of the council is observed fully. The council has the right to punish an offender by levying fine or by ostracizing the man from the community.

Contemporary Situation

So far we discussed the customary polity of the Jatapu which is timidly functioning as a result of introduction of *Panchayat raj* system, a pan-Indian, statutory political institution at village level and upwards to the extent of state level.

In the traditional system the village Panchayat was a powerful body as the authority rested on the hands of economically stronger group of people, and this continued for generation together as the post of the village chief i.e. *saonta* and the village priest i.e. *jani* were hereditary. They were treated as the representatives of God or supernatural power. The people believed in superstitions. Therefore, whenever they violated the norms of the society then automatically they would become morally weak and considered themselves guilty out of fear of punishment from the supernatural power. Thus they found only a reconciliation of their sinful acts by expiation as per the advice of the *saonta* and *jani*. Thus in the structure of traditional customary policy we find presence of both secular and sacred heads to deal with the breach of norms of the society but their domain of operation is different. The sacred head is consulted mainly when breach of taboos and ritual aspects are discussed and he at that time wields maximum power. His decision is final. Whereas the secular head deals with the breach of other customary norms and gives the verdicts. The inclusion of other knowledgeable persons who are usually aged and experienced has given a character of decentralization of customary polity which probably has been infused at a later date.

Then gradually the world view and the philosophy of life of the people changed due to exposure to outsiders. The establishment of civil and criminal courts and of the police and awareness of these machineries further led to the decline of the importance of customary polity. Moreover, the introduction of Panchayati Raj system once again makes a limitation of the power of the customary polity. This is very well proved by synchronic study of fringe and remote villages. It is observed that the people of the fringe area almost ignore the customary polity and take the help of court or police as the case may be, for any type of disputes and litigation of properties. It is found that some cases of land disputes of Adapatiguda village which is situated at the fringe are pending in the Civil Court of Rayagada whereas no such cases are found from the Bankili village which is 40 Kms. away from the town.

It is further observed that the function of *Mandali Panchayati* is less pronounced than that of the *Gram Panchayati*. In fact *Mandali Panchayati* is out of the memory of the young generation. It is true for both the fringe and remote villages.

Another observation is that the person who is holding power in the customary polity i.e. the *saonta,* has been elected as the *panch* or the *sarpanch* of the statutory panchayat. Thus there is a little change in functioning of the statutory panchayat. Similar picture was found in case of the Khairwar tribe of Suruja district of Madhya Pradesh in my earlier study. This is perhaps because of the fact that the common mass are not fully aware of the changes. It is also observed that in some villages where some of the common masses are aware of this election of the *panch* or the *sarpanch* on the basis of adult franchise, there arises group conflict and factionalisms, as it is observed during my earlier study of the Khairwar at village Singibahar of Tapkara Block in the district of Rayagada, M.P. At this juncture, it may briefly be mentioned that this is reflected in the politics of our national level. It is observed that somehow the people try to stick to the power, it is either by forming a separate party or by defection. Structure remaining the same, even the persons are unchanged.

Lastly, it is observed that though the power and jurisdiction of the customary polity of the Jatapu is decreasing and being replaced by the statutory *Panchayat Raj* system, yet they are not ignoring in their customary laws on which the society is build up.

16

CHANGES AND PERSISTENCE IN THE POLITICAL ORGANIZATION OF THE MALAYALIS OF KALRAYAN HILLS

S. LOURDUSAMY

Introduction

The Malayalis of Kalrayan Hills are a caste turned Scheduled Tribe of Tamilnadu. They live in the hills since more than six centuries. For most part they lived under the rules of Jagirdars. The Jagirdars are feudatory lords who assumed power in the name of their family deity, Kariraman. In 1976-1977, the last of the Jagirdar rule was abolished. With that the theocratic system came to an irreversible halt. All too sudden the Malayalis and their hill-country were exposed to alien administrative machineries of the Government and hitherto larger, heterogenous cultures of the neighbours. The Malayalis had to adjust themselves and live with the new world altogether. What has been effected by the abolition of the old and by the introduction of a new political order, what still remains of the old and why, if any, are some of the questions that rise in the face of changed conditions. This study examines the old and the new political orders and their significance for the Malayalis and the policy makers. The study is based on the findings of field work conducted in 1975-1976, when the last of the Jagir-land was still under the old system, and again during a re-visit to the area in January, 1990.

The People and their Genesis

Folklores and traditional practices speak of their origin from the sacred city of Kanchipuram, Tamilnadu, and their settlement with the Vedars, the original inhabitant tribes of the hills. The Malayalis were originally of the Vellala caste. They were also known as the Karalans, a synonym for the Vellala. When the Muhammadan rule was dominant in Southern India they migrated to the hills. By their counts the migration must have taken place between 12th and 15th centuries. The tradition also says that they mingled with the Vedars, and settled down with them there. For this reason they are rather known as tribals by marriage (V. Rajalakshmi, 1989). Today they are commonly known as Malayalis, meaning 'the inhabitants of hills', and are enlisted as a Scheduled Tribe.

Their social and religious customs are not much different from those of the Hindu-Tamils of the plains. However, what characterises them as the Malayalis and as different from the Tamils of the plains is the institution of Jagirdar, a metaphor for the present day course of their history and identity.

Until the Tamilnadu Government took over, the life of the Malayalis had been dominated by the rules of the Jagirdars; the land and its natural resources belonged none other than to the Jagirdars. The people could cultivate as much land as they want, but the right of purchase and sale of forest produce was the prerogative of the Jagirdars. They paid poll tax for residing in the hills and plough tax for cultivating the land. They had also to render their services and pay full respect and obedience to the Jagirdars. All this was done through a score of officials appointed by the Jagirdars, who in turn enjoyed enormous privileges and rights. Their social, economic, religious, political and cultural life was infused with the single institution of Jagirdars. Such being the case of the Malayalis, an understanding as to when and why such an institution began and how it survived for so long is called for here.

The Origin of the Political Organization

There are at least two traditions that are in parts historically accountable. The one is the Jagirdari-system and the other is the theocratic origin. What concerns the Jagirdari-system, is not fully clear as to when it took roots in this place. Tracing from various sources, it seems to have begun here about 600 years ago from the Muhammadan Emperors who used to give Jagir, a land assignment, to the Jagirdars in lieu of salary for their Kavali service rendered to the emperor. "A Jagirdar was a civil or military servant who was paid his salary by an order which authorized him to realize the amount due to him by collecting the land revenue of the area assessed to yield the exact amount" (Sharma, 1951 : 76). In the beginning the Jagirdars had no rights over the land, but were only assigned the postion of the royal officers in order to collect tax from their respective Jagirs (Sharma, 1951 : 76).

At the time of Vijayanagar empire, Palagars or Palayagarars (the name by which the people still call the Jagirdars), who were posted at Jagir-lands were used to meet with troubles from jungle tribes (Nilakanta Sastri, 1958 : 298). When the British took over this area from the Nawab of Arcot it was noted that the Jagirdars had gradually assumed right over the land and exercised lordship over the people. There existed a hereditary form of the Kavali system. According to this system the Kavalgars, who were known as the Palagars, kept a service of watch and guard against robbers. For the service rendered to their people they levied contributions and took from all property a quota of all crops grown in the village, a rate on houses, a tax on professions and a transit duty on articles transported by the roads. All these formed a bulk of their demands. The Kavalgars later assumed the leadership of the Kavali organization, levied extraction of all kinds from their countrymen, and thus installed themselves as the proprietors of the area they looked after (Imperial Gazeetter, 1886 : 75-76).

The State of affair had continued right into the first half of this century. The Jagirdars enjoyed the title deeds of Inam Estate over the Jagir-lands for a small Quit-Rent on the basis of revenues they collected from the people. For instance, as per information in 1976 from the Jagirdar of Jadayakaundan Jagir, the Quit-Rent he used to pay for an area of about 99.8 sq. miles was Rs. 1036.00 per annum. In this way the Jagirdars had maintained a long tradition upto 1977. Until recently the Malayali-folks did not know this side of the story.

According to an another tradition, which is widely known among the Malayalis, the story begins with five brothers from Kanchipuram. They had a family deity called Kariraman. When the Muhammadans persecuted the Hindus, their family deity found it uncomfortable to stay there and hence moved out to the hills. The five brothers followed him. They intermarried with the aboriginal Vedars and lived under theocracy. They divided the hills among themselves and settled down separately: the eldest brother settled down in Kollimalai of Salem district and called it Periannan Jagir, the youngest in Pachaimalai of Trichy district and called it Chinnannan Jagir, and the other three in Kalrayan Hills of South

Arcot district and called them Jadayakaundan Jagir, Kurumbakaundan Jagir and Aryakaundan Jagir. There are various explanations to their settlement patterns and naming of the five brothers and their respective hills.

Historically speaking a persecution had occurred about 1476; Muhammad III raided Kanchipuram, plundered its temple and slew all its priests (Nilakanta Sastri, 1958 : 247). Nothing is known about their migration. All the same, the Jagirdars being powerful their interpretation sticks to this day; they inherited the land of their family deity, and hence the land is theirs. This argument was used by the former Jagirdar of Jadayakaundan Jagir to claim the land as Inam estate (see High Court of Judicature, 1966).

Seen from the various traditions one can draw a conclusion that the political organization took its origin from combined incidents of a secular economic organization of past empires and of the interpolations of religious events and the submissiveness of the people. Of the five Jagirs the two in Kollimalai and Pachaimalai were taken over by the Government at an earlier peroid. The remaining three situated in South Arcot District, the area of this study, were taken over only in 1976-1977. This study was conducted among the Malayalis of Jadayakaundan Jagir as a sample for the study. This Jagir is special in that the transition from the old to the new is quick, drastic and more visible than in the others. With this background we shall now deal with the traditional political organization proper.

The Traditional Political Organization

It consists of hierarchical ranking as follows: At the top of the hierarchy is the Jagirdar or Palayakarar who is commonly addressed as *Durai,* i.e. Lord. Next only to *Durai* is *Garbari* or *Mandri,* meaning Minister. Almost equal in status with *Garbari* but one rank below in the hierarchy is the *Javundan* who is the official *Guru* of the Jagir. He is also the head of the functionaries mentioned below, and hence he is also called *Periyanattan.* Below him is a twin post of *Nattan* and *Moopan* who are incharge of each *Nadu* (province). At the lowest rung of the hierarchy are the *Kaundan* and *Kangani,* a twin post, who are village headmen. *Kanimagan* is a single post found in villages. His position is not well defined since he acts as the man of Jagirdar on the spot. Apart from these there are *Nambiars* (temple priests) and *Kodangis* (*Shamans*), who, though are concerned with the spiritual things, are under the control of the Jagirdar.

The positions and functions, the mode of assuming office, execution of duties, grant of rights and privileges, and the assumption of powers and authorities of these people are different as follows:

Jagirdar: He is believed to be one of the inheritors of Lord Kariraman. The Chinnathirupadhi temple, the temples at high mountain peaks and the objects of worship belong to him. He is the sole owner of the land and all that acrues from it. He is the author of the law of the land and his word is final and abiding in every affair of the land under his control.

The rank is hereditary, passed on from father to the eldest son. In the absence of a son, the brother next to the Jagirdar, or in his absence his brother's eldest son is the heir proper. Hence there are no competitions to the post. He is nominated according to the hereditary rules and ordained by *Garbari* and *Javundan* in the presence of the whole hill-nation. Once ordained he is Jagirdar for life.

His duties and functions include the following. He appoints and terminates all the officials and subordinates of secular and religious ranks at his will. He decides the dates for the festival at Chinnathirupadhi temple and for the village festivals. The festival at Chinnathirupadhi is conducted by him every year. He gives consent to every marriage; without his consent no marriage will take place. He protects his subjects from outsiders, settles criminal cases without approaching the court of law. He visits the villages once a while carried in a pallanquin by the respective villagers who host his princely visit. He uses the subordinates to serve him in the maintenance of law and order and to collect taxes. He allows his subordinates certain privileges according to his discretion.

The rights and privileges of the Jagirdar are unlimited. He is the owner of the forest produces such as the teak, sandle and black wood and all the timbers that have market value. He alone can sell them to any outsider he wills. He alone can buy the surplus crops from his people and market them outside. He owns the land

and hence anyone who lives and cultivates in the land has to pay tax to him. The tax comes in various forms: according to the changing nature of crops he receives around Rs. 10,000.00 per year from each *Nadu*. It comes in the form of tax on various issues as follows: *Manyavari*, a tax of prestige, paid by *Garbari* and *Javundan* once in five years is Rs. 25.00 per head; *Thirvai*, a tax on every married man is Rs. 3.25, excepting those who live in the village of the *Jagirdar* who pay Rs. 1.50 only. This concession is due to service they are bound to render to him whenever he needs them; Rs 1.50 as *Kavalivari*, a tax on every unmarried male above the age of 12; Rs 0.75 as plough tax on each plough one uses; Rs.5.00 as *Vazhavativari*, tax on a woman who does not live with her husband; Rs 1.25 as *Asaduvari*, a tax on widow Rs. 16.00 as water tax on one acre for three crops. There are varying amount of tax on grazing goats and sheep, and land tax on non-Malayali residents. Besides each village gives an average of 200 kg. of grains and gingely, 20 kg. of grams and tamarind, and a goat a year. Apart from this when a marriage takes place anywhere in the hill country he receives Rs 10.00 as marriage tax on every marriage. He punishes those who do not pay the taxes by refusing them the right to cultivate.

He receives the first produce of harvest from the people. He also receives gifts in the form of goats, pigs, ghee, fruits, honey and vegetables from each village on festive occasions or when auspicious events take place in his palace. A major amount of the turn-over from the collection at Chinnathirupadhi festival belongs to him. When people visit him or assemble in the palace he hosts a sumptuous meal and gives them money either as gift or on loan as the situation demands. In this way the Jagirdar is an all pervading figure in the life of the Malayalis.

Garbari : He is number two and next only to the Jagirdar in power, authority, status and possession. The post is also for life and hereditary. But if situation demands the *Garbari* could be anybody from the same lineage. For, if the Jagirdar is too young and the succeeding *Garbari* also is too young, which is a rare thing to happen, then someone from the same lineage is preferred. On assuming office he pays about Rs.5000.00 to the Jagirdar. This amount is treated as a status symbol.

The *Garbari* is the executive head or the agent of the people and the advisor to the Jagirdar. He sees to the execution of the law of the land; he controls the heads of the Nadus and the village in the name of Jagirdar. As advisor and counsellor he plays the role of the mediator between the people and the Jagirdar. It is he or together with the Jagirdar who is eligible to hear and pass judgements on incidents of crime, disputes over village boundaries and village properties such as the valuable timbers. Should he happen to be present during a *Sangyam*, a type of village Panchayat, he presides over it overruling the authorised functionaries below him. And his Judgements are final. It is he who can trace out the successor by the principles of hereditary rites and nominate him to the princely rank of Jagirdar. There is no ordination of Jagirdar without his presence.

He enjoys enormous respect from the people. He heads the festival at Chinnathirupadhi along with *Jagridar* and *Javundan*. For every marriage he is paid Rs 3.00. If he is present at a marriage he receives new clothes and a sum of Rs.10 or more. When he settles a dispute he is paid at least Rs.100.00. He has a major share in the total receipt of Chinnathirapadhi festival. He may also demand the service of his villagers for daily work at home and in his fields.

Javundan: He is the third ranking single person holding the office for life with the combination of material and spiritual roles. The post is hereditary, but anyone from the same lineage can be nominated to the office. His nomination is done by Jagirdar in consultaion with the *Garbari*. On assuming office he too pays a large amount to Jagirdar as a status symbol. The amount is anything like Rs.3000 or more. He enjoys the respect and reverene as does the *Garbari* and the freedom to intervene in most matters of the hill people excepting those to be referred to the *Jagirdar* and the *Garbari*.

As a spiritual leader he is the official *Guru* of the hill country. By virtue of his rank he officiates the princely ordination and puts the princely *Pottu* on the forehead of the Jagirdar-elect. He also officiates the expiation ceremonies in the house of Jagirdar and leads the annual festival at Chinnathirupadhi together with Jagirdar and *Garbari*. He officiates marriages and declares the couple as married. He is paid around Rs.10- per marriage. He is invited before ploughing and sowing to bless the fields. Should a non-Malayali enter any of their houses or someone enters their house with foot-wears on, the house is said to be polluted. Then the *Javundan* is called to remove the impurity from that house.He is paid around Rs.10-for that service. During the festival at Chinnathirupathi he receives from Jagirdar a small share of the total receipt.

In his political role, he assists the *Garbari*. He visits each Nadu regularly to see if the customary laws of their land are carried out effectively by the subordinate office holders. When a message from the *Jagirdar-Garbari* level needs to be carried to the entire land he is the official mouthpiece. He does it with the assistance of *Nattans* and the *Moopans*. He also hears complains against the *Nattans* and *Moopans* and reports them to the *Jagirdar* and the *Garbari* effecting actions against unwanted elements. He supervises the collection of annual revenues due to the Jagirdar from every *Nadu* and village. Should he happen to be present when a village *Sangyam* is in progress the matters are referred to him and his verdict is accepted even if the respective *Nattan* and *Moopan* disagree. He is paid in cash for his role in the *Sangyam*.

Nattan and Moopan: These are twin posts. The *Nattan* is the head and the *Moopan* is his assistant who carries out the order. Each Nadu has one *Nattan* and one *Moopan*. Thus there are four *Nattans* and four *Moopans* in this *Jagir*. They are by tradition hereditary but in practice anyone from the same lineage can vie for the posts. They are appointed by the Jagirdar in the months of, April-May. Usually the ones who offer more money to the Jagirdar are appointed and the sum amounts to more than Rs.1000.00 each. These posts are held for one year, and they can be re-appointed for any number of years.

Their main job is to collect the annual tax and any such income due to Jagirdar from their respective Nadu and submit them to the Jagirdar. They preside over the meetings within the Nadu and settle disputes especially in matters of tax, sharing of land for disaforestation, forest products etc. They preside over the *Sangyam* if the matter concerns the entire Nadu. They also help the *Javundan* in matters of ethical behaviours and social conducts. It is they who arrange marriages, fix dates and officiate them. There will be no marriage without them and any such marriage is illegal and invalid. The duty of the *Nattan* and *Moopan* is to get the unmarried girls and the widows married to anyone they decide. They can break any marriage and rearrange it as they decide. Their power is so great that if a man has an eye on a married girl, he has only to pay a lump sum of money to the *Nattan* and *Moopan* who then will declare the earlier marriage as invalid and get her married to the desiring party. If one does not want to live together in wedlock the *Nattan* and *Moopan* can grant divorce and extract fine from the party seeking divorce. Thus, their role is very extensive ranging from collecting tax to social conduct.

For all the services they render their remunerations are fabulous. First of all they enjoy obedience from the people. They are paid Rs.70 for every marriage as *Palupadi* of which Rs.10.00 is given to the Jagirdar and the rest goes to them. They also receive or demand new clothes from the bridegroom's party. They extract even more depending on their relationship with the parties concerned. People oblige them in order to avoid future harassments. They also enforce fine on illegal marriages, elopements or when one refuses to marry a girl or a boy proposed by them. While collecting taxes for the Jagirdar they also extract from the people some share for themselves. As heads of Nadu they are exempted from yearly poll-tax for life except for the tax they pay once in five years as status symbol.

Kaundan and Kangani: The *Kaundan* is the head and the *Kangani* is the one who actually executes the duty of the twin office. In the order of hierarchy they are the lowest functionaries who execute the law of the *Jagirdar* at the village level. Each Village has a *Kaundan* and *Kangani.* As village-headman their powers and influence are limited to their own village. They take their orders from the *Nattan* and *Moopan* and are directly responsible to them. Anybody can become the *Kaundan* and *Kangani* provided he is a good natured man, able to control the village situation and can speak with the philosophical bent of mind. They are chosen by the villagers in consultation with the respective *Nattan-Moopan* and the *Kangani,* and approved by the Jagirdar. This office is held for three years and they may be re-elected.

Their job is to assist the *Nattan* and the *Moopan* in collecting revenues from their village. It is their duty to provide labourers to the *Jagirdar* and the *Garbari* whenever they need. This is expected of the people who live near or in the village of the *Jagirdar* and the *Garbari.* They conduct village festivals once a year. All the managements such as decorations of the temple, amusements, etc.are done by them. They also conduct the *Sangyam* to settle disputes over village trifles and report crimes and serious matters to the Jagirdar or to the *Garbari* or to the *Nattan-Moopan* as the case may be. They also collect temple tax and keep village accounts. They carry gifts to the Jagirdar on festive occasions and speak for the village of their needs or of their complaints.

They are exempted from annual poll-tax for life except for once in five years. They get a sumptuous meal and at times few rupees whenever they conduct the *Sangyam*. On Pongal day, one of the most important festivals of the Malayalis, each house gives them a quantity of paddy freely. They enjoy a high status and recognition in the village.

Kanimagan: This is a single-man post found frequently in villages. The post is very ambiguous; he acts as a liaison man between the Jagirdar and the rest of the functionaries especially the *Nattan-Moopan* and the *Kaundan-Kangani*. The post is hereditary but anyone from the same lineage may be appointed. He is chosen by the *Nattan-Moopan* and the *Kaundan-Kangani* and approved by the Jagirdar. The post is renewed every year, but usually one continues for long unless he is judged unfit. He can be dismissed at anytime on the recommendation of the *Nattan-Moopan* and the *Kaundan-Kangani*. He is supposed to have the knowledge of the assessment of land each one cultivates and the income of every family. His assistance is important in the taxation. Besides, when the *Sangyam* is called for, it is his duty to inform the villagers and collect the fine imposed on a member. His remunerations are meagre, left to the good will of the authority and the villagers. Together with the *Nattan* and *Moopan* the *Kanimagan* plays an important role in changing the *Kaundan* and *Kangani*.

Temple Priests: There are temple priests of first category known as the *Nambiars*. They have no direct political function, but they are meant to care for the spiritual welfare of the people and in this way they make the institution of the *Jagirdar* complete. There are nine temples belonging to the *Jagirdar* and each one has a *Nambiar* appointed by him. They are hereditary and for life. There are also village temples erected by the people. Each temple has two to five priests to conduct worship. These priests help the spiritual needs in the local level. They are usually hereditary and approved by the Jagirdar. They are lower than the *Nambiars* in status and function.

Kodangi: He is the self made sooth-sayer, exorcist, healer and shaman found almost in every village. He has no recognised place in the hierarchy. All the same he enjoys the approval of the Jagirdar and the patronage of the people. They are usually hereditary. But one's service may be terminated if one is considered as dangerous to the interest of the Jagirdar. As people say, there are good and bad ones and both are useful in cases of mental, physical and psychic ailment, bad fortune, etc. People give them cash and kind whenever they perform rituals and worship for them.

Karnam: The Jagirdar maintains a *Karnam* from the plains to keep his records. His job is to keep accounts of the revenues according to which the Quit-Rent was to be paid to the Government. He usually goes around each village and makes assessment of revenues. He is paid by the Jagirdar from the revenue collected from the people. For every marriage conducted in the villages he is also paid Rs.3.00 from the parties contracting marriage. Besides, when he visits the villages he also makes his own demand from the people in kind and cash.

From what has been described above, the crisis of the political organization of the Malayalis may be summarised as follows: The traditional political organization is rooted in the economic expedition of past chieftains at the head of which Jagirdar exercised his lordship of theocratic virtues with the assistance of subordinates. The subordinates were endowed with powers and status to control and direct every aspect of the life of the people and the ecology of the hill-nation even if it overran the will of the common people. Being cut off from the rest of the world, such a system helped to maintain unity and harmony within, and created and maintained an identity of their own as the Malayalis.

Ever since the institution of Jagirdar was abolished, the area and the people are placed directly under the care and administration of South Arcot District, Tamilnadu. Before law and in the eyes of public the Jagirdar is now neither the head of the people nor the proprietor of the land and its produce. His prerogatives to nominate office bearers, to collect tax, to command anyone and to demand anything from his tribesmen, and his ultimate consent and verdict on social, economic, cultural, religious, civil and cirminal affairs do not exist anymore, and if any, is a weightless and unwarranted bad case. Apart from the political and economic deprivation, the traditional and ethnic pompousness accorded to him by being carried on palanquin during the feast at his own Chinnathirupadhi-temple, and any such public expression of respect and honour due to the tirbal chief is suspended. He is now a private man, at par with his tribes men. For the Malayalis the place that the Jagirdar occupied for centuries is now made vacant and irreplaceable. Be it a vacuum in sovereign leadership or a step towards democarcy, this is a major change in the politcal life of the Malayalis.

By the same stroke, the *Garbari, Javundan, Nattan-Moopan* and the *Kaundan-Kangani* are not only abolished but also made disfunctional. The ex-*Garbari* died, and with him the name has become extinct. The *Javundan* has become a mere family priest of the Jagirdar. In the event of purification and marriage ceremonies people call rather a Brahmin from the plains than the *Javundan*. In matters of revenue collection and land distribution the *Manayakaran,* a Government official has taken the place of the *Nattan-Moopan*. In ethical and moral, social and relgious matters the *Nattan-Moopan* have been replaced by the *Kaundan-Kangani* who, notwithstanding the abolition of the hierarchies, heads the affairs of the village in traditional fashion. Thus, all the officials too have become private persons living with the past accretion of name and prestige that have now no more than local eminence. Thus the society has lost another group of leadership.

Changes in the traditional political organization have effected changes in the overall life pattern and in the economy of the people. Some consider the abolition of the Jagirdar system a blessing. For, in the past, for any small offence the officials used to charge a goat or chicken and even extract money from the people. They used to interfere in the practice of marriage as mentioned earlier. This is no more the case. People in the plains, i.e. adjoining the village of Jagirdar, are no more obliged to render their service to the Jagirdar at his will. They are also happy because in former times the Jagirdar would not allow his people to go to civil or criminal courts when needed, or to sell land or to marry out with non-Malayalis. Now there are no such restrictions on them. Any developmental work by outside agencies was unheard of at the time of Jagirdar. Now there are schools with free education and hostels, a bus route running from one end to the other end of the hills, free supply of electricity for one bulb for each house in many villages, one primary health centre for every seven villages run by the Danish International Development Association, and subsidy on fertilisers, seeds and cattles, etc.

The other side of the story is that the people prefer the Jagirdar system for the following reasons: in the past, land was free and left to individual's capacity to disafforestate any amount of land for a meagre tax, and to build houses in the place of their choice. They could cultivate all kinds of millets, grams, vegetables and staple food. There were enough of grazing grounds for the cattle, fire-wood for cooking and wood for furnitures, building houses and cattle sheds. This is not the case anymore. The Forest Department has taken over much of the land for forestry leaving only small amount of wet and waste land to be distributed among the people. The land distribution is done by the Government, and those who have money and influence are able to get it though with great difficulties and long waiting. As a matter of fact some have upto 40-50 acres of land whereas many have two or three acres. Forest goods were once open to the people, but now, as the people complain, wood like sandle, rose, etc., are smuggled than available to them. Thus, the benefits they lost through the takeover by the Government are the forest, the centre of their life, and for this reason they would prefer the Jagirdar system.

Change in life pattern and economy has affected their soical and moral life too; in the first place, they are used to work whole day in the hills, but now they have nowhere to go. Remaining at home brings social and moral problems such as divorce, drunkeness, indebtedness and service as labourers. Due to land distribution, parity between rich and poor has crept in. Consequently everyone cares for one's own family, and the community aspect is wading away. In the past barter system was predominant and thus goods rotated within the society. But now many merchants have taken to trade here and the goods are sold out. Many political ideologies have spread in the interest of power politics so much so MLAs take part in their marriage ceremonies.

Amidst such chaotic situation people adjust themselves in obvious ways: the Jagirdar is visited whenever possible especially on occasions when they need his financial help as loan. He also exercises some influence among the Government officers especially when it comes to distribution of land, in case of court cases as they have none so well-informed as the Jagirdar. He listens to their grievances against the Government officers. They seek his help against outsiders and in case of crimes committed by themselves to get his help to be freed from the criminal cases. He hosts them good meal on auspicious occasions in his house or family, and on the feast days at Chinnathirupathi. He still leads the feast there and he is respected as the custodian of the deity. He still commands respect as the owner of all the big temples and as a rich man and all that go with it. This is a symptom of their longing for the institution though only for economic reasons.

The non-Malayalis run in many places shops, tea stalls and general stores. The Malayalis approach them in times of need. They help the Malayalis with loan, in the purchase of land, fertilisers and cattles and all household goods. The Malayalis offer to them on occasions like Pongal, etc. a similar respect in the form of gifts and courtesy visits as they used to do to the Jagirdar. In this way the outsiders play the substitute for the Jagirdar. This is one form of persistence.

In general the changes are drastic but the persistence is thin as it is too early to determine the course the society will take in the course of changing situation.

References

Baliga, B.S. 1962 : *Gazetteer of India, South Arcot District*, Madras.

High Court of Madras 1966 : *High Court of Judicature at Madras, Special Oriental Jurisdiction.*

Hunter, W.W. 1886 : *Imperial Gazetteer of India*, Trubner, London.

Rajalakshmi, V. 1989 : Tribals by Marriage, *Indian Express*, Madurai, Saturday, May 20, Express Weekend.

Sastri, Nilakanta 1958 : *A History of South India*, Oxford University Press, India.

1964 : *The History and Culture of the Tamils*, Calcutta.

Sharma, Jagdish S. 1970 : *India since the Advent of the British*, S.Chand, Delhi.

Sharma, Sri Ram 1951 : *Mughal Government and Administration*, Kind Kittab, Bombay.

Venkataraman, S.R. 1951 : Malyalees, in *Tribes* (ed.) Thakkar Bapa, Government House, Delhi.

17

POLITICAL SYSTEM OF THE GONDS

S.G. DEOGAONKAR

Rise of Political Institutions in Tribal Communities

"The primitive society is atomistic and individualistic and the only bonds that knit the people into social, groupings are those of kinship". This was mentioned by Morgan, Maine and some others, concluding that there was nothing like a 'Government' in primitive society. As their life became complicated, situations arose in which chiefs and leaders were created to meet the needs. Morgan was of the opinion that during the process of evolution of political structures monarchy came quite late as a centralized form. In India, among the Naga tribes, the *Sema* and *Konyak* Nagas had very strong monarchist inclinations. Even, there were elders' councils to assist them. The tribal councils existed and exercised a lot of social control and to a large extent played the role of political structures with functions like regulation of relationship, settling disputes etc. However, conscious political activity was not observed.

Kinship was a factor responsible for maintaining the cohesion of the society and serving the purpose which can be viewed as a political one. Radcliffe-Brown considers marriage and kinship system as an arrangement which enables persons to live together and co-operate with one another in an orderly social life. In a tribal social structure the proximate generations are never equal and this maintains the solidarity of the group. He also maintains that the generations immediately senior to one's own is responsible for one's education and training resulting in the need for the maintenance of its authority. This gives rise to obedience to the senior generations and naturally to the oldest person(s). While endogamy at the tribal level maintains the solidarity of the group, exogamy at the *clan/gotra* level helps to maintain sound genetical characteristics.

For a tribal society, the survival of the group is more important than that of the individual. However, the individual may not always realize this, and ought to be taught to adhere to the norms of behaviour necessary for social survival. Radcliffe-Brown opines that this is assured through the fear of supernatural control and punishment. To him, religion is meant to create the feeling of dependence on society and thereby obtain the individual's concurrence with social norms, which ultimately aims at social survival. Durkheim states that the two aspects of religion viz., beliefs and rites, constitute the static part and the dynamic part respectively and the Gods and deities are symbolic of society. He feels that the religious belief and notions originate from the group mind at the social functions and festivals, when to use Rousseau's term the 'real wills' are at the highest ebb and generate the 'general will' which is always in the interest of the whole community. Hence religion is the recognition of the moral and physical superiority of the community over the individual. The direction and the lead in religious matter is provided by the priest or the *Pujari* or *Bhagat* etc. and this results in his acquiring a status and effecting obedience which stimulates political obedience.

Norms of behaviour and the mores accepted by the society become the cementing material for the stability and survival of the tribal community. All these norms and mores become the precursers of law and are adhered to by all. Those who break them and fall out are punished. This function is to be entrusted to some person or body of persons. The clan-chief or the chief of the tribe, a body of elders or religious leader perform this function. The initial functions are related to the maintenance and growth of the tribe, but as the concept of property dawns, as the barter transactions grow and as the economy as such grows, the decision-making functions also grow and become more complicated. The community ownership gives way at least to some extent to family and individual ownership giving rise to the institution of inheritance. As a result, the nature and scope of functions of the tribal chief or the council also grows. The nature of functions now becomes more secular and the control on the society is not only social, but even economic, as the decision makers are now balancing the economic interest of the individuals which are growing everyday. The collective wisdom of the community as represented by the chief or by the council (who is/ are very close to all the individuals in the community and live the same life as their equals), settles the issues and applies the new rules involving norms, while making decisions.

In these primitive decision-making and regulating structures there is an absolute integration of functions viz. of law-making administering and judicial decision-making. As a result, these three functions are not identified and are performed in the same body, at the same place and in the presence of whole community members. With settled cultivation and territorial foundations more functions are created, protection from outside territorial groups being the most important one. This naturally gives rise to two things, the first one being military preparedness and warning attitudes and the second one of the identity of the tribal group as an entity separate from all other external groups. This awareness in the tribal community and the rise of the consciousness of their ethnic group within a defined territory, and, the growth of the military power are the political attributes which now convert the ethnic tribal groups into a political society and the tribal chief or the tribal councils automatically become the supreme political authority within the tribal political system. The armed strength or the prestige of the ruling group or the ability to protect their community decides the political cohesion as a tribal nation. The customary law based on the norms and mores becomes the law of the land. There are some political units specially in the simpler societies who have only a council of elders which co-ordinates the collective action of the sub-groups in their society. Thus many primitive societies had no chiefs or headmen. In some tribes the political units had a centralized organization headed by a chief or a king. While the Naga tribes (particularly the Sema and the Konyak) had strong monarchist inclinations though their chiefs, were assisted by elder's councils. It is observed that the Institution of the chief or the king was a product of necessity in tribes where emergencies and contingencies always arose. In middle India the village-councils were more powerful but suffered a setback during the British regime. The Gonds in India who constitute a major tribal group, had a political organization based on perfect equality and had chieftains and kings who were superior only so far as the political functions were concerned. However, the village-level councils were maintained and had positive role in administration. It will be rewarding to trace the growth and structure of the political institutions of the Gonds with special reference to the Gonds from the Vidarbha region of Maharashtra.

The Political System of Gonds

The Gonds, one of the largest of the Indian tribes, show an elaborate political system. Traditionally they had a well-knit social organization which formed the basis of social cohesion. The political superstructure had its base in the social organization. Though the Vidarbha pattern in this context is given it is more or less similar in the Gonds elsewhere.

The organization of the Gond community is based on the principle of fundamental equality of all Gond clans within the clans of all clan members. The Gond village community is basically free association of equals. Hence, class differences are absent and even the relations between phratries and clans (irrespective of exogamy) is based on equality of status. Prof. C. von-Furer-Haimendorf points out that this segmentary organization based on phratries and clans is without territorial implications and is concerned mainly with the regulation of marriage and with the *persapen* cult. He further points out that the feudal system among the Gond is however having a territorial and political basis with a hierarchy of feudal chieftains, who occupy a place in a rank system additional to their ascribed status as members of their clan and phratry, and cuts at right angles across a vertical division into pharatries. Clan and-sub-clans divide a Raj-Gond society horizontally into a small aristocratic class of *Raja* and other chiefly families and the great mass of commoners (Furer Haimendrof, 1979 : 122).

The principles of equality is also reflected in the fact that in the Gondi language there is no specific honorific term for class distinction, no status indicating terms of address and even the commonest Gond calls his Raja or any one from the Royal household in the second persons of the singular (*ibid*: 123). Similar is the case among the Madiya Gonds of the Gadchiroli district as their is no specific honorific term for their Raja. After immigration of the Gond to Chandrapur and later into Mandla a new kind of physical grouping of houses, which was associated with the concept of fort, was the beginning of a socio-political organization called 'Garh' (or *gadh*) which might have originated in Chandrapur or Mandla and Dr. Behram Mehta considers the 'fort' and the 'Garh' as the important landmarks in the emergence of feudalism among the Gonds (1984 : 618).

Establishment of the Gond Kingdom of Chandrapur dates back to 1247 A.D. when a warrior called Col. Bhill collected some warriors and established his influence in the Shirpur, Manikgarh area. During those years the Yadav Kings of Deogiri had lost their empire and *Nag Vanshi* Mana Kings of Vairagadh were also destabilised. Col.Bhil who was a Raj-Gond, conquered the big fort of the Manikgarh from the Mana Kings and established the Gond Kingdom. He made Bhika alias Bhim Ballal-Singh from the Atram clan who hailed from Movad (Dist. Adilabad, Andhra Pradesh) the first Gond King (Rajurkar, 1982 : 108-113). He made Shirpur as his capital but ruled from Movad. Between 1247 to 1751, all the twenty three Gond rulers who ruled in the area, were from the same lineage. The capital was shifted to Ballarshah (Ballarpur) in 1322 A.D. and later to Chandrapur (Chanda) in 1497 A.D. when the Gond King Hirshah was ruling (*ibid*).The emblem of the Gond Kingdom depicts a lion sitting over an elephant. The principal Gond Kingdoms in the Gondwana area were as follows:

1. Gadh Mandla -- North Gondwana

2. Deogadh and Nagpur -- Central Gondwana

3. Chandrapur -- South Gondwana.

On the northern slope of the Satpuda there was a Gond Kingdom named Kherla besides petty Gond Naiks inn Melghat, styling themselves as Rajas (Gazetteer of India, 1956-66).

The Gond Raja Hir Shah ruled between 1497 to 1572 A.D. with his capital at Chandrapur. He built the fort, temple of Lord Mahadeo, a lake and reformed administration. He established seventeen zamindaris, out of which the Aheri Zamindari was the largest in size (2603 Sq. miles). One Kok Shah was made the first

Zamindar of Aheri, as he succeeded in suppressing the rebellion of Sadho and Mula in the Surja Gadh area. This Kok Shah was also from the Atram clan.

The administration under the Gonds was broadly similar under the Gond Kings of Nagpur, Deogadh and Chandrapur. These were mainly feudal systems. They built forts at the capital and other important places. Subordinate local chiefs who exercised considerable power were called the *Rajas, Rais,* and the *Thakurs.* The Maharaja held small domain and the surrounding area was under the local chiefs like the Rais or Rajas, who were under the military strength of the Maharaja. The Thakurs made contribution in cash and kind and provided troops for the service of the Raja.

The local chiefs were called Thakurs, who took cognizance of the petty crimes, could levy fines and confiscate property. The structure of the Gond Kingdom at Gadh-Mandla and Deogadh was common and there were modifications elsewhere. In case of Chandrapur (Chanda) the basis was the same, but the Rajas were a little more powerful and possessed a territorial domain where they exercised direct authority.

In Deogadh, Nagpur and Chanda there were officers known as the Deshmukhas, Despandes, Huddars, Muharirs, and the Waradpandes for land revenue administration. The administration was centralized under them. The administration under Chandrapur Kings was similar, but the Zamindars were powerful (*ibid* : 59 60)

The Gond Raja of Chandrapur was the highest authority on the tribal heads even from the Additional district. The Raja Akbar Shah of Chandrapur as a direct descendant of the Gond King of Chanda was considered the supreme tribal authority and even after the loss of empire as rulers he maintained his prestige within the tribal community upto 1941 A.D. During his visits, he presided over Panchayat meetings to settle disputes which could not be settled by the local community. (Furer-Haimendrof. 1979 : 125). However, after the breaking of the Hyderabad State, this influence dropped in the Adilabad area. In recent past the Gond Rajas at Chandrapur have lost all influence and the only influential

Gond 'Maharaja' is the Zamindar at Aheri, who still maintains his feudal position among the Gonds from the Aheri Zamindari area, which includes the present Etapalli and Aheri tahsils and parts of Sironcha tehsil. One of the reasons is that the Gonds of this area are still much backward and illiterate and the Etapalli tahsil is the habitat of the Madiya Gonds who are classified as the primitive tribals and are much orthodox and tradition oriented. The feudal structure under the Maharaja of Aheri is still surviving, while in Chandrapur-- Manikgadh area, there is a lot of modernization of the Gonds due to the impact of industrialization and urbanization.

Under the Aheri Zamindari area, the traditional political chief was the Aheri Zamindar or the Raja of Aheri, who had an *Adivasi Sabha* or a council. The whole area was divided into four *patties* (regions) with a Sindhia as the head of each *patti*. Each *patti* was a track consisting of about fifty to hundred villages. Each village was headed by a Gaita or a Patel and also had a Panchayat. He could lodge report and complaints to the Sindhia. The Sindhia had full control over the *patti* and acted as a judge and also as *pujari*. The Gaita of the villages was also known as a *Bhumiya* if he performed religious duty. After the establishment of the tribal Panchayat by the British Government in 1949 under the Notified Tribal Areas Rules, the judicial functions of the traditional tribal chiefs was lost and the tribal Panchayats became more powerful alongwith the Gaita, who used to preside over the Panchayat. This position was more or less the same even among the Adilabad Gonds in the adjoining area of Andhra Pradesh.

The tribal Panchayat and its chief in this area are the important even today, as they settle many local problems and issues. Matters relating to marriage, divorce etc. are settled in these councils. The bride-price is settled and its performance is assured. A girl or a woman who runs away from her father's/ husband' house and 'enters' another man's house, has to appear before these Panchayats to answer queries or complaints after which the decisions are made and implemented through penalties in kind or cash or compensation. Decisions on social and cultural issues, religious matters, social functions and festivals are taken and the Panchayat or its chief can call the village community for action. The *pujari* (also called *perma* or *bhagat*) is also consulted if necessary. These councils and their chiefs report to the Sindhia of the *patti* in socio-cultural and religious matters, and they in turn report to their Raja of Aheri. The author has seen the Gaitas and Sindhias sitting in the Durbar of the Raja of Aheri and discussing social problems including differences and quarrels between the persons from the same village or different villages Community problems facing the village community,the tribals in the area very rarely carry their quarrels connecting behaviour against community norms and even against cultural and religious matter to the court specially when both the parties are from their own community.

The changing style of the traditional political leadership in the area is also worth noting. The present Raja's uncle Kirtimantrao Maharaj was a Minister in the old Madhya Pradesh Government. The Raja of Aheri viz. Raje Vishweshwar Rao Maharaja was a member of the Legislative Assembly in Maharashtra for three terms and the later he became the Member of Parliament.

His son Satyawan Rao is presently Member of the Legislative Assembly and throughout his political career he was with the opposition parties. His nephew Dharmarao-Baba Atram is an active worker of the Congrees-I and for some time he was the President of the Gadchiroli district Congress-I unit. It is interesting to note that in the outgoing Legislative Assembly all the M.L.A.s from the Gadchiroli district (all tribals) were from the opposition parties. The Aheri Raja popularly called as the Zamindar has also established Dharmarao Shikshan Mandal in 1958, and it is running thirty two educational institutions in the area which includes two senior colleges, (including a science college) two junior colleges, six hostels and the rest schools. This has given a new dimension to his leadership and has contributed to spread of education in the tribal area. However, this Raja has not encouraged much the development of communications and industries in the interior of tribal areas though he has consistently opposed the liquor consumption by tribals and the opening of liquor shops in the tribal areas. He himself is a strict teatotaller. The prominence of tribal leadership in this area in the socio-cultural sphere is demonstrably visible on the occasion of the Dussera, when the tribals from the area assemble at his palace and pay their respect in the traditional manner.

Among the Gonds from Maharashtra, the Aheri Zaminder is probably the only Chief who is still an active feudal Raja and is performing functions pertaining to socio-cultural and religious aspects of the tribal community in the area. Hence some details have been given above with a view to project a model of tribal political system which at once is reminiscent of the erstwhile sprawling Gond Kingdom of Chandrapur and also one which shows the political change of the traditional political chiefs due to education and modernisation. Raja Vishweshwar Rao is himself English educated, who had his education in Fergueson College, Pune and Hislop College, Nagpur. He can speak fluently in English and equally fluently in the Madiya-Gondi language which is the tribal dialect of the tribals from the area. He is Raj-Gond and himself practises and presides over the tribal population of the Zamindar which also practises the *Persa Pen* cult. However, along with the traditional *pujas* and rituals he has started worshipping Sai Baba (Shirdi) since the last thirteen to fifteen years. On the eve of the Dussera day, there is a grand procession of the 'Palkhi' (palanquin) of Sai Baba in which the Zamindar, members of his household, a few non-tribals reciting the bhajans and thousands of the Gonds participate and more through the streets of Aheri. On the Dussera day the traditional rituals and procession are followed. This change by way of an addition to worship through the Zamindar is a significant stage in the acculturation of the Gonds, because any change in the religious aspects of a primitive tribal community of the Madiya Gonds has high significance. This also indicates the persistence of his hold on their mind not only as a traditional leader but also as a moderniser. In politics his influence still carries 'a vote bank' though his nephew who is a leader of Congress-I (and whom he loves very much) is a potential competitor for carrying tribal votes. Either way, the household as such, does have a political influence on the tribal attitudes, which may bring out a modern political edition of the traditional, feudal, political imprints of the Aheri Zamindar of the Gonds.

References

Deogaonkar, S.G. 1982 : Media of Bhamragad, New Delhi, Inter-India Pub.

	1988	:	*Political Anthropology*, Allahabad, Kitab-Mahal.
Furer-Haimendorf,	1979	:	*The Gonds of Andhra Pradesh*, C. von New Delhi, Vikas Pub. House.
Mehta, B.H.	1984	:	*Gonds of Central Indian Highlands*, New Delhi, Concept Pub. Co. Vol. I, II.
Nadgonde, G.D.	1979	:	*Bharatiya Adivasi*, Pune, Continental Prakashan.
Rajurkar, A.J.	1982	:	*Chandrapurcha-Itihas* Chandrapur, Mahakali Prakashan.
Gazetteer of India	1973	:	*Maharashtra State --Chandrapur District* Maharastra State Gazetteers, (Revised Ed.), Bombay, Maharashtra State.
	1966	:	*Nagpur District. Bombay*, Maharashtra State.

18

THE DRAMATURGY OF POWER AND POLITICS IN A TRIBAL REGION

H.L. SHUKLA

I

Historically, there is ample evidence to suggest that cohesive tribal groups, with almost homogenous aspirations and grievances, have participated in a host of modern movements (Halba movement of Bastar 1774-9) and conflicts (The Naxalite Movement in Bastar 1986 onwards). It would seem, therefore, that the tribal people (often despite being ill-organised and poorly armed) are capable of waging a conflict of detachment and containment forcing the national Governments to disperse their concentrated mobile armed forces in occupation of regions which sometimes have fierce traditions of independence.

This relatively homogeneous group within the complex of tribal society of Bastar will form the focus of the following considerations for two reasons :

1. Four decades of Independence ought to allow an interim stock taking as to whether projections of development in Bastar have been realised or not;

2. The analysis of administration important in this connection, may produce findings relevant for the other regions of the country as well. But why to introduce the dual concept of "myth and ideology" here? My intervention is to show that statements

referring to an obviously tangible and quantitatively measurable object like public administration only gain in depth and explanatory capacity when they are rooted in the history and psychology of their environment.

Any action, institution, or social phenomenon can be analysed from two different perspectives of interest; on the one hand with regard to manifest objectives, tasks and consequences, but on the other also in relation to latent and subjective interpretations of the reality concerned. One could also say that each reality possesses two levels, the level of "strategic rationality" and the level of "symbolic mystification". However, the two levels are difficult to separate from each other; they exercise a mutual influence on one another. Thus administration, too, has an instrumental and a symbolic function; on the one hand the carrying out of functions and on the other the representation of the power of the State. The following remarks proceed from the assumption that in tribal Madhya Pradesh symbolic function of the administration is more important than in our socio-political system, indeed that it makes itself independent and overshadows the instrumental function.

A decisive part in the perception of the administration by the population is played by what is termed "myth" in literature, i.e. a conviction shared by a large group of people which is not questioned and conveys a particular significance to events and actions. It is noted that idealisation of the administration that interests us in this connection. This is as it were secularized definition of the concept of myth, required to be complemented in the special case of Bastar by the traditional, religious myth that is part of the ethical foundation of a tribal society.

Every society has its myths. We are not concerned here to distinguish between these myths and legends and folk tales; what is important is to note that these myths are not merely stories, but reality, that is, that they determine collective and individual life.

Myth and magic are,--without wronging present-day Bastar,--still more intensively present in this country than elsewhere, and also determine the life of today. At the same time, we must not relapse into the mistake of the simplifying dichotomy of (a) the traditional knowledge of Bastar is symbolic, non-critical (i.e. sacralized by the authority of the ancestors) and esoteric (enshrined in myths and transformed into rites for the initiated); and that (b) the modern science is discursive, critical (*i..e..* subjected to methodological scrutiny). rational and public.

The reality in each case is a mixture of the two extreme descriptions, though with different weighted components.

My topic would be considerably easier to deal with if in fact the development of India had taken place as scholars pictured it around 1950. At that time, thought was bound within the absolute polarity of tradition and modernity, and was only able to imagine development in this unilinear direction--from tradition to modernisation. This notion, hardly questioned at the time--from which arose prescriptions for development policy was based on considerations desired from the history of ideas on the process of evolution that took place in our cultural domain, and which were at an early stage conceived in terms of contrasting pairs: community and society, traditionality and rationality, tribe and non-tribe, primitive and civilized. What could befall the country better than to emulate this development? Must it too not progress from the agrarian to the industrial economy, from personal communication to that of media, from feudal to political democracy, from direct social control to indirect bureaucratic, and finally from myth to ideology? Many more such dichotomies could be quoted from the literature. Together they amount to a conception of development that is limited to the most faithful politicians of this country. Can that type of development be achieved by the State Government? Must they not collapse beneath the might of the exaggerated expectations of a quickening population?

How were these aspirations to be channelled and at the same time constructed into a provincial and administration system capable of functioning? In order to answer these questions, it is essential to make a condensed survey of the most important dimensions of colonial rule and their consequences beyond independence.

II

The national awakening of the tribes of India and the urge for an administrative organisation of national territories began when India was a British colony. The colonial doctrines were rapidly developed as justification for the "Civilizing mission", for politico-administrative rule, economic exploitation and cultural domination. But colonialism endeavoured to convince those who most closely came within its sphere of influence--for example via the school system and the mission of the inferiority of their own tradition and culture; thus it brought about a deformation of the individual, a splitting of tied personality factors that are still active today.

It was the middle class, numerically small though it was as a rule, that determined politics. It produced politicians who were in power for a long time. The acme of the "Civilising mission" was to be the adaption of the model of western democracy. But had democracy been practised under the colonial system? Or was it not rather suppression, manipulation and contempt of people thought inferior to the colonial matter? This simple question was asked only by a few critical spirits in the country.

Some Indian scholars express the view that the unity of India was "brought about" by the British during their colonial domination. M.N. Srinivas, for example, asserts that India was first made a single political entity by the British who brought with them modern technology, knowledge and administrative skills (quoted from Kluyev, 1981:110). Such a point of view is perhaps engendered by the tense national relations in modern India and the idealisation of the times of the Empire which are already in the post. But the unity of colonial India was only stable as the power of the parent State, and the stability of that power, in turn, depended on how the British managed to keep India internally divided.

What was decisive was the emergence of a "new elite" seeking a break through into the future between colonial socialisation and "traditional" forms of rule. It wishes to be "modern" and propogates, within the inherited limits--whether geographical or institutional in nature, a specific kind of nationalism, in which, as yet, no notion of the nationality exists in an accepted form, where no unity can so far be achieved--the individual still finds more security in the family, the tribe, the caste, the religion, the language, the region--prefigurations of unity are created.

III

The expectations of the population placed in Independence were, as if particularly important for our perspective of investigation satisfied largely by a rapid expansion of the formal education system and an inflamation of the administrative apparatus. Whilst under colonial could attend a modern school as auxiliary staff were required for the administration, the educational system acquired with Independence the quality of a central emanicipatory agency: it was regarded as the most important investment for rapid growth of the economy, and at the same time as an instrument with which the new values of the nation to be constructed, were to be transmitted as efficiently as possible to the new generation (Harrison, 1960 : 209).

In the process, a proper myth of the power of education developed which took hold of mainly the rural-population, who saw the dawn of a better future (at least for the next generation) and so put pressure on the Government to build more and more schools, more colleges, more universities. These aspirations, moreover, were largely fulfilled after Independence. The examples of brilliant careers made a powerful impression in the villages from which the holders of these offices originated. These perceptions led to the Government to provide quite a good amount in the budgets on the education sector alone. Even today, there are State Governments that grant all students (regardless of the income position of the parental home) a state bursary about twice as high as the legal minimum wage (Dinaman Times, 21 Sept, 1990).

Now, let us turn to the administration: although it might have been assumed that the administration, would have been subjected to a *thorough-going-reform* on the achieving of Independence, this was not the case. After Independence, the "elites" began by making themselves comfortable and enjoying the power that had come into their hands. The institutions, laws, and modes of behaviour of the colonial power were in some cases preserved, despite the fact that the colonial administration was designed more to ensure "law and order" than development. The first thing to be recorded is the rapid expansion of the public service: in only one decade, from 1960 to 1970, the number of civil servants atleast doubled, a significant amount, according to the financial state of the State concerned, goes to the maintenance of the civil service alone (including teachers). The State thus becomes the largest employer.

The vision of the pupil is one-track: any-one who has turned his back on the agrarian structure of the village and made his way through school has a right to a post in the administration. Even well-paid posts in industry appear to pupils questioned in the matter less attractive than administrative activities, even at the lowest level. It is thus not surprising that hundreds of young applicants enter for the entrance examination for every post advertised. This "Concours d' entree" (to take an example from Bastar) thus acquires the nature of an initiation rate such as was customary for boys and girls in traditional society, but is now gradually losing importance. If this parallel may be taken as meaningful, it becomes explicable how entry into the public service is viewed by the office-holder primary as a source of authority, status and prestige.

The civil service appears the incarnation of modernity, the avantegarde of knowledge, and of socio-economic progress. The population, conditioned by the past colonial rule to passivity, trusts the administration and expects from it the solution of their problems--an administration that acts in the official language (which may not always be understood by the majority of population) and produces more and more written paper, something unaccustomed in a society of oral communication.

This admiration is at the same time directly functional for the modes of behaviour of the civil servants. The civil servant sometimes sees himself as incumbent of the position of power, and not as executor of a service towards society always. The society on its part does not always measure the civil service according to its efficiency, but glorifies its members because they represent the myth of urbanity and affluence. The bureaucrats further reinforce this facade of prestige--as the Canadian sociologist ALF Schuwiz has expressed it in the African context, "by concealing the discrepancy between a post they wish to overcome and a future they cannot yet achieve behind a kind of "*ritual modernism*": the careful cultivation of status symbols (official car and housing), the stylisation of their external appearance (dark suit and tie, even in the highest temperatures), excessive stress on procedure and details, high-sounding speeches on official occasions. In this way it is possible to conceal relative incompetence and reluctance to make decisions." (1974 : 271-273).

In some respects, this picture may appear much exaggerated, but it does indicate how in India a new stratum has developed that lays claim for itself to the legitimacy of public action. There is no clear consensus among scholars whether this is to be designated a self-contained, or even parasitic, "class of country" (c.f. Bhanjdeo, 1965).

How, however, can this administrative stratum develop further in future? From this perspective, it would appear to cast a glance at the Oraons in Chattisgarh, who may be taken as paradigmatic for such an "elite culture" amongst the tribal societies. The Oraon is a dominant tribe of Chattisgarh. Out of their total population of 2,83,073 in the State of Madhya Pradesh, 2,81,459 live mainly in Surguja and Raigarh districts. The Oraons have come under the influence of British missionaries. While the total number of the Christian Oraons in Raigarh was reported as 47, 517 in 1931, their number has increased to the tune of 87, 516 in 1961. In 1931, there were no Oraon Christians in Surguja, their number in 1961 was 5,498 (Shukla, 1985 : 58-60).

The "Oraons" were used preferentially by the British Colonial administration as auxiliaries in the administration, judicial and educational systems, and were thus able to rapidly rise to leading positions. This state of privilege would not be worthy of special stressing had it not been able to be maintained beyond Independence. This is to be attributed to a strategy of "dramaturgy of power." This group is tightly knit by numerous family and professional ties, and so appears to outsiders as a powerful block. The Oraons never cease to demonstrate their significance to the outside world by most impressive sites and manifestations. splendid Church services and processions, baptisms, weddings and funerals with hundreds of participants, an elaborate sartorial order, and stilted manners. These occasions further, strengthen the inner cohesion of the group and create a myth externally.

Without wanting to carry the analysis of the ceremony too far, the following can be deduced from it: where an administrative elite succeeds in combining universalist values with particularist ones, its position is stabilised towards the outside world. Universalist values can be the tradition of norms of the legal system, the ethic of the civil service as most faithful servant of the State, equality of opportunity in access to the educational system; and at the same time these values are instrumentalised for the maintaining of collective and family privilege, whose most important instruments are the educational system and the civil service.

In contrast take the example of the Baiga tribe. Many of the Baiga norms and their enforcement are concerned with maintaining the integrity of the tribe on the one hand, and its prestige on the other (Elwin, 1939 : 196). The preservation of group solidarity through the maintenance of group integrity and prestige both explains and aids in maintaining the Baiga endogamous relations, rules of commensality, and concepts of pollution. Thus, he could not be alienated and remained backward in the game of power-politics.

An "elite culture" as self-contained as this (Christian Oraon) is not to be found in other districts of Madhya Pradesh, and the differences in other respects are also to be found: the "Oraons" are at most indirectly concerned in the political power in the country in the narrower sense, and apart from strategically important, they have no important share in the economic power. In other Indian states the picture is a different one.

IV

First of all, the close relation between the *administration* and the *political system* is to be stressed (Subramaniam, 1977). The assumption that the inherited western democratic institutions could provide a foundation for the formation of public life in India, was soon shown to be not true.

The political democracy was taken to a one-party system, often given the appearance of legitimation by recourse to traditional patterns of conflict resolution. In such an atmosphere, some civil servants were not able to remain neutral always; they sometimes got politicized and integrated into the political ruling complex. Now that the old politicians with their regional and ethnic backing, have long been eliminated, the administration has in fact gained in actual importance. It can today be said that the administrative competences that were trained in the years after Independence, and the goodwill of these holders of office to do something for the development of their States, have not been properly used. These political processes had two facets: they created an extreme centralisation of these processes of decision making and a "departicipation", that is, the institutional possibilities for the participation of the broad mass of the population in political decisions was drastically reduced, and thus the "political arena" made smaller. The administration is integrated into this *rhetoric* of dominance; indeed, it has become one of the main instruments--beside the party--of the preservation of status *quo*. This must be remembered when internal phenomena of the administration are considered in isolation and frequently criticised too mercilessly. An administration can only be as good as its political environment permits.

V

Any meaningful tribal policy can only be fashioned with a proper understanding of the historic processes of reaction between so called tribal and higher societies and in the context of our political administrative environment.

Thus when India became independent, the desire to integrate the tribals with the rest of the country was a strong motive with the policy makers. However, the bureaucratic set up sometimes created hurdles against this policy of outright integration. In many places the bureaucracy has only added to this insecurity. The opening of schools, hospitals and cooperative societies agree with the bureaucratic penchant for statistics, but it does not remedy the basic situation of insecurity caused by the alienation of land and forest rights.

In the ever-green forest of Bastar, the problem was aggravated by many external factors. At first the ruling party tried to bring the ruler into the fold of the party and thus net all the Assembly seats from the area. What exactly caused the split between him and the party will not be known. While this political arena was being staged to the concern of the administration and sometimes amusement of the general public, another and a great upheaval was going on within Bastar. The administration perhaps prodded by some unsympathetic civil servants and unimaginative politicians went on extending its sway into the heart of the tribal preserve, disregarding the tribal hierarchy. This sometimes resulted in violent incidents (Shukla, 1990).

The tribal attitude toward the administration is one of annoyance or indifference. They do not understand its function, and they are suspicious of the motives of the civil servants. It seems difficult for them to think of the Governnment in a helpful role. The administration is sometimes thought of as a necessary evil, an annoyance, and not as an instrument of progress (Jay, 1970 : 237).

This indifference toward the Government might have made them Naxalities.

The Andhra group of Naxalites has been intensified all over Bastar within a few years. A stage has now been reached when there could be a severe conflict if the relations between the administration and the tribes are completely broken. Here, in Bastar, the lack of much public support and cooperation has created difficulty in the proper functioning of intelligence services, the backbone of preventive and investigative work.

The relationships abstracted by the Dorlas from particular tactics and organizational methods propagated by the Naxalites (such as the night foray, the ambush, hit and run, and infiltration and attack from behind) appear to have had structurally similar parallels in the Gond culture. One recognizable parallel being the fact that the Dorlas still hunt annually and as hunters they exhibit the ability to stalk, camouflage themselves, attack with surprise and deploy weaponry in groups (Blunt, 1795). All these techniques represent a potential paradigm for conflict. When the Bastar tribes became upset within the nature and pace of change (many of which they could neither understand nor adjust to), they attempted to change forcibly those groups whom they felt most threatened by, i.e. civil servants and usurers. Using traditional weapons and tactics, they hoped they could reduce the pace and ameliorate the effects of change. Concurrent with these attempts were attacks on the institutions of the State, which the tribes saw as supporting the change.

VI

Particular attention should be given to demands linked to the problem of the administration and territorial autonomy of tribes. Together with economic demands a new dimension has been added to the tribals awakening by consciousness of their linguistic and political demands. The emergence of small groups of the tribal literate and a thin layer of middle class elements among various tribes has given the movement a new political complexion. The tribal language often forms the function of the new movement.

In the area where the Gonds live there are also signs of development of the national process. In October, 1968 an Adivasi Conference of the Bastar district, convened by a local unit of political party and leaders of some other organisation adopted a resolution on setting up an autonomous region for the Gonds with a separate Assembly and a Council of Ministers. A conference of a political party in Chhattisgarh area reaffirmed the demand. The movement of the Gonds, who live in the territories of several States, is patchy at present; it has not become a mass movement, but it's future, according to researchers, may be promising (Singh, 1983).

In the early 20th century, in the areas populated by the Bhils, attempts were made to start a movement for a *Bhil-Raj*, but they quickly subsided. In the 1960s there were numerous mass movements by the Bhils for improving their economic situation and for food assistance in bad years, and demonstrated against action of the officials and the police. In 1969 a demand was made to set up a separate State of *Bhilisthan* or *Bhil-Pradesh*. This demand is repeated from time to time and is acquiring more supporters (Kulkarni, 1975 : 97-8).

Analysing the character of national process in the post-Independence years in Madhya Pradesh, one should expect a more persistent struggle by these peoples for their rights and interests. This is supported by the experience of the peoples of Assam and other States of East India, where some ethnic groups have achieved the setting up of separate administrative units in their territories and have speeded up the awakening of national consciousness. The development of economic ties, the implementation of community development projects, political campaigns, the gradual expansion of primary education, and the activities of educational organisation aimed at the standardisation of the tribal languages and the expansion of their social functions (Shukla, 1985) all facilitate the awakening of national life and the victory over the isolation of the tribal people of Madhya Pradesh.

VII

What, then, of the relationship between the *administration* and the *economy* ? The Indian Government is pledged to overcome the heritage of the colonial era; all efforts should be directed towards constructing a national economy. The result should be an economic system based on the resources of the country and leading to an interdependence of the economic sectors (*e.g.*. financing of industrialisation from agricultural). This objective whose desirability no-one is likely to question, was to be achieved by Central Planning. Particularly corresponding efforts were made, although pragmatic adaptations are the rule. Now I am not of the opinion that such investments are basically to be judged negatively as far as their effects are concerned; but in the meantime many instances have shown that the eagerly awaited positive effects have not taken place--in particular, no significant contribution towards reducing unemployment, and no stimulating influence on the domestic economy, e.g. skilled trades and minor industry. The sectoral strategies of the goal of "economic development" reveal emphasis on economic growth (i.e. increasing the statistical per-capita income) at all costs. Here particular efforts continue to be made in the industrial area, the expansion of which is supported by a generous promotion policy. It is thus inevitable that this sector is mainly in the hands of foreign concerns, which are not guided by national economic interests.

It is no different in the services sector located in tribal regions (banks, transport, apart from small commerical and repair businesses), in which the non-tribal continuity is particularly evident. With this "modern sector" subject to non-tribal influence there contrasts a divided agrarian sector: a substance area with partial local marketing, and the agricultural export sector mostly organised in family economics. Agricultural policy concentrates on the latter sub-sector because it promises high fiscal yields, and thus fails to reduce the dependence on fluctuating market prices.

Diversification of agriculture and a regulated internal marketing of basic foodstuffs are still in their infancy.

While the new agricultural technology appears to be accentuating regional contradictions, it seems to be intensifying inequalities within the tribal regions and villages themselves. The village communities in Madhya Pradesh are now divided in two distinct groups--those who can avail themselves of the opportunity brought in by modern farm practices, and those who cannot take the opportunity because of their poor economic condition. It would appear, therefore, that the purchase of inputs is correlative to economic status. Concurrent with this increase in the standard of living of the village rich has been their increasing awareness of political realities. Communities like the Bhatras and the Halbas in Bastar are not only dominant traditionally, but their ethnic rules do not prohibit intimate association with the land. They, therefore, enjoy a great deal of freedom from upper caste domination and also possess the inherited skills to substantially improve the techniques of agricultural production. Consequently they have begun to assert themselves politically.

There is evidence to suggest that the values, norms and orientations of the tribal elite, which has emerged as a result of changes in the land tenure laws, and in agricultural production, are very different from those of the traditional elite. The traditional relationship between ethnic groups, economic status and power has been disrupted with the advent of *Panchyat Raj,* such that the middle strata groups have now acquired a position of dominance in village affairs. While one segment of the population has steadily lost control of the most basic means of agricultural production and development--land--another has developed into an affluent and assertive tribal elite. Thus new elite, however, with its preferences for western practices has tended to ignore traditional modes of reciprocity and thus has become more power oriented and less development oriented. These changes provide some explanation of the intensity of tribal/Naxalite vengeance upon local civil servants. In analysing the pre-conditions of the Naxalite upsurge, an understanding of the decay of local handicrafts is also of special significance.

Though the main cause of alienation of the tribe might be political, it however, operates because of the psychological, social and cultural conflicts between the two contrasting world views of the non-tribals and the tribal. Having been given a peripheral view of the non-tribal's culture through non-tribal education, the tribal evaluates his own culture superficially and thus develops a "marginal personality". Moreover, the tools with which he evalutes it are also supplied by the non-tribal. Consequently, he is not rejecting his own culture and language in favour of Hindi to which we know he has a marginal access. What has gone wrong with the tribes ?

Have the political leadership and the administration failed in this country ? An increasing number of voices are saying that this is so. Never before were the central Indian tribes so thoroughly and insolently exploited as since the Independence of the country.

Has the "elite" dodged its responsibility? No doubt, it will submit its arguments, e.g. the market situation and adverse climate conditions; but it will not be able to claim that it lacks economic thinking or management capacity. For in the "modern sector" it has given plenty of proof of these qualities: by beginnings in the Indianisation of the economy, the expansion of the state enterprises, participation in foreign firms, the forcing of alien elements out of business life, new fields of action have resulted, not to mention possibilities of private investment; which are mostly rented to foreign experts. The civil servants have had a rich share in these sources.

It is quite obvious that conflicts of interest and a decline in administrative efficiency can result from this. There is a reference to a "*Politico-administrative -economic complex*" in India today. I will refrain from deriving further conclusions from this. Just one remark more. "Every election manifesto claims that it will eradicate corruption". Our whole system is now jeopardised. The trio mentioned above has punctured the country.

VIII

If, to conclude, we wish to make an analytical summary, the following points present themselves.

(a) The administrative system of tribal India must be analysed, beyond its instrumental function, also as to its symbolic functions. Such an analysis reveals that the mystification of the administration prevents the proper performance of its functions and public control (for which reason, by the way, jurisdiction relating to administration, in tribal regions is highly underdeveloped).

(b) This administrative system is largely an immediate consequence of colonial rule, and thus manifests itself in "passive adaptive acculturation" or adoption of an alien structure of administration without relation to the tribal social system.

(c) This imitative borrowing is, in addition, a "lagging emulation" (Friedl, 1964) i.e. a social group that acquires new wealth and status (in this case the new tribal elite) tends, in the process of imitation of a group with higher prestige (in this case western culture) to adopt aspects and in particular to stress those that are historically no longer so topical.

(d) At the sametime, the old values are still present in Indian society in administrative action, too, especially in the relation of the civil servant to the citizen--but they conflict with the imported values.

The dozen of administrative research in developing countries, Fredl W. Riggs (1964) terms this "*Polynormativism*", pointing out that a dilemma can arise: the new rules do not yet meet with general social acceptance, and in such a situation the actors can tend to feel free of all norms, and to merely pursue their own short-term personal interests by exploiting their position of power.

How can this unsatisfactory situation be overcome? We demand a radical thinking in India against the "myth of administrative modernisation." We oppose the uncritical adoption of western models of administration, which all too often, have only reinforced mental and material dependence. Each continent and every country must find its own path on the basis of its own culture, even if this is a painful process. We demand the recollection of Indian values. The administrative system must grow from the society by integrating the individual and the social group, the process of premature bureaucratisation since independence has helped much in the rapid development of Indian tribes.

We should reject the blind importing of alien models for the development of Indian tribes. This may be an important impetus for the future of Indian tribes. An exaggerated idealisation and sacralisation of public administration is not calculated to solve the acute problems of the aboriginal tribes. Only those who strive for self-reliant development are also capable of intercultural communication, the promotion of the administration in tribal zones is only meaningful with this in view.

References

Bhanjdeo, P.C. 1965 : *I Pravir, the Adivasi God.* Raipur.

Blunt, Captain J.C. 1795 : "A Narrative", The Hindoos Vol. II, London 1835.

Elwin, V. 1939 : *The Baiga.* London

Friedl, E. 1964 : "Lagging Emulation in Post-Peasant Society". *American Anthropologist*, Vol. 66, 569-586.

Harrison, S.S. 1960 : *India : The Most Dangerous Decades* . Princeton.

Jay, E. J. 1970 : *A Tribal Village in Middle India.* Calcutta.

Kluyey, B.I. 1981 : *India: National and Language Problem.* New Delhi.

Kulkarni, S.D. 1975 : Justice Delayed or Denied. *Economic and Political Weekly,* 10 : 4

Riggs, F.W. 1964 : *Administration in Developing countries: The Theory of Prismatic Society.* Boston.

Schwarz, A n.d. : Mythe et realite bureaucratics Africaines, Revue Canadienne des Etudes Africaines, 2. 255-84.

Shukla, H.L. 1985 : *Language, Ethnicity and History.* Delhi.

1985 : *Socio-cultural Approach To Tribal Languages.* Delhi.

1985 : *Social History of Chhattisgarh.* Delhi.

1986 : *Tribal Heritage of Madhya Pradesh.* Delhi.

1987 : *Dictionary of Tribal Languages.* Delhi.

1988 : *Tribal History: A New Interpretation.* Delhi.

1990 : *Tribal Rebellions in Colonial India : People's History of Bastar.* Delhi.

Singh, K.S. (Ed.) 1983 : *Tribal Movements in India.* 2. Delhi.

Subramaniam, V. 1977 : "Politicized Administration: a Socio-historical analysis". *International Reveiw of Administrative Sciences*. 43 : 297-308.

The Pandey Commission Report on Bastar Palace Rebellion (Unpublished)

19

THE AUTHORITY STRUCTURE IN THE NICOBARESE SOCIETY

T.N. PANDIT
A. JUSTIN

The Nicobar islands which lie South of the Andaman islands, consist of altogether twenty two large and small islands, out of which only twelve are inhabited. The most northerly island of the group is Car Nicobar which is about 230 kms. from Port Blair. It is about 120 kms. away from Little Andmana. Chowra, Teressa, Bompuka, Katchal, Kamorta, Nan-cowry and Trinket form the Central group of Nicobar islands; which in the Southern group are Pulo Milo, Little Nicobar, Kondul, Great Nicobar etc. The last and largest island in the Nicobars is Great Nicobar. The uninhabited islands in the Central and Southern groups are Batti Maly, Tillangchong, Meroe, Trak, Treis, Menchal and Kabra respectively. The Nicobars stretch over 54 kms with an aggregate area of about 1644.5 sq. kms.

The Nicobar Archipelago is inhabited by two tribes, the Nicobarese and the Shompen. The formers are spread over on the twelve islands with a major concentration in Car Nicobar, while the latter inhabit the interior areas of Great Nicobar. Both the Nicobarese and the Shompen are of the Mongoloid origin. Unlike the latter who are averse to close social intercourse with the outside people, the former live in settled villages tending herds of domestic pig and growing coconut plantations. The Nicobarese have consequently been exposed to various forces of change. The Shompen, however, are very shy and lead a semi-nomadic life based on hunting and food-gathering and having very little interaction with other communites. They continue to live in relative isolation, having a sort of symbiotic relationship with the Nicobarese in some parts of Great Nicobar.

There is islandwise variation in the spoken dialects, though most of them can understand and converse in the Car Nicobarese langauge. Also there are noteworthy variations in their cultural and soical practices, but nonetheless they share a basic cultural tradition. The most important single influence on the social economic, political and religious life of the people is attributed to Christianity. Prior to the advent of Christianity the Nicobar islanders were animists. According to 1981 census the population of the Nicobarese is 21,172 and about two third of the Nicobarese population lives in Car Nicobar, which the main administration headquarters for the entire Nicobar islands, quite a few of them have settled down on semi-permanent basis in Port Blair and in other areas of the Andamans. About one hundred fifty Nicobarese families from Car Nicobar were brought to Little Andaman in the early 1970's under the rehabilitation programme.

This paper concern itself with the study of authority structure in the Nicobarese society, for instance, the power structure in a *tuhet*- maximal lineage, the decision maker, the power of *tuhet* head, the roles of village headman and island chief, church leaders, educated people and Government functionaries so on and so forth.

The concept of authority is used in many a way and is frequently well associated with power, influence and leadership. Yet a distinction may be drawn here between 'power' and 'authority'. Authority is power which is legitimized. It has been defined in the International Encyclopaedia of Social Science volume 1 (1968: 474) as a capacity which is innate or acquired for exercising ascendancy over a group. From this, it is meant a manifestation of power. Yet this view is not free from criticism in as much as authority is not a capacity. It is a relationship. It is neither innate nor a matter of ascendancy. Thereby it can not be confused with competence in the sense that authority becomes a power phenomenon which is a sanctioned power and an institutionalized power. It is used in variety of ways which can be viewed accordingly as assessed below:

1. as a property of person or office, especially the right to issue orders,

2. a relationship between the superiors and other subordinates such that both incumbents perceive the relationship as legitimate,

3. a quality of a communication by virtue of which it is accepted and respected. There could be countless variations on any of these but the phenomenon of authority is basic to human behaviour.

The authority structure in the Nicobarese society can be characterized by the congruency or diffused and fragmented nature of their multiple layers of authority patterns, as practised in a *tuhet*--maximal lineage group, village and island council, at a village church political sphere, Ellon Hinengo Limited (EHL) and finally the influence of educated people and other Government officials. Each of these has a varying number of individuals who in one context or another function as leaders. Thus, the instituion of customary laws among the Nicobarese is run by elderly recognised and influential individual or body and enforced by authority.

The Tuhet

Before describing the power structure in a *tuhet* it is very pertinent to understand the word, *tuhet,* in a broader sense. According to the people of Car Nicobar, it is the unit of social life whereas the nuclear and joint family are the units in other Nicobar islands both in the central and southern groups of Nicobar. The *tuhet* consists of a maximal lineage group which is recognised specifically under a particular name like *Hecho* of Kakana village. This provides a very important social identity of its lineage members. Recent investigation shows that it is not necessary for a large lineage group to reside only in the primary homestead. Some of the lineage members are occupying different areas of the village.

A homestead, as defined in Notes and Queries on Anthropology, is a single habitation, the occupants of which constitute a household (1974 : 64). Although the houses and huts of a large lineage group as stated before, are found scattered in separate areas of the village, they have no specific recognition and bear no separate identity as a *tuhet*. They form clusters of homesteads but are recognised as under a particular *tuhet* for instance, *Hecho*. Thereby a cluster of houses or homestead cannot be taken a *tuhet* itself. In their common parlance a *tuhet* not only denotes the main house, but also the large lineage group residing in their individual houses and huts, which are either built adjacent to the primary homestead or even in their horticultural garden and plantations of the *tuhet* found in different areas of the village.

Thus it is clear from the above explanation that the word, *tuhet* is appropriate to indicate the large extended joint family as prevalent on Car Nicobar. The *tuhet* and *Kinem* or *mirooto* are synonymous. When a population in a *tuhet* increases or a major dispute occurs over the use of land, property, plantations and other conflicts a large lineage group separates to form a *kinem* or *mirooto* of the same parental *tuhet*. In fact, *kinem* or *mirooto* is the outcome of a *tuhet* where some lineage members separate themselves from the other lineage group of the same *tuhet*; thus a new *tuhet* is formed bearing separate identity. The affiliation of such *tuhet* is known as *kinem* or *mirooto*.

The range of relationship within a *tuhet* is not genealogically restricted to the descendants themselves, but also includes adopted children. It is the custom of the *tuhet* to adopt the children of *inlom* son and daughter and relatives too. The *inlom* means rule of residence where the bridegroom comes to live in his wife's *tuhet* or vise versa. A *tuhet* is exogamous in character and family is patrilineal but the residence pattern may be either patrilocal or matrilocal.

Selection and Tenure of the Head

The Nicobarese stress the personal qualities of the head of the *tuhet* responsible for this heritage. They recall his character, ability, profound knowledge of customary laws and the qualities of administrative leadership to control and command order in a large group and above all his seniority in terms of age. Generally the *tuhet* head holds his office for a life time. The vacancy in the authority structure of the *tuhet* occurs only after death. This hierarchical structure of authority in a *tuhet* forges a kind of "we feeling", oneness and unity which operate through various roles and network of their relationship based on kind ties.

A village has a number of *tuhets* with head known as *marooto* or ma kuo *tuhet*. He is the deciding authority who organizes all important matters, political, economic, social and other practical purposes. He is assisted by various family heads of the *tuhet*. The head of the *tuhet* has judicial and executive authority within the *tuhet*. He has jurisdiction to hear cases and to conclude them too. As head he has means of commanding and compelling the lineage members to concede to the demands of the *tuhet*. The power and the authority of the *tuhet* head lies in fulfilling the obligations, duties, needs and demands of the *tuhet*. The lineage members have to fulfil all those obligations, duties etc. first and then their own day-to-day requirements, because traditionally an individual of a family residing within the *tuhet* has to rear pigs and poultry, raise horticultural garden, plantation etc. to facilitate the organization of many a traditional festival, cultural and recreational activities, Church festivals and other special occasions. Lavish feasts are routined with the Nicobarese. A family manages its own economic affairs not because of the order and command of the head but because it has to meet its own needs and requirements as described before. The reason is that the head of the *tuhet* does not demand any of their earnings and production every day except on festive occasion, All family members of the *tuhet* fall under the general guidance and control of their head.

The head have both policy-making and administrative roles, he has certain measures of authority. He can impose his will even against the resistance of lineage members in ways which are prescribed by customary law. Severe sanctions are imposed on disobedience. The guilty person has the right to appeal against the decision of the *tuhet* head; dissensions are generally allowed within the authority structure of the *tuhet*. The head is bound by the concrete prescriptions of the traditional norms and orders which are held to be binding on the person in authority as well as the other subordinates. Although the head of the *tuhet* is free to make decisions yet the judicial powers of the former within the *tuhet* administrative network are normally appropriated and his action or judgement is strictly bound by tradition.

Prestige and property are the two major elements which determine the distribution of power within the structure of authority in the Nicobarese society. Although usufructuary rights to use the available economic resources and its allocation are the prime economic interest as stressed by the *tuhet* norms, and is usually remain with the lineage group, but the corporate rights of the lineage members are more difficult to define especially when analysed in relation to the rights of the *tuhet* head and his offsprings.

The head is usually concerned with the control of land use, coconut plantation and the rights of into yield but he cannot sabotage the interest of the lineage members.

As the head of the *tuhet* he is expected to administer the customary law in the real service of the lineage members and not for his personal gain. He has to imbibe discipline within the *tuhet's* sphere without which the labour and support of the lineage members is not possible. There is a collective responsibility and is binding to every one; obedience is owed to the *tuhet's* norms and its order and demands are usually fulfilled. It may be worth mentioning here that whenever a linaeage member is committing a serious offence and punishment or fine is imposed, it is usually his *tuhet's* responsibility to pay the fine of pigs or throw a feast as the case may be. In this way the corporate rights of an individual can be ascertained in relation to the head of the *tuhet,* because under the *tuhet* law there is no individual ownership and whatever is available within their resources belongs to the *tuhet,* though all carry usufructuary rights.

The customary laws and norms of the *tuhet* are as old as the people themselves. In view of the tradition the head of the *tuhet* cannot have a complete hold over the entire resources of the *tuhet*. According to the norms of the *tuhet,* no individual family of the *tuhet* can dispose of land or property, coconut and arecanut plantation, or livestock. In the native language these are known as *in la len rom inlinen*. The law of inheritance is lineage ownership, thereby none of the lineage members can alienate the *inlinen* of the *tuhet*. The lineage members are treated as assets, and access to the *inlinen* is generally open to all but under the control of the head of the *tuhet*. There is centralized political authority within the *tuhet* which is vested in the head.

As it is obvious from the access to the economic resources of the *tuhet* that an individual or family is allowed a right over things such as horticultural products, catch from fishing, *copra*-making and other things produced by him or his family. There are, however, usufructuary rights over the use of land. In fact, there is no recognized property right to an individual. The distribution of coconut and arecanut plantations is governed by the convention of the *tuhet*, and is also determined by the kind of labour or products and amount of service rendered to the *tuhet*.

Generally the head of the *tuhet* can not interfere in any individual enterprise or in the use and disposal of horticultural products. An individual has the right to accumulate coconuts for making copra, but he has to take internal consumption into account, first ensuring that there is enough coconut for domestic purposes and for feeding the pigs and fowls. In order to balance the resources the head of the *tuhet* has power to curb the sale of copra and betelnut, although the plantation had been allocated to a particular lineage member. In this way the head can exercise his authority to certain extent.

Additional powers and rights are entrusted to the labourious lineage members because they are the keels of the *tuhet* in all practical purposes. The head usually seeks their advice in making decision like slaughtering of pigs, plucking coconuts from a specific plantation, and so on. It is also their duty to see that no one is plucking coconuts from the plantation allotted to a particular member or family. Their words usually count more than the words of others. It has been observed that their opinions are usually agreed to the end. Within a well-organized *tuhet* and family every individual enjoys a common share in the use of land, cocounts, arecanuts, pandanus and herds of pigs. As a member of the same lineage group, the head carries such usufructuary rights and works hard too meet his own requirements, with the cooperation and mutual aid of all the families residing in the same domicile. The characteristic feature of the *tuhet* is unity, fraternity and a sense of belonging to the *tuhet* where in the individual interests are subordinate to those of the *tuhet*.

Yet there is fear, however, that the lineage group within the *tuhet* is likely to be weakened when hereditary wealth or property produces a new social stratification within the authority structure of the *tuhet*. They may lose its corporate character through the dispersion of the lineage group, that is, when they no longer meet together frequently and have fewer interests in common. The rise of feudalism is often ascribed to the failure of the head of the *tuhet* to provide sufficient security for the lineage. Such kinds of things have occurred in some *tuhets* with stresses and strains, especially with regard to the uneven distribution of coconut and arecanut plantation among the lineage members. As such the unequal distribution of wealth, prestige and power in a *tuhet* leads to coercion and conflict. The point worth noting here is that it happens frequently as observed in some *tuhets* that the usufructuary rights pass to the head of *tuhet* and his offsprings so that it is they who ultimately hold rights of ownership. This manifests that they have a good deal of hold in the authority pattern right from the head of the *tuhet* to the offsprings who can apply their respective powers to the subordinate lineage members.

Nevertheless, it has not been uncommon also for all lineage members to achieve powers and rights and even to rise to the highest position. It may be mentioned here that lineage system has hereditary leadership in the past. Generally succession to the office of the *tuhet* is primogeniture and based on descent through male line. The rights and powers are usually acquired by descent. But of late adopted children of the *inlom* are even entitled to the same property. By dint of hard work, sincerity and the capacity to control and command such persons can become the head of the *tuhet*. Thus, a person of character and ability can enjoy good hold of powers and rights.

The head plays the most leading role in public affairs. He is responsible for a large number of public tasks, associated with the functioning and order of the village council, church and traditional festivals and other important Government official works from time to time. Affairs like organization of festivals, management of church activities, cleaning public places etc. are assigned to him by order of the village council for which he holds the superior authority. The head has means of compelling the lineage group to work, contribute and thus fulfills the order of person in authority. So the legal norm is formally acknowledged within a *tuhet*, whatever may be the inconsistencies and contradictions that appear in the actual relations among lineage members, they still consider themselves to be a united group of the *tuhet* and essential ingredients of the *tuhet*. In the same line the order and command of the head of the *tuhet* is obeyed and fulfilled. The most threatening factors to the unity of the lineage group are the impact of education, material gain and other heritable property, nature of their present occupation, expansion of population through natural increase and other external forces seem likely to disintegrate the lineage group as well power structure of the *tuhet*.

Village Council

Long before the introduction of British India rule, the village administration of the Nicobarese rested on the institution of captainship. Since the inception the captain is performing all the three main functions of the traditional form of Government in the Nicobarese society. The three main functions are legislative, judicial and executive. The traditional administrative structure usually concerns itself with the protection of the society from external forces, the maintenance of internal order, the organization of complex activities affecting the welfare of the society, the validation and maintenance of the structure of authority in the society. According to the Nicobarese the village council which is considered as the guardian of law, prescribes the customary laws, and is organized on certain levels of social control and authority. Customary laws and order are established and executed with the help of village and island councils.

It may be worth mentioning here that the maintenance of the chiefs or captains' has been encouraged steadily by all the foreign suzerains for their own political convenience and interest. The custom was started by the Portuguese in the seventh century, A.D. and had been carried by the Danes, the Austrean and the British in succession. In the eyes of the people a man so appointed by the foreign suzerain, is looked upon merely as an interpreter for communication with the suzerain without any social standing or power unless he is a chief or elder naturally. Other persons, besides the chief and the elders, who have certain political power, are the witch-finders and sorcerers. (A & N Gazetteer, 1909 : 52).

It is obvious as such that the political organization of the Nicobarese, in the remote past, was influenced in one way or the other, by the then British Administration in particular and of late the Andman and Nicobar Administration in general. The headman of a village and island is referred to as *ma* (Captain) and *kui* (Chief Captain) respectively. Apparently they have learnt the terms through many a contact with travellers and incorporated the concept of the captain-the chief authority on a ship. While tracing the historical and evolutionary perspective of the authority structure in the Nicobares society, it is essential to mention the roles of witch-finders and sorcerers as well as the wealthy man which may provide important clues in understanding the political system that existed three or four decades back.

The witch-finders and sorcerers are believed to be well-versed in divination. They can control the movement of spirits and also have powers to recognize the malevolent and benevolent spirits. They can invoke a benevolent spirit to drive away the offending one from the village habitat. In case of sickness they are immediately sent for. Whenever a person is possessed by an evil spirit, the witch-doctor can smell out the offending spirit. They also ascertain the type of spirit which has influenced a person. They make propitiations to invoke the spirit to release itself from the sick man's body. These help the sorcerers and witch-doctors to command a high respect in the society and enjoy a good deal of authority as practised in the remote past.

Generally a witch-finder is feared because he can harm anyone even to the extent of causing a person to get sick and die. Thus the emergence of 'ceremonial killings' or devil murders took place in the horizon of authority structure. This might have attracted the attention of the then British Administration. But it was one of the natives named Patungsu, who pleaded that the custom of awarding the death penalty to the culprit be abolished. The source of strength of the chieftains came from such different attributes as sheer economic power. This is to say that wealth makes difference and thus elevate a wealthy person from the echelon of the society which was common in the distant date. The emergnce of the present pattern of authority is ascribed to the conscious efforts of a few elderly and educated people keeping in view to preserve the society from external forces, maintenance of internal order and so on as described before. It can be analysed in brief that the present authority structure in the Nicobarese society is the outgrowth of a long-drawn conflict between secular and religious leadership.

On each island there are a number of villages. Several *tuhets* have heads known as *ma rooto* or *ma kno tuhet*, who organize all important political, economic and other practical activities. It is from among the heads of the *tuhet* that they nominate villagewise, the first, second and third captains. The village captains and all the heads of the *tuhet*, taken together, constitute the village council. The village council is reported to have effective power, in the distant past. It was usually in the hands of a wealthy man. It is thus obvious that the possession of wealth was one of the primary factors to make a man a captain or chief as the case may be. The village council in its basic form, was functioning even before the outbreak of World War II, according to aged people of Car Nicobars, while the island council came into existence soon after World War II was over.

Island Council

The emergence of the Island Council into the horizon of the authority structure in the Nicobarese society can be attributed to John Richardson Hachevka, the then a young Nicobarese missionary. At the beginning, even before the outbreak of World War II, the Nicobarese in general treated him as an anti-element of the society. He was a menace to the traditional beliefs and practices of the people, because it was he who superimposed the practices of Christianity. Although he was able to convert some young people to Christianity but their number was almost negligible. When the islands was under the Japanese occupation during the year 1942-45 John Richardson Hachevka showed a very courageous leadership to his own people. They began to realize that they had discarded the right person, who had love for them and could speak for the entire community. When the World War II was over, a mass conversion to Christianity took place. The entire Nicobarese were much impressed by his works and leadership, even during the war he showed a remarkable intellect and qualities of leadership and love for his own community. He exercised a wise and beneficent influence among Nicobarese and wielded a strong influence at the administrative level too. According to the aged people the Japanese were not able to lay their hands on him because of his wit and courageousness. In the same manner the most wealthy Nicobarese started to like him and obey his order. They not only obeyed his order but also expressed their desire that John Richardson Hachevka could steer the entire community towards the paths of progress. Thus at the initiation of John Richardson the Island Council came into existence.

Of late, each island has its own chief captain. The chief has an assistant referred to as vice-chief captain. The Island Council consists of the island chief, vice-chief captain, all the first, second and third headmen of various villages,the counsellor, Pradesh Council members and Home Minister's Advisory Committee Members and also the Bishop, who act as an adviser and religious head. Thus the Bishop is also a very important official member of the Island Council. In brief, the hierarchy of authority as prevalent on Car Nicobar, is the chief captain, vice-chief captain, the first, second and third captain, and the heads of the *tuhets*. As supplements to this hierarchy the functionaries of the church like the village presbyter, recognised elderly persons, pastorates, Mothers' Union and the Bishop at the top are acting. The political functionaries like the counsellors and councillors of the territorial council are also included in this panel.

Selection and Tenure

According to Weber the primary source of status in all primitive societies is wealth. Possession of wealth alone is often sufficient to make a man a 'chief'. In addition to this, according to different circumstances, the attribution of hereditary charisma or the mere fact of birth may be more prominent than wealth as such (1947 : 414). This applies to the selection and tenure of the chief and headmen of various villages in the Nicobarese society. According to elderly people it was suggested by Bishop John Richardson Nachevka that the village headmen and chief should be wealthy persons, preferably landowner. The reason behind this was that the captains and chiefs looked after, or actually herded the people. Economic privileges, the power of command and controlling authority on relevant matters, seniority in age, proper knowledge and experience of customary law and qualities of adminstrative leadership were particularly taken into account as criteria for captainship and chieftainship.

As a rule, the village captaincy is a hereditary post. The tenure of office is for life time. Succession to the office of the village headman is based on descent, the rights and powers are usually acquired through descent. If viewed accordingly the selection for the post of village headman is limited to members of the same lineage group. He is usually assisted in all practical purposes by the second and the third captains as well as the representatives from each of the *tuhet* in the village.

The villagers and islanders have the right to dethrone the headman or the chief (as the case may be) by common consent if they prove to be inefficient or misuse their responsibilities. Under such circumstances all the villagers assemble together to formally remove the headman or chief as the case may be. Such rare cases have taken place in the distant past.

It is said that the first committee meeting of the Island Council was held at Seti village. It was held soon after World War II under able guidance of Bishop John Richardson Hachevka. Thus, Seti village was the main headquarters of the Island Council. Its primacy was due to its being the original settlement from where the entire population dispersed to different parts of the island. Evidence also shows that the very first chief captain of the island was Thomas Hala-any-pa of Seti village. After his death, as per the customary law, the next chief had to be selected from among the lineage members of Thomas Hala-any-pa, Unfortunately there was no suitable person from the very same lineage. Who was capable of holding the supreme post of the island chief. Thereby the succession went to another village, i.e. Mus. Fred Tun was elected after Hala-any-pa. Later he himself stepped down voluntarily due to old age. After Fred Tun, Edward Kuchat of Kakana was appointed by the Island Council and is still continuing in office till date. This, if analysed from the above, is in contrast to the custom of appointing persons from the parental village only. It may be mentioned here that the main objective of the first committee meeting of the Island Council was to elect the chief captian of the Island and its official members.

Both the village and Island Councils are found in existence in other Nicobar islands but not in a very orgainsed form. Even today the councils on the central and southern islands are not as active and effective on these lines as in Car Nicobar. The advent of 'Rani' into the political orgainzation of the central Nicobarese can be traced back from Mewalal, the then Tahsildar of Nancowry. It was at the time when Laxman Rao took charge of Government administrative work of Nancowry island, a Nicobarese woman named Islond deserted her husband and came to live with Laxman Rao. A child was born to her, the present Rani Laxmi. After some years Islon was married to Mewalal. As an administrator's wife, she gained political recognition and thus the title 'Rani' came in vogue. Usually people began to bring cases of disputes of different kinds to her to solve. Thus from this day onwards the word 'Rani' crept into the central Nicobarese Political Orgainzation. Even today her daughter Rani Laxmi commands respect from the people. As Rani and arbiter, she acts as a liaison authority between Nicobarese of various islands, and as a link and spokeperson between islanders and administration. Her grand daughter, Aiysha obtained the important appointment as Member of Pradesh Council by means of heredity. Janga of Katchal island also recognised as Rani. Later when she died, her son Abu Saul was elected as chief captain. Also there a few women who consider themselves as Rani. Mention may be made of Mary Ann Minaji. It appears that women enjoy the same degree of equality as men in the structure of authority as prevalent on Central Nicobars.

Powers and Functions

The word or command of the village council is the law, and the council official members themselves are the *Kam honka* (judges), comprising the various *tuhet* heads and recognized elderly persons. The role of the village presbyter is also important in guiding and influencing the village council. The Government administrator does not interfere with village council affairs, nevertheless, maintains contact over relevant issues. If there is a serious murder offence, for example, the latter brings it to the notice of the former. They rarely go to lawcourt (established by Andaman & Nicobar Administration) for justice, because the village council is incharge of general affairs, such as settling disputes and correcting wrongs -for instance theft, abusive language, quarrels, adultery and other soical offences connected with the breach of norm and custom. By implication it has the power of making laws and imposing penalties or punishment on disobedience among the people and *tuhets,* intra-village and inter-village as well. It exercises its authority to facilitate the organisation of church festivals, cultural and recreational activities, cleaning of the village area and so on. For all external and internal purposes the village captain is the head of the village council and representative of his village both at the official and non-official level.

The village captains have no special privileges and rights in personal matters but are treated with respect on account of the responsibilities discharged by them. There is no special law to safeguard their interest, though an attack upon the village headmen is considered as a grave offence and is dealt with according to customary procedure. The village do not derive any wealth from office. Even as arbiters in disputes and offences they do not receive any remuneration. All the expenditure of the village headmen is borne by their respective *tuhets* according to available resources. And the people themselves take pride in their traditional political institution. Thus the village council occupies a prominent place in all administrative, political, judical matters, and religious affairs and other important issues.

The chieftain holds the highest position and keeps control over the society members. They speak of the chief as a person of much importance and is treated with more respect than the other ordinary people. Sufficient powers are given to him, although he is not allowed to do anything against the interest of the community as a whole. But in most of the cases the order and command of the chieftain is the law, and every one has to obey it. He has the power to enforce law and to dispense justice on matters which the village headmen cannnot settle at village council level. The latter consults the former in adjudicating grave offences pertaining to social crime, illicit sexual union, separation, breaching the rule of tribal endogamy and so on. The assembly of the former and the latter together form the island council. The sanctity of traditional norms is taken into consideration in enforcing a decision. The island council head (the chief) and his assistant (vice-chief captain) have no special rights, but they hold the most prominent position in the power structure. Like the village captains both the chief and vice-chief captain receive no remuneration or wealth from his office not even in kinds. But their economic priviliges and status are drawn entirely from the resources of their *tuhet.*

The jurisdiction of the village council extends over social offences infringing the traditional code. For quarrels and petty conflicts, disputes over land boundary and property, horticultural activities, theft, adultery and so on the people generally go to the village council. It is very powerful. None of the people take their cases to the courts of law established by the government. The council settles all such cases except murder, which is rare, and is referred to the courts of law for decisions. The council's main aim is to see that cases are mutually settled. Whenever a case is to be judged, the village council usually sits in the community house or the house of the first, second and third captain which is traditionally fixed for such hearings and this is known as *chouck kam honka*. There is no fixed session for the village council. If there is any immediate issue for discussion, then deliberations are conducted in the evening.

The Government administrator has to approach the village headman in all matters concerning administration and welfare of the people. This is very essential both at island and village council level. The village council is organized on very sound lines. It receives guidance from the village church presbyter. Also there is great involvement by recognised and eminent elderly persons. Traditional solidarity is functioning very effectively, with all its elaborate machinery, assembling not only to settle disputes and right offences but also to make arrangements for constructive activities. For instance it arranges and provides financial assistance for patients with their attendants to go to Port Blair or the mainland, as the case may be, for medical treatment. Sometimes financial assistance is provided to needy students for higher studies at Port Blair or on the mainland. Like the village council there is no fixed programme for the island council. Traditionally the deliberations were conducted in Seti village but of late there has been a shift to the Ellon Hinengo Limited (EHL) complex.

Law and Justice

It is obvious from the above explanations that the village council is responsible for day-to-day organizational, administrative and judicial affairs within its framework. It is characteristically coercive in the application of law and justice, so that community can continue to function in an orderly manner on the basis of rules so maintained. The international Encyclopaedia of the Social Science (9 :74) defines law as one of the devices by means of which men can reconcile their actual activities and behaviour with the ideal principles that they have come to accept, in a way that is not painful or revolting to their sensibilities and in a way which allows ordered social life to continue.

It has been observed that whenever complaints of various offences are brought to the notice of the traditional council, the village headmen do not take action until an assembly is held. As the judicial authority head, the village first captain presides over the assembly with second and third captains, all *tuhet* heads and recognized elderly persons as advisers. At the time of deciding the case, the intention and grievances of the offender and aggrieved respectively are taken into account. There is much free discussion and all office bearers of the council have an equal opportunity to express their views and arguments in deciding the *kuo* or punishment as the case may be. After weighing their argument, the first Captain announces the *kuo* to the offender on .the common consent of the council members. Hence the final decisions is usuallv unanimous.

It may be worth mentioning here that a *kuo* is indeed in the native common parlance. It is a warning applied to an offender not to repeat and to commit the same blunder, crime or social offence. And if he does so he will be liable to be excommunicated, thrashed, fined or made to host a feast and banned from drinking toddy as the case may be. He is made to take an oath and to check his unbecoming behaviour and habits. *Kuo* is generally applied when the offender makes a plea to be pardoned or when an amicable settlement is made between parties by the headmen without imposing any thrashing, fine or punishment.

In the distant past death penalty by some sort of crucifixion was awarded to persons charged with serious offences such as theft, habitual adultery, murder, and public annoyance. It was a customary law prevalent in Car Nicobar. This old custom of awarding death penalty to the culprit was abolished by a person named Patunagsu of Tapoiming village. He pleaded for the abolition of crucifying the offender because if it continued their numbers would reduce. He suggested the idea of reconciliation.

It is thus obvious that the imposition of fine or feast, thrash and excommunication etc., do evolve in the decision-making process. It is why the offender is made even today to throw a feast to appease the sentiments of the aggrieved party. Besides giving a feast, as stressed by the present chief, it was also suggested by the people of Perka village, Car Nicobar to distribute a portion of pork to all village council members as the penalty for misconduct. Another suggestion was to pay a fine in the form of pigs to the bereaved party as a substitute for a feast, in order to compensate his grief. As a rule, no feast is organized when the culprit has to pay a fine in terms of pigs to the concerned party. The proposal of Patungsu and the residents of Perka village was accepted by all and in this way the old custom of awarding the death penalty to the culprit was abolished.

It was a customary, among the Nicobarese of Katchal, Nancowry, Trinket and Teressa etc., to stage a stick fight called *ma lung* or *pumon* in settling disputes. A person eloped with another's wife, the deserted husband challenged the accused to a fight with sticks about two inches in diameter and twelve feet long, at an appointed time and place. They wore helment of padded cloth and coconut husk. With the wooden stick they used to strike each other, till one got defeated and the matter was settled. Land disputes, too, were settled through stick fights. The headman used to interfere only after the defeat of one and reconciled both parties. The defeated party had to pay several pigs and feast to all the villagers who came to attend the assembly. The application of such customary law in settling disputes and other social offences has gradually been diminished in the Central Nicobar Islands. Of late they are trying to adopt the village council as prevalent in Car Nicobar.

The normal punishment, according to tradition, is to impose a fine in terms of pigs which are highly valued among the people. For seduction and habitual adultery the punishment is flogging, and a fine of pigs. At times a grand feast is thrown to the village council members and the island council whenever a grave offence is committed. Slaughtering pigs, destroying one's large sea faring canoe, land property, coconut and arecanut plantation are considered as grave offence and giving a feast etc., are accepted as compensations for grief by an aggrieved party. In cases of petty quarrels and conflicts *kuo* is applied to the guilty individual as discussed earlier. For minor offences like dishonesty and abusive language, when committed again and again by the same offender, corporal punishment and a fine are imposed. As for theft, exaction of the stolen item is the most widespread punishment used. For eve-teasing and molestation, thrashing or sometimes a fine is imposed, as prevalent in Car Nicobar even these days.

The excommunication of an offender can be decided by the village council and the village church presbyter. The influence of the presbyter at the village level has been very instrumental in rendering decision. Both as pastor and religious head at village level, he also functions as an adviser in awarding punishment from time to time according to social pressures. Generally excommunication is imposed upon those who elope with the wives of others, or who breaks the rule of tribal endogamy. Although imprisonment is strikingly absent among the Nicobarese, nevertheless, the sanction for persistent and dangerous antisocial activity by witch-doctors is generally exile or death. After the cessation of the death penalty expatriation, for a year or so, for instance, from Car Nicobar to Port Blair is awarded to witches who are caught red-handed by the people. Also some form of banishment is imposed on a violator who does not act on the advice of the council. But this is not an exile in the proper sense of the term, since the offender is sanctioned to stay and attend to various domestic chores in a *tuhet* other than his own. According to the decision it could be any *tuhet* of the office bearers, his stay is purely temporary and is not allowed any kind of liberty.

It may be noted here that little changes have occurred in their jurisprudence since the death penalty and stick fights have been abolished. There is no denying the fact that the head of the village council is still powerful in mediating and settling a dispute or offence as per traditional practice. In the same manner the chief of the island can exercise his judicial powers in awarding various nature of offence.

The Impact of Christianity

The impact of christianity has brought many a change in the authority structure of the Nicobarese society. It has become a part of their life. The role of Bishop, as head of the Andaman and Nicobar Dicocese of Church of North India (CNI), is noteworthy. He not only functions as the head of the religious institution but also the main administrative head of the entire church activities. He is assisted by archdeacon, presbyters, deacons, catechists and lay vicars besides the Mothers' Union and pastorates. As an overall incharge of the diocese administration, he also acts as an adviser and arbiter on serious matters. In brief the Bishop's interference as a religious head carries equal power with that of the chief Captain and counsellor both at the official and non-official level. He not only projects himself as a Bishop but also brings important issues to the notice of the Government, thus superseding the island chief, village headmen and even the counsellor in all respects.

The historical evidence of the Bishop's involvement in the power structure of the Nicobarese society, can be traced back from John Richardson Hackevka era. It has been pointed out that from the very beginning of his career as a Christian missionary, he showed a remarkable intellect and qualities of leadership and love for his own community. He dedicated his life as a school teacher, compounder, catechist, tahsildar and so on. It was he, who gave the Nicobarese language, the variant form of Roman script. In the later part of his life Bishop John Richardson Hachevka perpetuated his leadership by patronising the village headmen along with a group of young educated Nicobarese missionary workers. Thus it may be recalled that the first Nicobarese Bishop, J.R. Hachevka, was entrusted different assignments during the pre and post-Independence period as already stated. The authorities of Church of North India (CNI) consecrated him as the first Nicobarese Bishop in St. Paul's Church Cathedral, Calcutta, on 15th January, 1950. Because of his sincere devotion and loyal service to his own people, he was appointed as a member of the Chief Commissioner's Advisory Committee by the Andaman and Nicobar Administration, and later nominated as the first Member of Parliament in 1952 to represent the people of these islands.

Thus this recognition after 1947 has also helped to increase Bishop Richardson's personal influence and prestige among the Nicobarese and accelerated the quicker spread of the Christianity.

His unique and tremendous contribution for the growth of the society has labelled him as the modern architect of the Nicobarese, who bears the beacon light. The Government of India conferred on him both the Padmashree and the Padma Bhushan in 1965 and 1975 respectively, in recognition of his meritorious service for the upliftment of his own community. Padma Shree award was also conferred on Edward Kuchat in early 1990, the second Nicobarese to receive such award. After a close analytical study of the first Nicobarese Bishop's position, influence and prestige, the current Bishop is tryinng hard to follow suit, functioning in a parallel role at all levels, on the Island Council and territorial council too. Since the induction of the Nicobarese as members of the Advisory Committee, young educated captains are gradually emerging into the horizon of the power structure.

Other Factors of Change

The change in various aspects of the authority structure in the Nicobarese society is directly and indirectly attributed to education. This holds true in as much as educated people have the tools to gain better opportunities, influence, prestige and have, indeed, access to various sources both at the official and non-official levels. The effects of modern civilization are a threat to the elderly people in general and the power structure in particular. Thereby change is also being experienced in all the authority structure. As a result, the election of first, second and third village-wise captains through secret ballot papers was conducted for the first time in 1978. The present order of captainship is a combination of elderly, recognised and young educated persons. Unlike the past, the current term of captainship is five years. The authority structure is undergoing change with the growth of political consciousness after the induction of the Nicobarese as advisory committee members and counsellors at the territorial level. The traditional political organization has been influenced by the Andaman and Nicobar Administration, Ellon Hinengo Limited (EHL) and Manulo Matai Limited (MML). The traditional political structure faces a new threat posed by the growth of individualism. A sharp observation by T.N. Pandit is worth quoting in the context. The trend towards higher education is increasing, with better facilities and opportunities being provided by the Government. This will, in due course, give rise to an educated elite that would in proper time become the political elite and may supplant the traditional leadership (1976 : 5).

At a much recent date there is a conscious effort on the part of the young educated Nicobarese to present their grievances and difficulties to the concerned administration and for channelizing these, of late, they have formed a registered association called Nicobarese Employees Welfare Association, popularly known as Manulo Inkuken Nicobarese. Any Nicobarese who is over 18 years of age can become a member, upon the payment of rupee one as admission fee and rupee one as monthly subscription. The central executive committee of the Association consists of a President, Vice President, General Secretary, three Organising Secretaries, one Joint Secretary, a Treasurer and four other members. The term of the central executive committee is for a period of three years. The main aim of the Association is to organise and unite the Nicobarese who are working in different parts of the Andaman and Nicobar Islands and elsewhere in the country. Its general function is to uplift the socio-economic condition of the people in general and to present relevant matters to the administration. The Association also helps to develop social harmony with other communities through sports and other cultural activities. On the whole, it has no concern with political activities but the older Nicobarese are afraid of it in general and the authority structure in particular for its growth and control over the education.

These days the educated Nicobarese youth are absorbing the values of other cultures. Thus the impact of cultural contact has resulted in both evil as well as favourable consequences. This has in one way or the other, influenced their outlook and the political structure of the island too. With the fast increasing awareness of education a new trend was introduced recently to elect village captains. This proves that literacy is largely responsible for the emergence of political modernization in the Nicobarese society.

Young educated Nicobarese are making a conscious effort to give a new shape to the power structure, to influence the election of various village captains, island chiefs and vice-chief captains as stated before. Here 'modernization' means what has been conceptualized by S.C. Dube, as the transformation of a traditional society in economic socio-political spheres with an increasing absorption of the elements of modern science and technology (Mishra; 1980 : 1). There by the election of first, second and third captains villagewise through secret ballot papers has been conducted for the first time as mentioned before. That now the tenure of office is restricted to five years unlike yesteryears which was hereditary and for lifetime. The number of candidates bearing different symbols like a canoe, cane basket, cross bow and arrow, but, and beehive houses is restricted to five in each village. All villagers above the age of fifteen are entitled to vote. A special election committee consisting of influential persons like the Bishop, Chief and Vice-chief captain, Home Minister, Advisory Committee members and presbyter is constituted in this connection. This is assisted by a sub-commitee of twenty educated persons. It is thus obvious that the present terms and conditions of captainship are unlike those of the past. Now people opt for those who can speak for and represent the community by raising relevant issues before the administration.

The most relevant change, which have occurred in early 1980, is ascribed to the introduction of the territorial council by the Andaman and Nicobar administration. It may be noted here that this Advisory Committee was introduced among the people quite a few years after Independence. Among the village headmen, two captains were nominated in the Advisory Commitees, one for the Chief Commissioner and the other for the Home Minister. However, although the territorial council has been formed, yet the Home Minister Advisory Committee is still functioning. It is significant that the present member is a female. Under the able guidance of the counsellor at the top, four other Members of Pardesh Council (MPC) have been appointed, two of them from Car Nicobar and one each from Katchal and Nancowry islands, to represent the community of different islands. Unfortunately, there is not even a single Nicobarese from the southern group of Nicobar island on the territorial council. In the village council of *Kam honka* (judges), which is more informal than formal, the role and function of the counsellor amounts to very little. This does not mean a degradation of his political status, but as spokesman for the entire community in all external matters, both to the Government and non-official agencies, he holds an important position, playing a parallel role, if not superseding, the chief captain and the Bishop as well.

It has also been observed that the two registered co-operative societies of the people possess an undoubted political influence, which sometimes causes negative reaction in the overall process of development. An under-current of resentment is descernable among a section of young educated people. It is a fact that they have rendered useful service to the islanders, who, these days realize the importance of money and the value of their local commodities. But due to the monopolistic rights and the service they extend, the Nicobarese cannot protest against any fault.

Although both co-operative societies are now completely owned by the Nicobarese but the management activities are in the hands of the some non-Nicobarese. The impact of the latter in guiding and controlling the general affairs of the people, is powerful. They sometimes function more as administrators than as central co-operative societies or firms. Thus, in spite of its continuity, tradition faces a threat. Given the pattern of change, individualism is bound to emerge from within the society. This would certainly affect the administrative structure at *tuhet*, village and island council level. Despite the presence of influential Nicobarese in the companies the grievances are not redressed.

Both co-operative societies have some political power in moulding the attitude of some elites of the village. They are the guiding factors in the authority structure and play a decisive role in political activities. They have monopoly in trading activities and occupy a prominent place in the power structure. These are the marketing society 'for the people, of the people, and by the people'. So, no one likes to criticize some of the activities for a variety of reasons. A few educated Nicobarese wish to curb political power of these co-operative societies, but it is of no avail. The head of village and island council as well should give serious thought on these issues since the future of Nicobar islands lies in the quality and ability of its leadership.

In the wake of modern civilization, the authority structure of the Nicobarese society is going through a crucial formative phase, where both conservative and progressive practices are simultaneously being followed; but they are very selective in areas of accepting any new changes. They are now politically conscious with the induction of the Nicobarese as Advisory Committee members and counsellor at the territorial level. The impact of education is also quite great.

It is worth mentioning here that a few educated Nicobarese are keen to contest for the position of the Member of Parliament in the elections. There was a clear indication with regard to this in 1984, but for some reason the candidate withdrew.

Finally, it is pertinent to note that the village and island councils are dealing with internal affairs quite satisfactorily. The interests of the people are well looked after, but when it comes to external matters, the chief and village headmen even the Bishop and counsellor, have sometimes failed to live upto the expectations of the people. This appears to be a draw back of the in-built democratic nature of the authority structure among the Nicobarese. But the danger that lurks in prosperity is likely to disintegrate the unity among lineage members, and village and island councils as well as the integrity of the Nicobarese Society as a whole. This may directly and indirectly affect the traditional authority structure of the society in the not too distant date.

Notes

The paper is based on experiences, observation and information drawn through various field works conducted in the Nicobar Archipelago. The authors are thankful to the Director General, Anthropological Survey of India, for the facilities extended in undertaking this work. They are also grateful to Shakeer Ahmed, Librarian who have rendered a very useful service as and whenever required to make the necessary references available. Sheetal did a stoic work with the typing of the manuscript for which we owe her thanks too.

References

Banton, Michael 1965 : *Political systems and Distribuion of Power*. London: Tavistock Publications.

Bonington, M.C.C. 1932 : *Census of India 1931: Andaman & Nicobar Islands*. Vol. 2 Calcutta.